Web Design
Complete Course

Joyce J. Evans

WILEY

Wiley Publishing, Inc.

Web Design Complete Course

Published by:
Wiley Publishing, Inc.
111 River Street
Hoboken, NJ 07030
www.wiley.com/compbooks

Published simultaneously in Canada

For general information on our other products and services or to obtain technical support please contact our Customer Care Department within the U.S. at 800-762-2974, outside the U.S. at 317-572-3993 or fax 317-572-4002.

Library of Congress Control Number: 2003101809

ISBN: 0-7645-3752-0

Manufactured in the United States of America

10 9 8 7 6 5 4 3 2 1

» Credits

Publisher: Barry Pruett

Project Editor: Kezia Endsley

Acquisitions Editor: Tom Heine

Editorial Manager: Rev Mengle

Technical Editor: Mary Rich

Interior Designers: Edwin Kwo
Daniela Richardson

Layout: Beth Brooks, Sean Decker, Kristin McMullan, Heather Pope

Production: Joyce Haughey, Susan Moritz, Dwight Ramsey, Regina Snyder

Special Help: Cricket Krengel

» Dedication

I'd like to dedicate this book to my family for their wonderful support and encouragement.

» Acknowledgments

It takes an entire crew of people to get a book into your hands. I'd like to thank my acquisitions editor, Tom Heine, for giving me the opportunity to write this book. I'd also like to thank my project editor, Kezia Endsley and my tech editor Mary Rich. I'd also like to thank my two private testers, Leroy Stanley and Brenda Lem, for doing last minute testing.

Much appreciation goes to Macromedia and their top shelf team of engineers and support staff for producing such a great program as Dreamweaver. Thanks also go to the hard working guys and gals who write the extensions for Dreamweaver that extend its capabilities so greatly. I'd also like to thank Donna Casey for her site design and session contributions.

» Bio

Joyce J. Evans is a dynamic communications professional, with a lifetime of experience in instructional design and human interaction. With over 10 years of experience in educational training, speaking, tutorial development, and Web design and usability, she faces every challenge with a genuine concern for the users. Joyce has written articles and tutorials for several online graphics magazines including Web Review and Graphic Design and is a trainer/speaker. Joyce founded, designed, and maintains the Idea Design Web site (www.je-ideadesign.com), a Web design studio. She also has a personal site (www.JoyceJEvans.com). Joyce can be reached at Joyce@JoyceJEvans.com.

» Table of Contents

Introduction

Understanding the Process

Web Design Complete Course is designed to walk you through all the design stages from planning a Web site to connecting to a database. Each session builds upon each other while you develop the stockimagenation site. You learn techniques that can be applied to your own Web site. You can also use this design and simply trade these images, logo, and so on for your own.

Web Design Complete Course is broken into manageable sessions that are also topic-related so that you can use this book as reference when you need to refresh your memory. The instructions are succinct. The sessions are taught in a way that beginners can understand but are also laced with intermediate skills right from the start.

Is This Book for You?

Absolutely, if you are serious about entering the field of Web design. It is not for the faint of heart. It is a beginner's book but the programs used are professional level and are full featured. It's very easy to skim an instruction and make a mistake. If you are willing to follow the instructions carefully and repeat them if you make a mistake, you'll be amazed at how fast you learn by doing. This book is written for today's new Web designers. You create a dynamic site using a database and other interactivity. The sample site can be viewed at www.stockimagenation.com

What's in This Book?

Web Design Complete Course is divided into parts, sessions, and tutorials. The parts are subject categories that contain sessions that in turn contain tutorials and discussions. Each tutorial focuses on a specific topic. They walk you through the steps for using specific features to create a portion of the stockimagenation Web site, that you develop throughout the book.

Each tutorial builds on the previous tutorials and it is assumed you have performed the previous tutorials and learned the skills taught in them. Each session does have a starter file, so you can jump in anywhere, but the text assumes you have learned all previous lessons.

I have found that most people I teach and help on a daily basis learn best by actually performing a project. It's a great way to get hands-on experience using the various tools. It's more interesting than reading about what each tool does and how to use it.

Here is an overview of what you'll find in each part:

> » **Confidence Builder.** You get a kick start into Web design by working through a hands-on exercise that gives you a taste of creating images, image compositions, and page layout as you design your first Web page.

> » **Part I: Course Setup.** This is a narrative section of the book. It contains introductory material about Web design. The only other narrative parts of this book are in the form of a few discussions sprinkled throughout the book. You do not need to read them to perform any of the tutorials. The discussions are more "geeky" and add additional insight into certain topics.

>> » **Web Design Basics** includes an overview of major topics that all aspiring Web designers need to know. Topics such as planning, making a flow chart, and presenting the client design comps and a contract are just a handful of the topics discussed.

>> » **Project Overview** explains the project that you create as you work through this course. It also discusses how to use the files on the CD-ROM.

» **Part II: Building the Site Imagery Using Fireworks MX.** You start off by creating the images you need for the design of the stockimagenation site. You learn how to bring the images into Fireworks and how to create your own.

> » **Session 1**, "Bringing Image Assets into Fireworks," starts off with a discussion of image basics and provides a quick tour of Fireworks. You quickly start to bring images into Fireworks from other sources.

> » **Session 2**, "Designing Image Compositions," focuses on an image composition, but you do other image manipulation as well. As you compose your images, you'll discover how easy they are to produce and manipulate in Fireworks. You learn how to use quite a few of Fireworks tools while putting together a composition for a CD cover. Stockimagenation offers CD collections; the cover you make in this session is for the "Watersports" collection.

> » **Session 3**, "Building the Site's Vector Images," begins with a basic discussion of color theory and then moves into making vector icons for the stockimagenation site. You also design the site layout for the home page and a details page.

> » **Session 4**, "Building the Site's Bitmap Images," teaches you how to remove the background from an image, add a border to a bitmap image (learn what a bitmap is), make a command to automate tasks, perform a batch process, and fade an image into a background.

> » **Session 5**, "Fireworks Animation," is an optional session on the CD that teaches you how to make some text animations in Fireworks. You learn about symbols, tweening, and the timing of an animation.

» **Part III: Finalizing the Images for Export.** You make the mockup or comp pages for the client and then slice, optimize, and export the images to use in a Web page.

> » **Session 6**, "Preparing the Mockups," covers adding images, text, and icons to the site's main pages. These can then be presented to the client for approval and then used in the site design. These are the approved designs so you continue using them to build the stockimagenation site.

> » **Session 7**, "Optimizing and Exporting Images for Use in Dreamweaver Layouts," explores how to intricately slice (divide) your designs and apply optimization settings. The decisions of whether to slice your document, and where and how to do so all contribute to how, and sometimes whether, users view your Web pages.

» **Part IV: Laying Out the Site Using Dreamweaver MX.** In this part you perform the most work. You make the actual Web pages and add the navigation and text structure as well as make a template to use for the site's remaining pages.

  » **Session 8**, "Setting Up the Site in Dreamweaver," includes a quick tour of Dreamweaver and covers how to set various preferences and define your local site. This is extremely important to utilizing Dreamweaver's powerful site-management tools.

  » **Session 9**, "HTML Page Structure," covers the ins and outs of building tables. A table in Dreamweaver is a container with rows, columns, and cells. Tables were originally made to hold data, but Web designers discovered they were great containers to aid in the placement of images.

  » **Session 10**, "Behaviors, Snippets, and Client-Side Scripting," uses some of Dreamweaver's most popular behaviors to build interactive rollover buttons for the site and to open a new browser window on demand. You also learn how to insert a dynamic date in your pages through the use of a custom script. Finally, you take a look at how the Snippets panel can be used to store code, scripts, and other content for use throughout all your sites

  » **Session 11**, "Using Cascading Style Sheets," covers Cascading Style Sheets, which are probably one of the most important tools to learn in Web development. As a specification set forth by the W3C World Wide Web Consortium, CSS is a standard designed to separate the visual presentation of content from the actual structural markup—a language used to render structured documents like HTML and XML on-screen, on paper, and verbally, in speech.

  » **Session 12**, "Building the Site's Snap Menus," shows you how to download and install extensions that add new functionality to Dreamweaver MX. You use layers and behaviors to script elements you built to appear and disappear on demand.

  » **Session 13**, "Automating with Library Items and Templates," covers how to use Library items to build page elements that are easily updated, allowing Macromedia Dreamweaver MX to do all the grunt work of maintaining accurate paths to images and files. You also learn how to work with Dreamweaver templates to add more pages to a site while maintaining a consistent, yet editable layout.

» **Part V: Building a Web Application in Dreamweaver.** In this part, you make the site dynamic so that information and images are returned to the browser on demand of the user. You also add a shopping cart so the user can purchase goods.

» **Session 14**, "Building Dynamic Web Pages," covers what you need to prepare to build dynamic Web pages. You learn the difference between local and remote testing of dynamic content. You define your Web and testing server locations and access methods. You also define a ColdFusion DSN (Data Source Name) locally (Windows) and/or remotely (Windows or Macintosh).

» **Session 15**, "Displaying Dynamic Data," covers how to build a *recordset*, which is a subset of information pulled from a database, and how to use it to dynamically display content in your page. Recordsets are created through *Structured Language Queries* (SQL) that ask for specific data from the tables of a database. As you work through the tutorials, you see just how easy it is to build SQL statements to display records returned by a search page; to display dynamic images, text, and links; and to request the server to build enough HTML structures to display the returned data.

» **Session 16**, "Adding a Shopping Cart," teaches you how to add a shopping cart to your Web site. You use a free extension for Dreamweaver that you can customize. You'll be amazed at how easy it is to set up a shopping cart for smaller sites.

» **Session 17**, "Before You Publish," walks you through some of the major testing stages prior to uploading the site to your server.

» **Part VI: Appendixes.** This part includes appendixes covering what's on the CD-ROM, Web design techniques, resources for finding more help, and more.

Confidence Builder

This confidence builder lets you get a feel for working with Fireworks and Dreamweaver. You also add a line of Flash text to the Web page. By working carefully through these tutorials, you'll quickly build your confidence as you see how easy it is to actually make a professional looking Web page. Many of the techniques used are discussed in more depth and detail throughout the book. Plus there are other things you can do to this page such as styling the text with Cascading Style Sheets and making a template of the site. These features and more are discussed in the book's project site at www.stockimagenation.com. So get started!

MATERIALS NEEDED
background.jpg, logo.gif, body.txt, spacer.gif, thumb1.jpg, and thumb2.jpg

TIME REQUIRED
30 minutes

Test Tutorial
» Making the Banner Shape in Fireworks

In this tutorial you make a custom shape that you later place an image inside of. The top banner or header for this Web site has a curve cut out of the rectangle to match the curve of the logo.

1. **Copy the ConfidenceTest folder from this book's CD-ROM to your hard drive.**
   Windows users need to unlock the files. Right-click, select Properties, deselect read-only, and close.

2. **Open Fireworks and choose File→New.**

3. **Type** 770 **in the Width field and** 200 **in the Height field.**
   The Resolution is probably already set at 72. But if it isn't, change it to 72.

4. **Click White to select it as the canvas color.**

5. **Click OK.**
   The document is a little larger than you need it to allow some working room. Because you are designing this Web page for a monitor resolution of 800x600, the top banner and logo should not exceed 760 pixels.

6. **Click the Rectangle tool.**

7. **Draw a rectangle any size in the document window.**
   Don't worry about the size; you change that next.

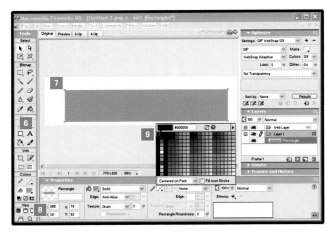

8. **From the Property inspector, change the width (W:) to** 655 **and the height (H:) to** 131. **Press Enter (Return) on your keyboard. Move onto the canvas if it's no longer there.**
   The fill and stroke color you see depend on your previous settings. If you don't see a stroke (a line around the rectangle), proceed to step 9. If you do see one, skip to step 10.

9. **Click the color box for the stroke (pencil icon in the Property inspector) and click a black swatch.**
   The actual color doesn't really matter because you are only using it so you can see the outline when you remove the fill color.

10. **Click the Fill color box and select the red circle with a slash in it to remove the fill.**

11. **Choose File→Import. Navigate to the ConfidenceTest folder you saved to your hard drive and open the source folder. Select** logo.gif **and click Open.**

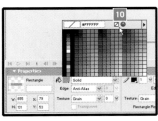

12. **Click in the document window.**
    You see a little two-cornered symbol in place of the cursor; click to place the image.

13. **Move the rectangle to the right and position the logo to the left.**
    It's okay if the rectangle goes off the canvas for now. You are going to work on the left side of the rectangle only.

14. **Select the Ellipse tool.**
    To access the Ellipse tool, click the little arrow below the Rectangle tool and choose Ellipse tool from the fly-out menu.

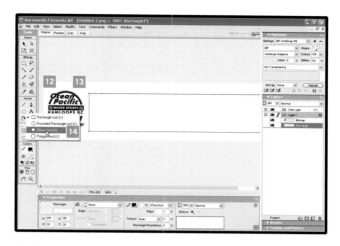

15. **Draw an ellipse of any size.**

16. **In the Property inspector, change the width (W) to** 120 **and the height (H) to** 137. **Press Enter (Return).**
    The logo was used simply to determine the size of the ellipse. If you move the ellipse you just resized over the logo it fits pretty close. You want the same curve as the logo to cut it out of the rectangle shape.

17. **Place half the ellipse over the rectangle.**

18. **The ellipse is still selected. Press the Shift key and click the rectangle to select both objects.**

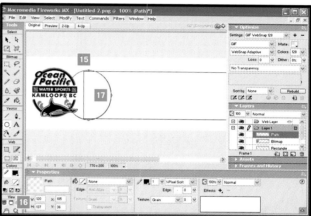

19. **Choose Modify→Combine Paths→Punch.**
    You are left with a shape that contours the logo shape.

20. **Choose File→Save As. Name your document** header.png **and navigate to stockimagenation/source files folder. Save your document.**
    A copy is saved in the source folder of ConfidenceTest_final folder, if you'd rather not save. You can leave this file open if you are proceeding to the next tutorial.

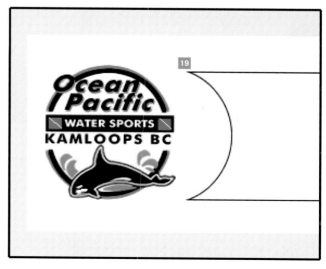

Test Tutorial
» Placing an Image Inside a Custom Shape

In this tutorial, you place an image inside of the shape you made in the previous tutorial. The image conforms to the shape. The image used is a composite, which you learn how to make in Session 2.

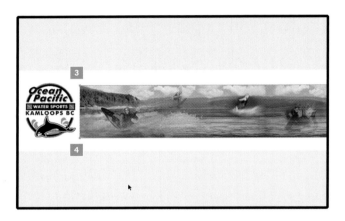

1. **Open** header.png **from the ConfidenceTest_final/source folder if you closed it.**

2. **Choose File→Import and navigate to the ConfidenceTest folder on this book's CD-ROM. Open the images folder and select** background.jpg. **Click Open.**

3. **Click in the document window.**
   You see a little two-cornered symbol; click to place the image.

4. **Move the image over the custom shape you just made.**
   When you imported the active tool automatically changed to the Pointer tool, allowing you to position the image without first selecting the Pointer tool.

5. **Choose Edit→Cut.**
   The image disappears, but don't worry about it; it's stored in memory.

6. **Select the rectangle.**

7. **Choose Edit→Paste Inside.**
   Your image is now placed inside the rectangle.

8. **Select the image.**
   Notice the cloverleaf symbol in the center. This shows that you have an image placed (or masked by the shape). Click and drag on the cloverleaf to see how you can re-position the image if you wanted to. Just be sure to put it back in place when you are done practicing.

9. Click the Effects button (+) in the Property inspector and select Shadow and Glow→Drop Shadow.

10. In the dialog box that opens use the default values. Click anywhere in the document to activate the effect.

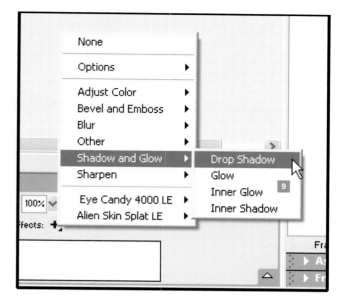

11. Move the shape next to the logo. Line it up so the fin goes into the shape area just a little.

12. Save and leave this document open for the next tutorial.

Test Tutorial

» Exporting the Banner Images

In this tutorial you slice the banner into two images. You then optimize the images to reduce the file size and export them for placement in a Dreamweaver layout.

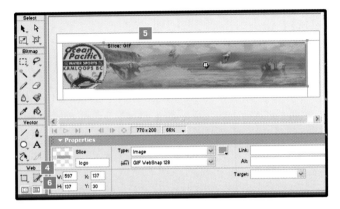

1. **Right-click (Control-click) the logo.**

2. **From the contextual menu, choose Insert Slice.**
   Notice the red lines added to your document. Fireworks places these lines that show where additional slices are made automatically on export (if you use this option). But this feature normally produces too many slices.

3. **Change the Slice name to logo.**
   When the slice is selected, you see a Slice field in the Property inspector. Highlight the default slice name and type **logo**.

4. **Select the Slice tool.**

5. **Draw a slice over the remaining part of the banner.**
   To draw, place your cursor next to the right side and top of the logo slice and drag to cover the rest of the banner.

6. **Notice the height of your slice in the Property inspector. It should be 137, the same as the logo. If it isn't, change the number and press Enter (Return).**

7. **Click the Expander arrow to open the Optimize panel if it isn't open already.**

8. **Select JPEG from the Export File Format list.**
   JPEG was selected because it's the best format to use for a photo with a lot of colors.

9. **Change the Quality to 70.**
   To change the Quality you can either highlight the number and type a new one or click the slider and drag to the desired number.

10. **Select the logo slice. In the Optimize panel change the Export File Format to GIF.**
    A GIF format was chosen because GIF is best for areas of flat color and for images with 256 or less colors in them. There is a tiny bit of the image in this slice but the optimization difference with the JPEG image next to it won't be noticeable.

11. **Change the number of colors to 128.**

12. **Choose File→Export.**

13. **Click the Save In arrow and navigate to the ConfidenceTest/site/images folder. Select it.**

14. **Click the arrow for Save as Type and choose Images Only.**
    You can export the entire table from Fireworks using the HTML and Images option but that isn't what you want to do here. You want to use the images only to place into a Dreamweaver layout.

15. **Click Include Areas without Slices to uncheck it.**
    The Export dialog box should look like this image.

16. **Click Save.**

Exporting Images for a Site

Whenever you export images for a site, export them into the root folder of the site. For instance, this site's name is ConfidenceTest. Also make a folder named Source at the same level as the site to save your Fireworks files into. The reason you save the source files at the same level as the site folder is so when you define the site in Dreamweaver, the source files won't show in the Assets panel and they won't automatically be uploaded when you upload the site. The reason you export directly into a folder in the root folder is to support editing Fireworks files directly from Dreamweaver. When you export, Fireworks writes a note that tells Dreamweaver where to find the source file. If you move it, you have to locate the file yourself. Storing the source files with the root just makes finding your images easier.

Test Tutorial
» Setting Up the Home Page in Dreamweaver

In this tutorial, you get the home page ready for its images and text. You set up the page properties and define the Dreamweaver site.

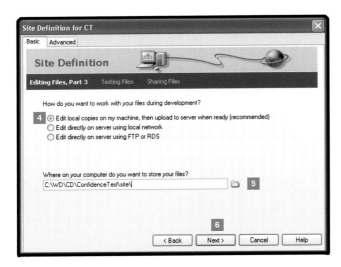

1. **Open Dreamweaver and choose Site→New Site. Click the Basic tab if it isn't already.**

2. **Enter** CT **for the site name and click Next.**

3. **In the Site Definition dialog box, check "No, I do not want to use a server technology" and click Next.**
   You set up a server technology later in this book.

4. **Select "Edit local copies on my machine, then upload to server when ready (recommended)" option.**

5. **Click the yellow folder and navigate to your ConfidenceTest folder. Choose site and click Select.**

6. **Click the Next button.**

7. **Click the arrow for the "How do you connect to your remote server" and select None. Click Next.**

8. **Click Done.**

9. **Choose File→New. Select General, Basic Page, and then click Create. Choose Modify→Page Properties.**

10. **Type** Ocean Pacific **for the document title.**

11. **Click the color box next to Background and click the white swatch.**
    This sets the background color of the entire document.

12. **Type** 0 **for all four margin fields.**

13. **Click OK.**

14. **Choose File→Save As. Save it in the site folder and name it** index.htm.
    This name is the document name, not the title of the page. You set up the title in Page properties.

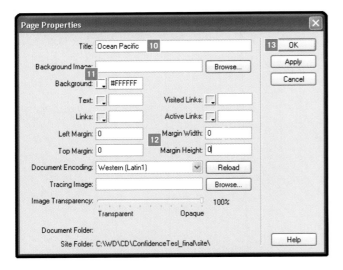

Test Tutorial

» Adding the Banner Images to the First Table

In this tutorial, you add the top logo and banner. You use two tables to control the layout's positioning. Modular tables make it easier to update the information and help the site load faster in a browser. The complete contents of a table have to load before the table renders. By using smaller tables, the users see your content faster.

1. **Click in the document window.**

2. **Click the Insert Table icon.**

3. **Fill in the following values in the Insert Table dialog box:**
   Rows: 1   Border: 0
   Columns: 2   Cell Padding: 0
   Width: 730 pixels   Cell Spacing: 0

4. **Click OK.**

5. **Click inside the first cell (left side) of the table.**

6. **Click the Insert Image icon in the Insert panel.**

7. **Navigate to the ConfidenceTest/site/images folder and select** logo.gif.

8. **Click OK.**

9. **Select the logo image. Press the right arrow key then the Tab key.**
   This places your cursor in the second column. You could have clicked it, but it probably collapsed. By doing it this way, you are assured of being in the correct column.

10. **Click the Insert Image icon and navigate to the ConfidenceTest/site/images folder. Select** banner.jpg.

11. **Click OK.**
    Notice that there is a whitespace between the logo and the banner. This happened because the table is larger than the images and there is extra space.

12. **Click the logo and press the left arrow key to place the cursor in front of the logo image.**

13. **Click the Insert Image icon and navigate to the ConfidenceTest/site/images folder. Select** spacer.gif.

14. **Type** 13 **in the width (W) field in the Property inspector and click anywhere in the document.**
    This is a transparent GIF spacer. It is 1 pixel by 1 pixel. By changing the width the image stretched to the necessary size. Notice now that the space between the images has also closed up.

15. **Choose File→Save.**

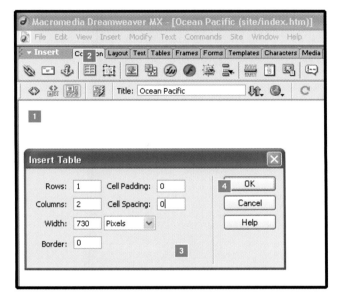

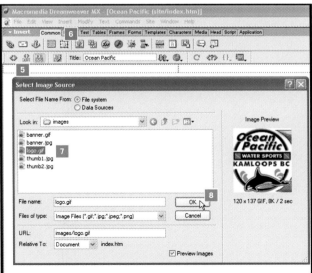

Test Tutorial

» Adding the Navigation Bar

In this tutorial, you add another table to hold the navigation bar for the site's main navigation.

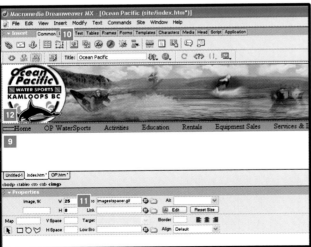

1. **Select the banner image and press the right arrow key.**
   This places your cursor outside the first table.

2. **Click the Insert Table icon and use these values:**
   Rows: 1
   Columns: 1
   Width: 730 pixels
   Border: 1
   Cell Padding: 0
   Cell Spacing: 0

3. **Click OK.**

4. **In the Property inspector, type #CC0000 in the Brdr Color field.**

5. **Click inside the table and select the `<table>` tag in the Tag Selector at the bottom of the document window.**

6. **Type #0AA794 in the Bg field in the Property inspector. It's the Bg with a color box next to it.**
   You just made a navigation bar without using an image. Next you add some text to use as links.

7. **Click inside the new table to place your cursor.**

8. **Type Home, OP WaterSports, Activities, Education, Rentals, Equipment Sales, Services & Info.**

9. **Place your cursor in front of the word *home*.**
   The number in the image shows where to place your cursor but the image shows the results after the image has been inserted.

10. **Click the Insert Image icon and navigate to the spacer.gif image. Open it.**

11. **Change the width of the spacer to 25.**

12. **Repeat steps 9-11 in front of each link name. Links are added later.**
    A faster way is to select the 25x1 spacer you placed in front of home and then paste it (Ctrl+V / Option+V) in front of each link name.

Test Tutorial

» Adding the Table for the Body Content

In this tutorial, you add another table to hold the body content and a couple more images.

1. **Place your cursor outside the last table.**
   If you aren't sure the cursor is in the correct place, then click inside the table and then press the Tab key.

2. **Click the Insert Table icon and use these values:**
   Rows: 1
   Columns: 1
   Width: 730 pixels
   Border: 0
   Cell Padding: 0
   Cell Spacing: 0

3. **Click OK.**

4. **Choose File→Open and navigate to the ConfidenceTest/site/images folder. Select** body.txt.

5. **Choose Edit→Select All (Ctrl+A / Option+A), and then Edit→Copy (Ctrl+C / Option+C).**

6. **Close the text document.**

7. **Place your cursor in the body table and choose Edit→Paste (Ctrl+V / Option+V).**

8. **Place your cursor in front of the word** *exhilarating* **and click the Insert Image icon.**

9. **Navigate to the ConfidenceTest/site/images folder. Select** thumb1.jpg **and click Open.**

10. **Place your cursor in front of the sentence,** *Where else . . .* **and click the Insert Image icon.**

11. **Navigate to the ConfidenceTest/site/images folder. Select** thumb2.jpg **and click Open.**
    It looks pretty bad right now but don't worry about it; you fix it in the following tutorial.

12. **Choose File→Save.**

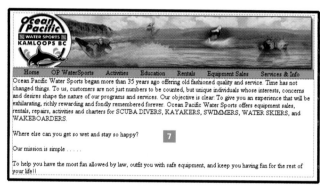

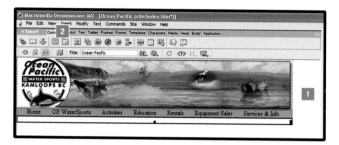

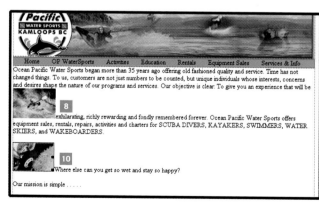

Test Tutorial

» Aligning the Small Images and Adding Flash Text

In this tutorial, you align the images in the body so they look better. You also add some more secondary navigation on the bottom of the page. You don't always have to make things directly in Flash to add a bit of "Flash" to your page. In this tutorial, you add a line of Flash text with a rollover right from Dreamweaver.

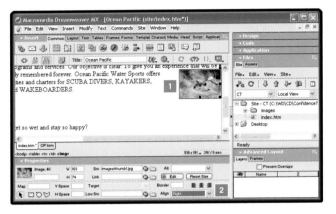

1. **Select the first image in the body.**

2. **In the Property inspector. Click the arrow for the Align field and select Right.**
   The image shows the picture moved already. In order to show the right alignment in the Property inspector, I had to select it, which moved the image.

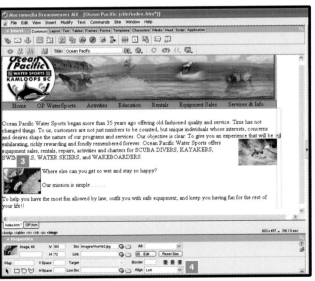

3. **Select the second image.**

4. **In the Property inspector, click the arrow for the Align field and select Left.**

5. **Place your cursor at the end of the body text and press Enter (Return).**

6. **Type** Feedback I Our Staff I Facilities I FAQ I Contact US.

7. **Select the entire line you just typed.**

8. **In the Property inspector, click the Align Center icon.**

9. **Highlight the word *Feedback*.**

10. **In the Link field of the Property inspector, type** javascript:;.
    This is a null link. You replace it with a real one when you finish the site or know the link.

11. **Repeat steps 9 and 10 for the rest of the bottom links.**
    Instead of typing **javascript:;** each time, you can click the drop-down menu for the link field and select it there.

12. **Click anywhere inside the body (don't select an image).**

13. **Click the** `<table>` **tag to select the table.**

14. **In the Property inspector, type** 25 **in the CellPad field.**
    You just added space around the edges of the entire body table. This removes the text and the images from the edges.

15. **Click at the end of the last line of body text and press Enter (Return).**

16. **Click the Center Align button in the Property Inspector.**

17. **In the Insert panel, click the Media category tab.**

18. **Click the Flash Text icon.**

19. **The Insert Flash Text dialog box opens; enter these values:**
    Font: Whatever you like (Staccato222 BT was used here)
    Size: 30 or whatever size is good for your font
    Color: #6699CC
    Rollover Color: #99CC99
    Test: Come On In The Waters Fine
    Link: javascript:;
    Bg Color: click the color box and select white
    Save As: comeonin

20. **Click OK.**

21. **Select the text and click the Edit button in the Property inspector. Change the word Water to Water's and click OK.**

22. **Choose File→Save.**

23. **Choose File→Preview in Browser.**
    View the results in your browser.

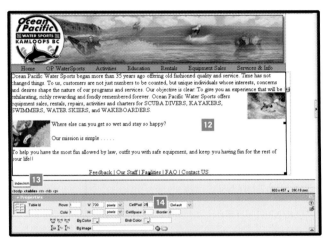

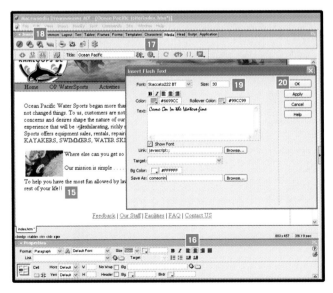

Part I
Course Setup

Web Design Basics

Web Design Overview

What is the role of a Web designer? Given the scope of such projects, from large-scale, corporate e-commerce sites to single-page, personal vanity sites, the skills, tasks, and tools of the Web designer can vary greatly. In some cases, the designer focuses on only one aspect of a project, for example, the graphic look and feel of the layout; in others, many hats are worn and the designer is responsible for several parts of the project, or even the entire process.

This book assumes that you are a one-person shop and wear all the hats. You're the person who sells the client the project, gathers the content, documents the goals and specifications of the project, creates graphics and layouts of pages, builds or obtains a database, and writes the code for both the front and back end. You get the client to sign off on each milestone and hold their hand as they waffle about functionality or nitpick about a single pixel of white space (may you never encounter this client!). You are also the one who readies the site for deployment, transfers it to a Web server, and even registers it with search engines to make the site easier to find online. In other words, you need to know a lot about the Web and have an expert set of software skills, right?

Well, yes, but I understand that you might be new to Web design or perhaps you've never tried Macromedia Fireworks or Dreamweaver. So I'm with you as you step through each part of the process. By the end of the book (and the project) you *will* know a lot and you *will* have an extensive set of skills you can use in your own projects to design graphics, develop code, and create very cool functionality.

So, where do you start? What are the steps to creating a Web site, whether personal or commercial? How do you know what software to use, where to host a site? If you're doing commercial work, what do you charge for your services? How do you know you are meeting your client's needs? How do you know when a project is a success? How do you make decisions about design, code, and technology?

When learning Web design and development, it's easy to be overwhelmed by the sheer amount of knowledge it takes to complete a project, but keep in mind that you can always hire others to help you with the tasks you don't know how to do yourself. To understand what you can do and what you cannot, each project begins by discussing the planning stage.

Project Planning and Web Design

Planning is the key to efficient workflow and to minimizing the need to revise any portion of a Web site project. Planning determines the site's success, whether it is a client's project or your own personal site. Resist the urge to skip over this part (and dive into the tutorials); careful planning can make the difference in how smoothly your project goes as well as how successful the resulting site is. Start by identifying and addressing the factors that affect a Web site.

Effective Web design results in the successful communication of a message to an intended audience. This seems like a simple and obvious observation, but when you consider that your site's message is one of many out there on the Web, how do you get the message—and your site—out? The key to successful design is to get your audience's attention and keep it long enough to get the desired response. Start by asking and answering these questions:

» What's the message? What do you want to say?

» Who cares and why? In other words, who is your audience and why will they come to your site?

» What is the desired audience response? What would you like your audience to do as a result of your message or content?

Your answers are the first step in planning your project, and with them, you are well on your way to designing an effective Web site.

What's the Message?

When a visitor comes to your site, he or she needs to be able to quickly recognize your message, starting with the nature of your site. What is the purpose of your site? Which of the three major categories does your project belong to?

» Is it informational or educational? This type of site could be a university, a non-profit organization, governmental, political, or even a personal site.

» Does it intend to entertain? The category can include magazine or e-zine sites, movie or music sites, hobby sites, clubs or communities, and personal pages.

» Will it market, sell, or persuade visitors? Arguably the most common site online seeks to sell something — even if it is only a point of view. This category includes the widest range of sites, from businesses to personal resumes.

Create a statement of purpose. You don't have to make it a lengthy process, just a sentence or two will do. The project site for this book is a fictitious company named *stockimagenation*, a business that sells digital imagery, including still and motion graphics, audio, and typographical fonts.

The mission statement for the stockimagenation site is: Stockimagenation seeks to provide high quality, affordable digital photographs, videos, audio, and typographical resources to a typically professional creative via downloadable files or on CD-ROM that are easily located, reviewed, and efficiently purchased.

Who Cares and Why?

So you have a message—who cares and why? This is where you define your audience by painting a picture of who they are, why they will come to your site, and why they need or want to know the information you are presenting. The means and methods of gathering and defining this information can vary. Large corporations might conduct focus groups; a "mom and pop" operation might ask existing customers or study the competition's site. As the designer, you might be able to get information from a client's existing collateral materials, such as brochures, business cards, and product packaging. For any project, you should identify the nature of your audience and the reasons why they would want to learn more about your message. Keep in mind that age, gender, and financial and geographical demographics affect the visual and functional design of a Web site as much as they would in a physical store. A clear understanding of the goals of your audience helps you organize the content of your site to meet their needs.

The stockimagenation site sells digital and physical product to creative professionals. The audience is technologically savvy, secure in purchasing online, and is likely shopping with a business account or credit card. They will want efficient means to locate, review, and purchase content by either downloading digital files or through the shipment of a CD-ROM.

Getting the Right Response

Now that you've determined your message and defined the audience, what do you want the visitor to do when he or she visits your site? Pin down what it is you want your site visitor to do and provide functionality to help them quickly meet their goals. Organize the site in easily understood sections. Build defined page regions for content and keep the regions consistent. Use visual clues to teach the visitor how to find content. Help the visitor navigate the site, understand where he or she is within the site, and provide a clear call to action. Is the visitor searching for a product? Make it easy to find and even easier to buy. Minimize the number of clicks it takes to meet a goal but keep it easy to make a decision—a task that is far harder to do successfully than it might seem.

You should consider site architecture, page layout, and navigational issues when considering how to get the response you want.

Site Architecture

A major step in designing your site starts with organizing its content into logical chunks or sections. Store organized content in folders for each section. Later, you'll develop navigation that incorporates the sections you've chosen. Obviously, the more content you have, the greater the need for organization and structure. A flow chart or site map is a useful step in the process of creating site structures, whether you use a pencil and paper to create it or purchase a computer program that helps you build a graphical representation.

Flowcharts and site maps help you determine the type of navigation you use for the site. There are several types of charting you can create. A site map displays the sections of the site; a functional flowchart indicates visitor action and site reaction. For large corporate sites, site maps and flowcharts are part of complex site requirements documentation; for smaller projects, just a site map might work.

Page Layout

To determine placement of content in your site pages, develop specific regions for specific types of content. First determine the parts of your page, for example, check out this layout.

The example may be the final page design or may simply diagram the regions required by the content. Start simple, perhaps with a pencil and paper, working small-scale and drawing quick thumbnail sketches of potential layout. When your designs reflect the needs of your project, open a Web graphics program like Macromedia Fireworks MX and re-create the layouts at a usable scale. Document key pages required by your project. The documentation and planning of page layout for a site is sometimes called a storyboard.

Remember to keep page regions consistent, both in location and in usage. This doesn't mean that page layouts cannot change within the site because they often do, typically when the type of content that you need to display changes. For example, the stockimagenation site's page layout changes drastically when a visitor clicks a link to display the details of any digital asset, but all catalogs use the same page layout.

Navigation

As a Web designer, your toughest job is to design effective navigation for your site. After you organize your content and set the goals of your site, you plan its navigation. After all, the content isn't very useful if the site visitor cannot find it! To a great extent, the navigation method you use should reflect the nature of your content and the type of actions that your visitors want to take. There are several models of navigation:

» **Linear.** Linear navigation moves from point A to point B to point C. To get back to point A from point C, you must first go back to point B. The most basic form of linear navigation uses the Forward and Back buttons of a Web browser.

» **Hub and Spoke.** This type of navigation is radial, with a clearly defined center. To get to the "arms" or "branches" of the site sections, the visitor must return to the center. A good example of this type of site is a portal or community-based site such as Yahoo's GeoCities (http://geocities.yahoo.com). The user can click to find member pages through directories, traveling outward along one "spoke" of the community. But to go to a different type community, the visitor must return to the center or "hub" to select a new spoke. "Breadcrumb" navigation is typically used to help the visitors keep their bearings within a site; as the visitor travels farther outward, the trail created grows, adding a new link at the end with each click.

» **Hierarchical.** The most commonly used navigational method today is hierarchical and is designed to teach the site visitor about the relationship of content to site sections through the use of color, typography, or sizing of link options. The menu system is available on all pages within a site, offering the visitor access to every section of the site from any page. In its most simple form, this type of system is created through the use of a main set of navigation links that are available on every page and a sub-set of links that are displayed for each section. More complex systems offer access to many levels of a site from all pages. "Drill-down" accessibility to content within sections is useful because it provides the site visitor with an abundance of information, understanding about the structure of the site, and also saves valuable real estate on the site's pages.

Concept and Design

Armed with documented information about your audience, goals, content structure and organization, and a clear idea of the type of navigation and page regions you'll need, it's time to develop a look and feel for your design. Graphic design is a creative process and it should support your site and convey your message to site visitors. The concept phase of the design explores the use of metaphor, color, and typography to set a mood for the site. For example, reserved colors, tabbed navigation, and classic typography is better suited for a bank's site than highly saturated color, graphics intensive image map navigation, and the use of comic or script fonts.

Try a search online for sites that have the same message or purpose as your project. You're likely to find that similar sites share similar themes, navigation methods, and colors schemes. Should you follow the pack? Of course not—you want to stand out, right? But keep in mind that standing out because your design is perfect and totally conveys your message is different than standing out because you used every color or font you had and your site looks like a neon sign! Use your research to focus your design.

Color

The overall intensity of color (saturation), contrast of light to dark (value), and selection of colors (harmonies or schemes) can be used to support a metaphor, to set a mood or tone for the site, and to control the "read" of the site interface and content.

There are many programs available designed just for creating color themes.

>> **ColorSchemer** (Windows only) on the CD or download from http://colorschemer.com/ (tutorial on the CD).

>> **ColorWrite** (all platforms) on the CD or download from www.adaptiveview.com/cw/download.html.

Site Requirements

Site requirements provide a means by which you can measure the success of the finished project. Requirements document the particulars of how and what is designed, developed, and deployed. Typically, in the scenario of the larger company or corporate client, site requirements are defined in-house, but for smaller businesses (or for your own project), defining the requirements becomes your job (even if the client doesn't initially expect it).

For a small project, you might be able to jot these down on a single sheet of paper; for larger projects, requirements can be a hefty, hundred-page document detailing every little aspect of design, development, and deployment.

Why bother? The answer is easy—when you have documented requirements, it is possible to know when you have met them. When nothing is written down, a project can lose focus, resulting in feature creep (increasing development time and cost). As an independent designer/developer, you want the requirements carefully specified, including as much detail as possible about the functionality required to complete the project. In some cases, you use information gathered to determine the nature and scope of a project, considering the following:

» Content

» Audience

» Design considerations

» Functionality

When determining methods for completing a project, you might also have to consider your budget, the timeline, your resources, and the technology used.

Content

One of the first (and often most difficult) tasks to complete is obtaining the content from the client. Determining the content gives you a place to start your project requirements. Reviewing the content allows you to decide site flow, navigation, and functional needs. When writing requirements and project contracts, be sure to include milestones that set dates for receiving content, including text copy, collateral graphics, existing code, and even databases. Specify formats for digital files you will need from the client. Work with your client to develop a coherent organization of the content based on what the client wants to deliver and what the audience will expect to find.

Audience

The next step in the planning process is to define the target audience. From the site content, you can extract a base of information about the average user. Client collateral, such as brochures, literature, and existing Web content can provide a starting point to learn more about the client or company's business and target audience. Ask your client to provide details about their customers to help fill in a profile of who the site visitor is likely to be. Although large corporations generally use market research obtained through companies that specialize in creating focus groups to gather feedback, a "mom-and-pop" site might simply query their existing customers, either through personal interaction or through an online survey. The more information you can get about the needs of the potential site visitor, the easier it will be to design layouts, navigation, and functionality to make the site a success.

Here are some points to consider when determining audience and some simple statements about the stockimagenation site's audience:

» *User Goals:* What is the visitor's purpose for coming to the site? What is he or she looking for? Are the visitors looking to be entertained or are they shopping? Are they trying to gain information?

Stockimagenation: The typical user comes to the site with a purpose. He or she is searching for an image, video clip, audio file, or font for use in a print, Web, or other project. They will want a search option and a catalog of assets. They may need one or many items and will want to review the items before purchase.

» *Demographics:* Are they young or old? Is the average visitor male or female? Are they employed? Do they spend a lot of money? Are they well educated? Do they all speak English or some other language or both?

Stockimagenation: The user is typically older than 18 and can be male or female. He or she is likely to have a high school or better education. The average customer speaks and reads English.

» *Technology Base:* Is the average user surfing from home? Do they have a fast connection to the Internet? Which computer platforms will they likely use? What is the average resolution and color-depth of their computer monitor? Is your average visitor "computer-savvy"? Do they feel comfortable shopping online?

Stockimagenation: Our average user is surfing from a home office or a company or corporation. He or she has a fast connection (DSL or T1 line). There is a higher than average percentage of Macintosh users because that platform is often used by print designers. Their computers are probably newer and faster than the average. The user monitor is better than average, with a higher resolution and greater color-depth. Because the users are technically savvy, their monitors will likely have a greater color depth and they will be able to set their computers to make use of it. They will expect to see the product quickly, efficiently, and at its best. They will be comfortable providing a credit card for purchases because they will know how to tell whether a site is digitally secure.

Design Considerations

Designing the look and feel of a Web site depends upon many factors. The client might come to you with a vision of how the new site should look, from color preferences to navigational methods. Sometimes it's hard for your clients to convey their vision to you but these same clients will be able to tell you what they *don't like* after you've finished! To avoid this inefficient method of design, try providing the clients with a useful worksheet that asks questions about their preferences, from sites they like and why to sites they don't and why not. Find out what their goals, demographics, and technology base are. They are, after all, the first member of the site's audience.

When creating the specifications for a design, here are some things to consider:

» Branding

» Size (pages, text, images)

» Color, value, and composition

» Connection speeds

» Target browsers

Branding

In many cases, a company has existing branding, from logos to specific color combinations. Large corporations often have rules about how the logo and colors can and cannot be used. For smaller projects, you may find that you are expected to create a logo and determine color choices—tempered, of course, by client preferences and audience feedback.

Logos are generally created with graphic software that makes use of *vectors*, mathematically defined lines and fills that are not resolution-dependent like a photograph. This is important because the file might be used in high-resolution projects such as a printed brochure and in low-resolution projects, such as a Web site. Good programs for designing a logo include Macromedia Freehand, Fireworks, or Adobe Illustrator. The stockimagenation logo was built with Fireworks MX.

Size

Designing for the Web has its challenges, especially if you come from a print background or have no graphic background. When you create a design for a printed project, every instance of that project looks the same no matter who sees it. The paper is always the same size. The colors are always the same colors. The typography is always the font you specified and always the same size. With Web design, your site can vary from user to user because there are so many variables, such as monitor resolution, color depth, and gamma settings. Even the user's computer platform and browser choices affect your designs. Size is an important factor for your project's page width, text size, and overall image sizes. All of these elements are affected by:

» The resolution, color depth, and gamma settings of the visitor's monitor.

» The type and version of the visitor's Web browser.

» The overall width preference of the visitor's Web browser.

» The visitors' individual settings for text sizes in their browser.

Browser and Platform Considerations

It's important to know before you begin which browsers need to be supported and tested on. Knowing which version browsers your site needs to look good in can alter your bid amount drastically. If you don't factor in the extra design time for workarounds, you take the loss or risk having an unhappy client. You can avoid many pitfalls and hassles by dealing with these types of issues before you begin any work.

For Web design, navigation is of utmost importance. If the users can't find what they are looking for, they will simply leave and check somewhere else. Another thing that print designers need to be conscious of is to use smaller columns of text for viewing. The stockimagenation site supports Netscape 4.79 and higher and IE6.

Hosting Solutions

The host you decide on is determined by your needs. Later in this book you see how to work with Crystaltech, the hosting company for stockimagenation. It gives you a feel for how to work with a host. Some of the things to consider when choosing a host include:

» How much traffic is anticipated (bandwidth requirements)

» Level of service needed (secure, ColdFusion MX server)

» Environment recommended by programmer (Windows NT or Unix)

» Site traffic reporting capabilities

<NOTE>

If you need to bring in outside help, do it now before you present your plan and bid. You need to factor in the cost of the services as well as know that the service you require can be done in the timeframe you outline for the client. If you wait, the person/firm may not be available and it may kill your budget if you "guessed" wrong.

Present the Plan and Contract

Before you start any design work other than a comp (sample of the page look and feel), put what you will do in writing. Be very specific about who is responsible for what and when the client is supposed to provide content is spelled out. Determine who is going to update the site. How many pages are needed, what features, what technologies are needed? Spell out what each deadline is and when payments are due. It's a good idea to get one third or one half of the payment up front. Much of your work will be done in the planning stages.

» Include approval stages. At each stage have the client sign off on it. Additional changes after approval results in increased cost. But that doesn't mean that additional features can't be added that were not in the original contract or addendums.

» Be specific; list the pages you are developing, and what will be included. Who does the copywriting; who does the proofreading?

» List the features the site will include such as illustrations, photos, animated GIFs, forms, rollovers, e-commerce, Java, JavaScript, database, or Flash. Get estimates from a specialist if you need to include a feature you can't create.

» Discuss eventualities ahead of time. For instance, when a *"change order"* comes through, and it almost always will, how will you charge? By the hour; per page? The client will normally think of a page or even section they want added.

» Have a design and production schedule. Allow time to test in various browsers and platforms. If you come from a print background, you'll be tempted to use the time you know it would take to do a print piece. Triple it for Web work; there are many more variables involved.

» Include deadlines for client to provide materials. Have a payment schedule.

» Plan for maintenance. If you do the maintenance, work out a fee structure. If you need to train their staff, budget in a consulting fee.

There are many great articles that deal with Internet law and contracts at www.ivanhoffman.com. Ivan is an attorney who specializes in Internet law.

Creating a Design Comp

Once you have a solid plan and a contract, you are ready to start your design. You need to develop your images and gather your assets first. You should have an idea of the type of navigation you are going to use from the planning stages. Because you are using Fireworks, you can do your comps right in it. Set up your document to the size of the site you are building. Because the current standard is 800 x 600 I recommend doing your homepage layout at 760x. Some points to consider when doing the design draft are:

» Keep all navigation and important things above the scroll or fold. You don't want people to have to scroll to know what the site is about.

» Avoid clutter.

» Use plenty of white space.

» Be aware of the focus; guide the users eye to the important features. They will begin scanning at the top left (that's why logos and branding appear here).

» Build for the future; design it so that it's easy to add categories.

» Limit the top level navigation to only the most core features of the site. The second level can have additional links.

» Use short names for the navigational links.

» Build a site map.

You most likely need to present the client with a couple rounds of design comps. For first round have three to five different options of the home page design only. Then get the client's feedback. The client will frequently like things from more than one design. By round three, the client should have settled on the design and sign off. Of course it doesn't always work out this way, but you have to determine how many rounds is too much.

Get the client's signature approval. A good way to do this is to make three copies of each major template page you are going to do and have the client sign two copies of each page. This way they and you have a viewable record of what was agreed upon.

You might even want to include an escape for the client and yourself at this point in the contract. If the client doesn't like anything you do and he or you wants to end the relationship, you need a provision in the contract. How will you be paid for the work you've done?

Project Overview

The Complete Course Project

Web Design Complete Course is written for the aspiring Web designer. It looks at the big picture and yet offers insight into using a specific tool when necessary. The goal of the book is to discuss the concepts and techniques of building a Web site, including planning, graphic design, code and content development, and deployment of a project, while offering practical and sound advice for using Macromedia Fireworks MX and Dreamweaver MX—industry standards for Web design.

You create the images needed for this site's design and lay it out in Dreamweaver. You add drop-down type menus, a design that doesn't fit "in the box" for that extra punch, and add a search engine to the site. You develop a dynamic site with an image catalog that can be searched, display the purchase info for individual images, and then add the capability to purchase the product. The browsers supported and tested in this book are Netscape 4.79, Internet Explorer 6, and Netscape 7.

Software Used

Fireworks MX is an image editor that you use to create, optimize, and export images. You can download a free, fully functional 30-day demo from www.macromedia.com. Installation instructions are on the Macromedia Web site.

Dreamweaver MX is a professional layout editor that you use to assemble your Web site. You can download a free, fully functional 30-day demo from www.macromedia.com. There are installation instructions on the Macromedia Web site.

ColdFusion MX is what you use to add *server-side scripting*—application logic that runs on the server before a page is returned to the user's Web browser. This enables you to build pages with dynamic or data-driven content.

Organize Your Files

On the CD with this book, you'll find a stockimagenation_site_start folder. You copy this to your hard drive and rename it stockimagenation. From here you can access new files needed for each session from the sessions folder on the CD when needed. Each session has a starter_files folder. In it is the `html` folder of the site. You can use these starter files at any time by dropping them into your defined root folder (stockimagenation). If you'd rather not overwrite your working folder but want to use a starter file (to troubleshoot), you can copy the starter file to your hard drive and define a new site (Session 8 tells you how to define a site). The stockimagenation_site folder contains the completed site files. The site is also live online at www.stockimagenation.com. There are a few working links in the menus. You can also use the search field with these words: flower, bird, turtle, mountain, shell.

Copy Files from the CD

By default, Windows makes files copied from a CD to your hard drive read-only, which means you can't edit or change these files. Once you copy them to your hard drive you can right-click and select Properties. Uncheck the read-only option.

When using Dreamweaver you can use the Site panel to drag files into your root. At the bottom of the root folder files, you see the rest of the files on your computer. Navigate to the CD and drag the files, into your root folder. The files are not locked using this method.

System Requirements for Windows 98, Windows 2000, Windows NT, Windows Me, or Windows XP

» PC with a Pentium III class III or 4 or better processor

» Version 4.0 or later of Netscape Navigator or Microsoft Internet Explorer

» At least 64MB of total RAM installed on your computer, 128MB recommended

» At least 280MB of free hard drive space

» A 256-color monitor with at least 800 x 600 resolution and a 16-bit video card

» A CD-ROM drive

System Requirements for Macintosh

» Macintosh OS computer with a G3 or G4 PowerPC processor running OS 9.1, OS 9.2, or OS X

» Mac OS Runtime for Java (MRJ) 2.2 or above (included on the Dreamweaver MX CD)

» Version 4.0 or later of Netscape Navigator or Microsoft Internet Explorer

» At least 96MB of total RAM installed on your computer, 128MB recommended

» At least 320MB of free hard drive space

» A 256-color monitor with at least 800 x 600 resolution and a 16-bit video card

» A CD-ROM drive

System Recommendations

Those are the minimum requirements that Macromedia lists. But here are real-world recommendations:

» Windows NT is about to be discontinued. Windows 2000 cannot work well without at least 128MBs of RAM. XP needs 256, or at the very least, 192.

» Netscape is up to 4.79. There is also Netscape 6.2. Most users of Windows Me, 2000, and XP are pestered until they have the latest version. That is up to somewhere in the 6.x range at this time.

» I doubt if there are even any consumer monitors available that can only handle 256 colors. Regardless, any site designer is going to need at least 24-bit capability in order to properly see the colors that are to be displayed on the site.

» Without a CD-ROM drive, the software cannot be installed.

» The only MacOS specific issues are RAM and what the monitor can handle.

» Any legacy Mac (using a Motorola 601, 603, 604 or variant CPU) will need to be at least 200 MHz and have at least 128MBs of RAM.

» Any G3-based PowerMac should have at least 192MBs of RAM.

» Any G4-based PowerMac should have at least 256MBs of RAM.

» MacOS X-based systems should have either the system limit or a minimum of 512MBs of RAM. Most PowerBooks can only take 384MBs of RAM.

» There are no Macintosh compatible monitors that have a maximum color depth of 256 colors.

Mac and PC Differences

For the most part, Dreamweaver looks and works the same for the Windows and the Macintosh operating systems. Mac users will be pleased to know that Dreamweaver for the Mac was written for the Mac and not for Windows and ported over. Counterpart of Windows Control (Ctrl) key is the Macintosh Command key (⌘).

Counterpart of Windows Alt key is Macintosh Option (Opt) key and is also marked as ALT on all newer Mac compatible keyboards. When opening files, Windows selection button is named Select, and on the Mac it's named Open. Windows on the PC close by clicking the close box in the upper-right corner. The close box on a Mac is in the upper-left corner. The Dreamweaver Site panel is called a Site Window on the Mac.

Part II

Building the Site Imagery Using Fireworks MX

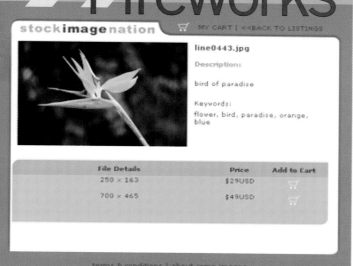

Bringing Image Assets into Fireworks

Discussion: **Image Basics**

Tutorial: **Getting Around in Fireworks**

Tutorial: **Obtaining Images from a Scanner**

Tutorial: **Obtaining Images from a Digital Camera**

Tutorial: **Importing Images from Other Applications**

About Fireworks

Fireworks was built from the ground up to be a tool to produce Web graphics. Because it was never meant for the print arena, it didn't have to be rewritten to be compatible with your needs as a Web designer. Fireworks excels at *scalable* vector graphics. This means that you can change their size without image degradation. This is especially important for logos you may want to print but more so for graphics you make for use in Flash. Most of what you do to a vector image in Fireworks is editable. When you save a file in the Fireworks native PNG format, you can open it at any time and change the properties and effects that have been applied to a vector image. You see in Session 2 that vector shapes can be used as masks (and are totally editable) and that you can apply effects even to raster (bitmap) images that remain editable. Get ready to fall in love with Fireworks. This first session shows you the Fireworks workspace briefly and then shows you how to get images from your scanner or digital camera into the Fireworks workspace.

TOOLS YOU'LL USE
File menu, scanner and digital camera options; File menu, Open and Import options

MATERIALS NEEDED
`collage.psd` and `Rose.fh10`

TIME REQUIRED
30 minutes if you haven't installed your scanner or camera software

Discussion

Image Basics

The two types of images you work with are vector and raster images. A vector object consists of paths, which are two points connected by a line. A vector graphic is generated using a mathematical process that basically says, "start a line here at x, y and draw it to a, b." Of course you don't see the calculations being made; they are all done behind the scenes. Every path has at least two points to yield a line segment; a path can be open (a line) or closed (lines connecting). It's the mathematical function that gives vectors their power.

A vector object retains its image quality no matter how big you stretch it because it simply re-calculates and redraws itself. This scalability makes vectors valuable Web objects. Vectors also give programs such as Flash their flexibility in resizing images on the fly.

Raster Images

Just in case you are coming from a vector-only world, here is a quick course in pixel-based images. Photographs are comprised of pixels, the smallest component part of a bitmapped image, also known as a raster image. Pixels are little squares of color resembling a mosaic composition, or a "grid of squares." The larger the image, the more pixels it contains. The more pixels it contains, the larger the file size is. Editing pixels involves adding, removing, or coloring individual pixels.

The pixels distinguish a bitmapped image from a vector image. Because vector objects are made up of a series of lines, they are fully scalable. Pixel images lose detail as they are scaled up because each image contains a set number of pixels. When you scale a bitmapped image up, Fireworks has to guess which pixels need to be re-sampled to "fake" the detail in the increased space. This stretching of pixels results in what is known as a "pixilated image."

Resolution

An image's resolution determines how many pixels there are per inch. The resolution of an image is determined when a scan is taken, or if you use a digital camera, you decide on the resolution before you shoot the image. The higher the resolution, the more pixels per inch, and the bigger the image can be without degradation. For images destined for the Web, higher resolution incurs larger file sizes.

Resolution-dependent images such as raster (bitmap) images have a set size; the height and width are fixed. If you change the image's size, you may distort it depending on the image data available. The higher the resolution of the original scan or digital file, the more image data there is to work with.

Image Formats

The time it takes for your Web site to load depends a great deal on the amount of images and their size. The two most widely used and the only two fully supported file formats for the Web are GIF and JPEG files. It's important to understand the differences so you know when to use which format, and to understand a bit about other common types of file formats you might run into.

GIF

GIF stands for Graphic Interchange Format, pronounced JIF. The GIF compression algorithm works better for line art (or any image with flat color) than with photographs. When you have images with 256 colors or fewer, there is no quality loss when the image is compressed because of the lossless compression scheme. The GIF format uses indexed color and is an 8-bit image file. Some of the advantages of GIF compression are:

» Small file sizes

» Animation capability

» Transparency

» Interlacing

The main disadvantage of GIF is that it supports only 256 colors.

GIFs use *lossless* compression (LZW), which results in no image degradation if the image is 256 colors or fewer. An LZW compression looks for patterns of data; when a new color is detected the file size increases.

Dithering is the process of simulating colors that don't exist in an image. Dithering gives the illusion of new colors by varying the pattern of dots of color. Two colors are mixed, giving the illusion of a third color.

Interlacing is an option for GIF files you are exporting for use on the Web. When a file is interlaced, it appears "blockie" or blurry until it loads, enabling the users to see a blurred copy while the image is loading. The alternative is that users cannot see anything until the entire image loads. The drawback is they need to fully load before they are clear.

Transparency is one of the coolest and most useful benefits of a GIF file. You can make the background transparent so that the rectangle edges don't show, giving the illusion of a shape cut out (it's still a rectangular image).

GIF files have the added benefit of supporting animation. An animated GIF file contains frames with different images that are all contained in one GIF animation. You add GIF animations to your Web page just like any other image file; no special treatment is required. No plug-in is required and all the major browsers support GIF animations.

JPEG

JPEG (PC file extension is .JPG) stands for Joint Photographic Expert Group. The JPEG compression algorithms work better for photographs than for line art. JPEG images deal with millions of colors. JPEG images are widely used for the Internet; it's most often used with images with more than 256 colors, with images with gradients, and with photos.

JPEGs use *lossy* compression, which removes information from the image. JPEGs are compressed and are decompressed when viewed, which can result in a longer loading time. You have control over quality settings in the Optimize panel—the higher the quality, the less compression is used. Don't JPEG a JPEG image, because it loses info each time and gets considerably worse after the second time.

Progressive JPEGs are similar to the GIF interlacing process. Images appear "blockie" and gradually become clear.

The following table describes some other file formats you might run into.

Table 1.1: Other File Formats

File Format	Description
PNG	PNG is an exciting alternative but at the present it is only partially supported by Netscape and IE. PNG files support full alpha channel and graduated transparency, which the browsers do not support yet.
TIFF	The Tagged Image Format is supported by about every application that can work with a bitmap. TIFF is an industry standard and accepted format for both the Mac and Windows platforms.
PSD	PSD is a Photoshop native file. Photoshop files typically contain layers, editable text, channels, masks, and more. These types of files are common. You can import or export a PSD Photoshop file.
EPS	The Encapsulated Post Script format, preferred by many service bureaus, is made up of text commands that a PostScript printer can understand.
AI	AI is the extension of a native Illustrator file, which you can open in Fireworks.

Tutorial
» Getting Around in Fireworks

This tutorial is for the readers who have never used Fireworks or Fireworks MX before. It's a brief primer about how to familiarize yourself with some of the terms and where to find things when you are given instructions in future sessions.

1. **Open Fireworks.**
   Fireworks will open with no blank document. You can choose to open a new blank file or open an image.

2. **Choose File→New to open a new document.**

3. **Type the height and width you'd like the document to be.**

4. **Leave the default resolution set to 72.**
   Making the resolution any higher will only increase the file size.

5. **In the Canvas Color area click the White or Transparent radio button for either of those options or click the Custom radio button to choose your own color.**
   To choose a custom color, click the color box and then click a swatch. You can also type in a hexadecimal number if you have one you want to use.

6. **Click OK.**

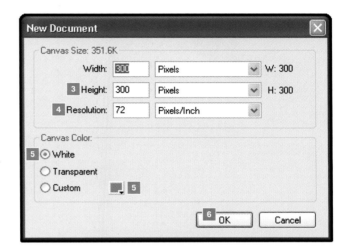

< N O T E >
Whenever an instruction wants you to use the menu bar, it starts with "choose menu name→menu option." For example, choose File→New.

Menu Bar

Document Window with blue canvas color

Title Bar

Object Drawn

Panel Groups

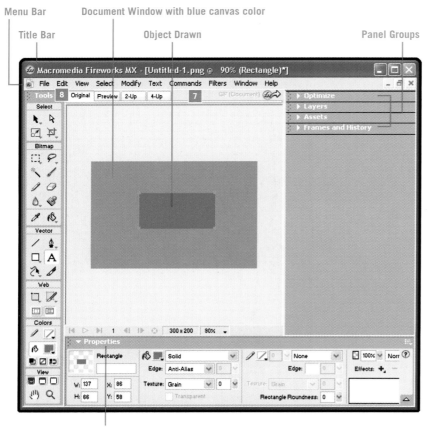

Property inspector

Gripper

Expander

Options pop-up menu

7. **Take the time to study the workspace for a moment.**
   The main areas are the document window, the tools panel, the menu bar, the Property inspector, and the panels.

8. **Take a look at the Tools panel.**
   Notice that it is divided into sections, selection tools, bitmap tools, vector tools, Web tools, and color tools.

9. **Click the Expander arrow (white triangle) on one of the panels.**
   This image shows some of the common features found in most panels. The table shows many of the functions found in the various panels.

Table 1.2: Common Features of Fireworks Panels

Function	Description
Options pop-up menu	Accessed by clicking the little icon in the top-right corner of the panel. This is a menu with additional options relative to that panel.
Slider controls	When a number is required for a percentage or a size, you can use the slider to select the number rather than typing one.
Color box	A square box with color in it. Click the box to change the color of whatever the color box is associated with, such as a stroke or fill. When you click in the color box, use the eyedropper to select a color from one of the swatches or from anywhere in the workspace. You can also type in a Hexadecimal number and press the Enter (Return) key.
Check boxes	If you see a check box and you want to select it, simply click it once. It's selected if you see a check mark. Click again to deselect it.
Edge options	Some of the panels give you the option to select an edge. A hard edge is a crisp sharp edge, which appears jagged if the object has any curves in it. Anti-aliased gives a softer edge. This edge combines with the background color to give a smoother appearance. The last option is Feather, whereby you choose how many pixels on the edge you want to feather.

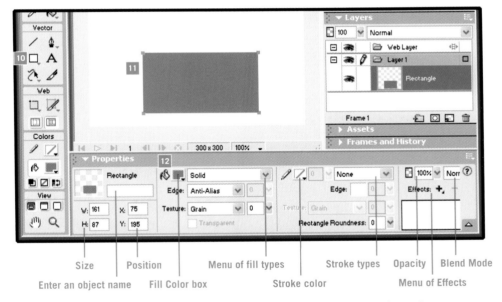

Size   Position   Menu of fill types   Stroke types   Opacity   Blend Mode

Enter an object name   Fill Color box   Stroke color   Menu of Effects

10. **Click the Rectangle tool in the Tools panel.**

11. **Click and drag anywhere in the document to draw a rectangle.**

12. **Notice the Property inspector.**

    The Property inspector changes as the tool selected or the object selected changes. Take note of some of the options available for a vector object; you see most of these options frequently.

13. **Right-click (or Control-click) the rectangle you drew.**

    This is a contextual menu, giving you easy access to many of the main menu commands. Additional options are often found here.

<NOTE>

The Property inspector lets you change attributes by either typing
new information into text boxes (such as the size of a font) or by
using a slider. If you use the slider, you can see the changes on-
screen right away. If you type in values, you have to press Enter
(Return on a Mac) to accept the settings.

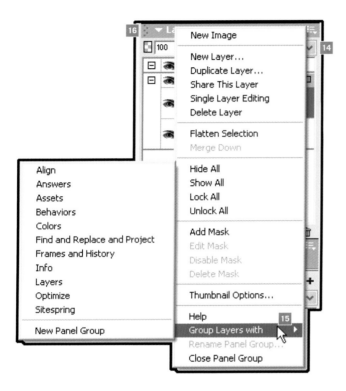

14. **Click the Layers Option pop-up menu.**

15. **Pass your mouse over Group Layers with option (but don't click
    anything).**
    Take note of the menu of options. This allows you to move
    your panels around or rearrange them to suit how you work.
    You can close a panel or a panel group or simply move them.

16. **Click and drag the Gripper to detach a panel/panel group from the
    docked area.**

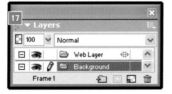

17. **To move the panel back, click and drag the Gripper, and move the
    panel back the docked area.**
    When you see a solid blue line, that's where it docks. Release
    the mouse when it's positioned where you want it. If you made
    changes and want to save your layout, then proceed to step 18.

18. **Choose Commands→Panel Layout Sets→Save Panel Layout.**
    Give the layout a name. Now you can use a command to
    retrieve a custom panel layout at any time.

Tutorial
» Obtaining Images from a Scanner

This tutorial is general because of the many variations in scanner software. You learn how to bring an image directly into Fireworks from your scanner. You also learn how to prepare your scanner and learn about some of the settings you need to be aware of.

1. **If you haven't installed your scanner software, you need to do that first.**
   Some scanners require that you have the scanner hooked up into the computer prior to installing the software.

<NOTE>
Your scanner may require the Photoshop Acquire plug-in (Macintosh needs it). Fireworks automatically looks for the Photoshop Acquire plug-ins in the Plug-ins folder within the Fireworks application folder. If you want to put the plug-in somewhere else, follow steps 2 through 5 to tell Fireworks where it is.

2. **Choose Edit→Preferences (Fireworks→Preferences).**
   Steps 2 through 5 only need to be done if you need to find the Acquire plug-in.

3. **Click the Folders tab.**

4. **Click the Browse button for Photoshop plug-ins.**

<NOTE>
Most Photoshop compatible plug-ins work with Fireworks, but if you install plug-ins into a Photoshop 6 or 7 plug-ins folder, Fireworks ignores them. Fireworks can use Photoshop 5.5 and earlier "native" plug-ins, but not the ones from versions 6 and 7. Therefore Fireworks simply ignores everything in the plug-ins folder of versions 6 and 7.

5. **Navigate to the folder where your Acquire plug-in is located and select it.**

6. **Click Open, and then click OK in the Preferences dialog box.**

7. **Be sure the scanner glass is free of dust or dirt.**

8. **Lay your artwork/photo or object on the scanner.**
   Try to place artwork as straight as possible so you don't have to do further editing to straighten it. You can even use objects on your scanner. Just be sure to protect your scanner glass from scratches. Use clear acetate to protect the glass from sharp objects or damp items.

Legal Issues

You may not scan and use copyright material or trademarked material. For instance, if you are scanning a crayon you need to remove the label or remove the markings in Fireworks. Removing markings isn't always enough. If you scan a shape that's easily identified as a trademarked item, you can't use it—period. As long as you are aware of this and don't violate others' copyrights and trademarks, you won't have any problems.

There are a lot of things you can scan in order to add interest to your layout. Just open your refrigerator, or go outdoors and start shooting with your camera. Of course, if you use a traditional camera, you need to get the film developed before you can scan! If you want that pinecone you just spotted, you can simply place it on your scanner and get almost instant gratification.

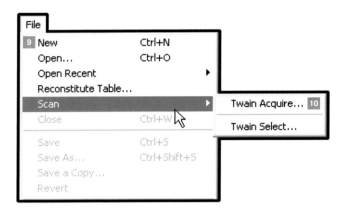

9. **Open Fireworks and choose File→Scan→Twain.**
Choose your scanner from the list. If you have installed digital camera drivers, they show up as well.

10. **Choose File→Scan→Twain Acquire→Import TWAIN Acquire.**
Your scanner interface opens automatically.

11. **Take a moment to get familiar with your scanner interface.**
The software shown comes with the Agfa SnapScan e50. The preview shows when the scanner first starts up. Notice the different file types to choose from.

<NOTE>
If you need more control over your images, consider getting a scanner that comes with SilverFast software (www.SilverFast.com) or one that is compatible with SilverFast. I found out after the fact that my scanner isn't compatible—time for a new scanner.

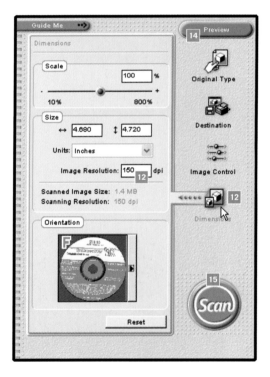

12. **Set the resolution at which you want to scan.**
Because monitors display at lower pixel levels, 150 is more than enough resolution for an image meant for the Web.

<NOTE>
Most scanner software has a list of types of images to choose from such as black and white, glossy, magazine, and so on. When you choose one of these presets, check the resolution; it may change to 300dpi. This is the default for images destined for print. Because you don't need that much resolution (higher file sizes), change it to 150dpi.

13. **Make any other adjustments needed.**
The adjustments you can make depend on your scanner software. Refer to its manual to learn of the different options.

14. **Check the Preview; you may have to click a button to see the preview of the scan.**

15. **Click Scan when you are ready to scan.**

16. **The image opens in Fireworks where you can edit, optimize, and export it.**

<NOTE>
I prefer to do my editing in an image editor rather than with scanner software. Some feel they have less work to do by fixing some things prior to a scan. The decision is yours.

Tutorial

» Obtaining Images from a Digital Camera

Digital cameras work very much like standard cameras except that the images are stored digitally rather than on film. A huge advantage of using digital cameras is that you don't have to wait for developing. If you have a tight deadline, you can shoot and get your images into your computer within minutes.

1. **Connect the cable that came with your camera into the camera and the computer.**
   Connecting to the computer through your camera uses your camera's batteries. If you have an AC adapter, use it for this purpose.

2. **Install your camera's software.**
   Refer to your user's manual.

3. **Refer to steps 2 through 5 in the previous tutorial to point Fireworks to the Acquire plug-in if you need it.**

4. **In Fireworks, choose File→Scan→Twain.**
   Choose your digital camera from the list

5. **Choose File→Scan→Twain Acquire→Import TWAIN Acquire.**
   Your image opens in Fireworks as a new document. The image is now ready to adjust however you like.

Using a Card Reader

I find using a card reader much easier and faster than plugging the camera into the computer. A card reader hooks up into your computer; then you simply insert your camera's memory card into it—no batteries. You then open Windows Explorer (or File Explorer on the Mac) and click the images folder from the new drive you see. Copy the list of images and paste into your photos folder (or wherever you keep your photos). Delete them from the card reader drive and they are removed from your memory card. You probably want to rename the images to something more meaningful than the default names. You can get card readers for a very reasonable price.

Tutorial
» Importing Images from Other Applications

Even if you only use Fireworks for your Web images, there might be times when a client gives you image source files from other applications, such as Photoshop or Illustrator. Fireworks plays very nicely with these applications.

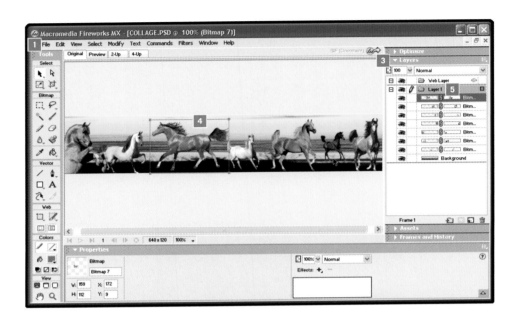

1. **Choose File→Open to open a Photoshop PSD file.**

2. **Navigate to the session1 folder and select the** `collage.psd` **file. Click Open.**

3. **Click the expander arrow to open the Layers panel.**
   In Photoshop each horse is on a different layer; each horse also has a mask applied. A mask covers areas you don't want seen. In Fireworks, each horse is now a separate selectable object.

4. **Select the brown center horse.**
   The cloverleaf indicates there is a mask.

5. **Notice in the Layers panel the link and the second icon with the word Bitmap next to it.**
   This is the Photoshop mask that stayed intact in Fireworks.

<N O T E>
If there were editable text in this image, it would remain editable. Many of Photoshop effects such as drop shadows and bevels stay intact as well. Basically, if Photoshop has effects compatible with Fireworks, they stay in Fireworks. There are some incompatible effects (such as the Liquify tool), which you have to change once you open a file in Fireworks.

6. **Choose File→Open and navigate to the session1 folder on the CD-ROM. Select the** `rose.fh10` **file and click Open.**
   This is a Freehand 10 file and the image is a vector so the Vector File Options dialog box opens.

7. **Look over the various options and accept the defaults by clicking OK.**

8. **Click OK on the Missing Fonts dialog box that opens.**
   You have the choice of replacing fonts when you see this dialog box.

9. **Pass your cursor over the rose.**
   Notice the red highlights. These indicate that the image is fully editable.

10. **Click the outside border of the rose.**
    Notice the blue outline; it shows all the points of the path. You can move each individual point (white rectangles) on the path if you want to.

11. **Close the image without saving.**
    Click the X in the top-right corner to close the image.

< T I P >
You can use other images from programs such as Illustrator EPS or AI files and maintain their editability.

» Session Review

Now it's time to see how much of this session you can remember. Try answering the questions first. You can then look up the referenced tutorial to find the answer.

1. Which type of image is best suited to 256 colors or fewer? ("Discussion: Image Basics")

2. Which type of image is best suited to photographs? ("Discussion: Image Basics")

3. Can you animate a JPEG image? ("Discussion: Image Basics")

4. How do you open a panel in Fireworks? ("Tutorial: Getting Around in Fireworks")

5. How do you create an edge that's not jagged? ("Tutorial: Getting Around in Fireworks")

6. Which plug-in do you need for scanning into Fireworks? ("Tutorial: Obtaining Images from a Scanner")

7. What is a good resolution for Web use? ("Tutorial: Obtaining Images from a Scanner")

8. What's a fast way to get images from your digital camera onto your computer? ("Tutorial: Obtaining Images from a Digital Camera")

9. How do you import a Photoshop file into Fireworks? ("Tutorial: Importing Images from Other Applications")

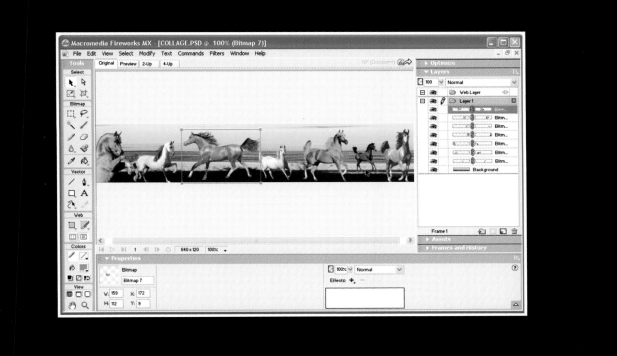

Designing Image Compositions

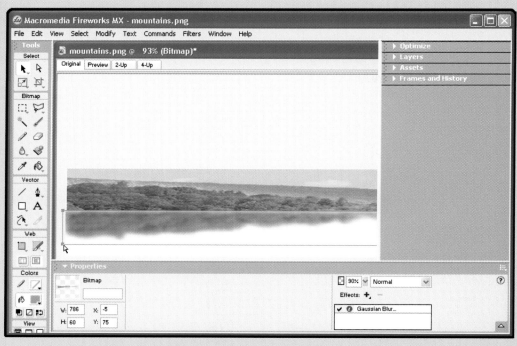

Image Creation in Fireworks

The main focus of this session is an image composition but you do other image manipulation as well. As you compose your images, you discover how easy they are to produce and manipulate in Fireworks. You also learn how to use quite a few of Fireworks tools while putting together a composition for a CD cover. Stockimagenation offers CD collections; the cover you make in this session is for the "Watersports" collection.

TOOLS YOU'LL USE
Polygon Lasso tool, Rectangle tool, Scale tool, Property inspector,
Dodge tool, Eraser tool

MATERIALS NEEDED
Files in the session2 folder on the CD-ROM:
dive.jpg, kayak.jpg, mountains.jpg, para_border.png,
splash.png, and water.png

TIME REQUIRED
90 minutes

Tutorial
» Preparing the Composition Background

If this is your first time using Fireworks, follow the steps listed here very carefully. You start out using very powerful bitmap-editing tools. You make your own background from two images cropped from larger images. I've done the cropping on these two but you crop the final image when you are done.

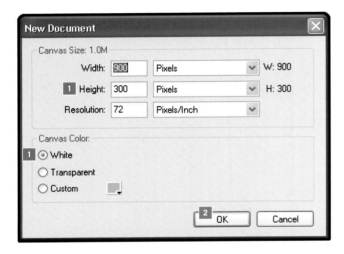

1. **In Fireworks, choose File→New and use these values:**
   Width: 900
   Height: 300
   Canvas Color: White

2. **Click OK.**

3. **Choose File→Import and navigate to the session2 folder. Select** mountains.jpg **and click Open. Click anywhere in the document to place the image.**

File Naming Conventions

It's good to establish a naming convention for your project. Random "descriptive" names generally end up creating a logistical nightmare. You keep all of your source files in the stockimagenation/source_files folder. They are also on the CD in the stockimagenation_site folder, which is the finished site. Keeping the source files in separate folders that correlate to the site's structure makes it easier to find an image.

The source files are also important for the way that Fireworks and Dreamweaver communicate. When you export an image from Fireworks into your root folder, Dreamweaver is told where to find the source image. This is important if you want to edit an image from within Dreamweaver. You see how this works in a later session.

Making Selections

You can make more than one selection at a time and you can add to a selection. For instance, if you make a selection with the Marquee tool, you can press the Shift key and make a selection somewhere else on the page using any of the selections tools.

If you make a selection that is too big or too small, you can refine the selection by adding to it or deleting from it. To add to a selection,

press the Shift key, click inside the current selection to set the first point, release the Shift key, and continue making your selection. End the selection by clicking the first point. To delete parts of a selection, press the Alt (Option) key and set the first point, and then click or draw to define the area you want removed. These techniques are also demonstrated on the selections.mov video file in the movies folder on the CD-ROM.

4. **Select the Polygon Lasso tool.**
   The Polygon Lasso tool is in the flyout menu of the Lasso tool. To access it, click the small arrow on the Lasso icon and select Polygon Lasso.

< N O T E >

The Lasso tool is a freeform selection tool that works fine for non-precise selections. Also notice the Marque tool (rectangle) and the Oval Marquee. These tools make rectangluar and oval selections.

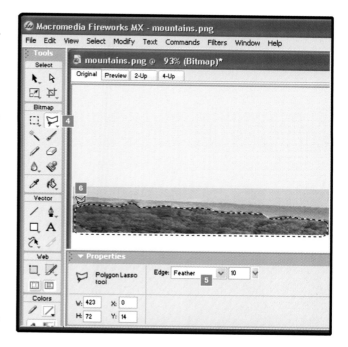

5. **In the Property inspector, click the drop-down menu for Edge and select Feather. Change the Amount of Feather to 10.**
   You must set the Edge properties prior to making the selection.

< N O T E >

If you select the Marquee tool, there is an additonal menu in the Property inspector—a field named Style. There are three choices: Normal: Drag to draw a selection.
Fixed Ratio: You enter a fixed height and width ratio.
Fixed Size: You enter the exact size you want the selection to be. Be sure to always check the values before drawing a selection. The last one you used remains selected the next time you use the tool.

6. **Click the left edge of the mountain. Continue clicking around the shape of the mountain. Close the selection by clicking the same place you started.** You see a moving dotted line (known as marching ants).

< T I P >

Refer to selections.mov movie in the movies folder of the CD-ROM if you've never made selections before and need some help.

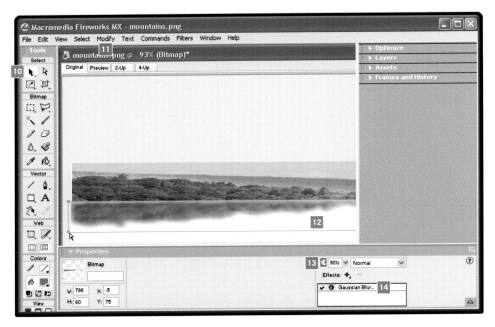

7. **Press Ctrl+C (⌘+C) to copy the mountains within the selection.**

8. **Press Ctrl+V (⌘+V) to paste the new copy of the mountains into the document.**

9. **Press Ctrl+D (⌘+D) to deselect the selection.**
   If you try to move the selection before you deselect it, it actually cuts the selection out of the image. This is not a bad thing, just not what you want to do here.

<NOTE>
The copy, paste, and deselect keyboard commands are used frequently and you may want to memorize their shortcuts.

10. **Select the Pointer tool and click the mountain to select the top copy.**

11. **Choose Modify→Transform→Flip Vertical.**
    You see the mountain flipped on top of the original mountain.

12. **Use the Pointer tool to drag the flipped mountain below the original.**
    This copy is a reflection in the water you add shortly. Because of the feathering of the selection, the reflection may be a bit shorter on the sides than the original mountain. To fix that, click the right side and drag the blue line until it matches up. Repeat for the left side. It's okay to go outside the document into the gray area.

13. **Change the Opacity in the Property inspector to 90%.**
    You can change the opacity of each individual object in Fireworks, not just an entire layer.

14. **Click the plus sign in the Property inspector next to Effects. Pass your cursor over Blur and select Gaussian Blur. Enter 2 for the blur amount and click OK.**

15. **Choose File→Import and navigate to the session2 folder. Select** water.jpg **and click Open.**

16. **Click the document to place the image.**
    The water is placed on top of everything.

17. **In the Layers panel, click and drag the top bitmap (the water) and move it to the bottom of the stack.**

    You know it's at the bottom when you see a dark line below the last bitmap image name. Release your mouse.

<TIP>

You can rename the objects in the Layers panel by double-clicking a name and typing in a new one.

18. **Use the Pointer tool to position the water directly under the original mountain.**

    The water is behind the reflection.

19. **Choose File→Save As. Navigate to the stockimagenation/source_files/CD_covers folder on your hard drive and save the file as** 001_wat.png.

<NOTE>

A copy of 001_wat.png is saved in the stockimagenation_site folder on the CD.

Effects and Filters

In Fireworks you can apply effects to your bitmap or vector images. These effects remain editable. To change the value of an effect, click the little i with a circle around it to open the dialog box. To see what your object looks like without the effect, just click the little check mark. This disables the effect until you click again to turn it on. If you decide you want to delete the effect, select the name and click the minus icon.

The Filter menu looks a lot like the list you see in the Effects menu. The difference is that the Filter menu applies filters that are permanent changes unless you use the Edit→Undo command (Ctrl+Z / Control+Z). Filters are for bitmap images. You can apply it to a vector object but it is converted to a bitmap first.

Tutorial
» Blending the First Image into the Background

In this tutorial you use some of the selection techniques you learned from the previous tutorial to remove bits of an image and to smooth the edges to blend into the background. You also use the Scale tool to make the image fit within the composition better.

Photodisc/Getty Images (www.gettyimages.com)

1. **With the** `001_wat.png` **file open, choose File→Import and navigate to the session2 folder. Select** `kayak.jpg` **and click Open.**

2. **Click in the document to place the image.**

3. **Select the Scale tool and drag in on a corner (this preserves the proportion of the image) square to make the image fit our background better.**
   Watch the Property inspector, and the width and height fields. Stop when you reach a width of about 207.

4. **Move the image so the water is at the left edge and the boat is near the bottom edge.**

5. **Double-click the image to accept the transformation.**
   Some of the water goes up into the mountain. You remove that next.

6. **Select the Polygon Lasso tool. In the Property inspector, change the Edge to Feather and 15.**

Photodisc/Getty Images (www.gettyimages.com)

7. **Make a selection where the water meets the mountain.**
   Start above the image in the mountain area then go around the board, the head, the paddle, and then down to the corner. Refer to the illustration when making your selection. Don't get close to the head or paddle because the feather will remove it.

8. **Press the delete key to remove the unwanted areas.**
   Notice in the image that there is still a bit of water around the paddle; you fix that.

<NOTE>
You can always add or subtract from your selection if needed. You can also deselect it (Ctrl+D / ⌘+D]) and start over.

9. **Press Ctrl+D (⌘+D) to turn off the selection. Click the Zoom tool and click the document a few times until you can see the paddle up close.**

10. **Select the Eraser tool.**

11. **In the Property inspector change the Size to 5, Edge to 2, and Shape to round.**

12. **Click around the edges of the paddle where you see white.**
    Don't get too close or you erase the paddle. You don't have to get every little bit, just the bulk of it.

13. **Choose File→Save As and save it in your stockimagenation/ source_files/CD_covers folder as** 002_wat.png.

14. **Choose Select→Select All.**

15. **Choose Modify→Flatten Selection.**

16. **Choose File→Save As** 003_wat.png **in the stockimagenation/ source_files/CD_covers folder.**
    It's a good idea to save your working files before flattening the image so you can go back and edit if you need to. You flatten the entire composition because the next technique needs it that way.

Photodisc/Getty Images (www.gettyimages.com)

Tutorial
» Using Layer Blending Modes to Blend an Image

In this tutorial you learn how to use the Layer Blend modes to combine images. The Blend modes interact with the objects below the selected object in different ways. You discover how powerful this tool can be.

Photodisc/Getty Images (www.gettyimages.com)

1. **Open the** 003_wat.png **file if you've closed it.**

2. **Choose File→Import and navigate to the session2 folder. Select** dive.jpg **and click Open.**
   Don't click the document just yet to place the image. Next you learn another way to place the image.

3. **Click and drag with the Import cursor. Drag a size that fits in the water area.**
   You want the man to be below the water line. You can always use the Scale icon and resize if you need to. The method of dragging the Import cursor determines how large the image is upon import.

4. **Position this image in the bottom-right corner.**

5. **With the image still selected, change the Layer blend mode to Multiply and the Opacity to 25% (or 35% if you want it to be more visible).**

6. **Click anywhere in the document to deselect the image.**
   Notice that the image has a distinct line on the left side.

7. **Select the Dodge tool from the flyout menu of the Blur tool.**

8. **In the Property inspector, set these values:**
   Size: 20
   Edge: 100
   Shape: Cirlce
   Range: Midtones
   Exposure: 100

9. **Click and drag along the left edge of the image several times until the edges blend into the background.**

   Be careful not to click too much or you remove too much color. If you used a higher opacity, you need to blend in the top edge.

   <TIP>
   If you accidentally remove too much color, just choose Edit➔Undo.

10. **Save the image as** `004_wat.png` **in your stockimagenation/source_files/CD_covers folder.**

Blending Modes

Blend modes give the appearance of pixels on one layer being "blended" with the pixels of another layer. The result is based on calculations Fireworks makes on the values, which are associated with the pixels. The values used in the calculations depend on the blend mode chosen; it could be hue, RGB values, brightness or the transparency of the pixels, depending on the Blending mode chosen. The layer on the bottom is the base layer. The layer on top with blending modes applied reacts differently with the base layer depending on the mode chosen.

Blend Mode	How it Works
Normal	No blend mode is applied.
Multiply	Multiples the base color by the blend color, resulting in a darker image.
Screen	The opposite of multiply, resulting in a washed out look.
Darken	Replaces pixels lighter than the blend color.
Lighten	Replaces pixels darker than the blend color.
Difference	The color with less brightness is subtracted from the color with more brightness.
Hue	Combines the hue value of the top layer of pixels with the luminance and saturation of the base layer of pixels. The effect is most noticeable when the values of the layers used are different.
Saturation	Combines the blend layer pixels with the luminance and hue value of the base layer.
Color	Blends the hue and saturation values of the top layer pixels and combines with the luminance of the base layer of pixels. Good for colorizing grayscale images.
Luminance	Reverse of Color mode. The resulting color is the hue and saturation values of the base layer and the luminance of the blend layer. The color of the base layer is unaffected.
Invert	Inverts the base color.
Tint	Adds gray to the base color.
Erase	Removes base color.

Tutorial
» Finishing the Composition

In this tutorial you finish the composition using techniques you used in the other tutorials.

Photodisc/Getty Images (www.gettyimages.com)

1. **Open the** 004_wat.png **file if you've closed it.**

2. **Choose File→Import and navigate to the session2 folder** para_boarder.png **and click Open.**

3. **Click the document to place the image.**

4. **Position the para-boarder near the top of the image.**

5. **Choose File→Import and navigate to the session2 folder. Select** splash.jpg **and click Open.**

6. **Click the document to place the image.**
   The water is placed below the man in the air. Don't resize it just yet; it's easier to make the selection if it's larger.

7. **Select the Polygon Lasso tool.**

8. **In the Property inspector, set the Edge to Feather and 20.**

9. **Make a selection around the water.**

10. **Press Ctrl+C (⌘+C) to copy what's inside the selection.**

11. **Press Ctrl+V (⌘+V) to paste what's inside the selection.**

12. **Press Ctrl+D (⌘+D) to deselect.**

13. **Use the Pointer tool to select and move the pasted water below the skier.**

14. **Delete the original image.**

Photodisc/Getty Images (www.gettyimages.com)

15. **Select the Scale tool and scale the water to fit.**

16. **Choose File→Import and navigate to the session2 folder. Select** ski.jpg **and click Open.**

Photodisc/Getty Images (www.gettyimages.com)

17. **Click in the document to place the image.**

18. **Select the Polygon Lasso tool and set the Feather to 15.**

19. **Draw a selection around the water skier.**
Make your selection close but not exact because the feather takes away some of the image.

20. **Press Ctrl+C (⌘+C) to copy what's inside the selection.**

21. **Press Ctrl+V (⌘+V) to paste what's inside the selection.**

22. **Press Ctrl+D (⌘+D) to deselect.**

23. **Place the skier near the back of the water.**
The reason you place him in the back is that he is too small to be a forward image. The farther away an object is, the smaller it is.

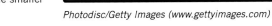

Photodisc/Getty Images (www.gettyimages.com)

24. **Select the Eraser tool and erase the ski rope.**

25. **Save the file as** 005_wat.png.

Photodisc/Getty Images (www.gettyimages.com)

» Session Review

Now it's time to see how much of this session you can remember. Try answering the question. If you are unsure of an answer or just want to check your work, look up the referenced tutorial to find the answer.

1. How do you access the Polygon Lasso tool if it isn't visible in the Tools panel? ("Tutorial: Preparing the Composition Background")

2. How do you change an object's opacity? ("Tutorial: Preparing the Composition Background")

3. Once you've applied an effect, is it editable? ("Tutorial: Preparing the Composition Background")

4. How do you rename an object? ("Tutorial: Preparing the Composition Background")

5. Which tool do you use to resize an object? ("Tutorial: Blending the First Image into the Background")

6. How do you make many objects into one flattened bitmap image? ("Tutorial: Blending the First Image into the Background")

7. What does the Dodge tool do? ("Tutorial: Blending the First Image into the Background")

8. What are the keyboard shortcuts for copy, paste, and deselect? ("Tutorial: Finishing the Composition")

9. What is the keyboard shortcut for paste? ("Tutorial: Finishing the Composition")

10. What is the keyboard shortcut for deselect? ("Tutorial: Finishing the Composition")

Building the Site's Vector Images

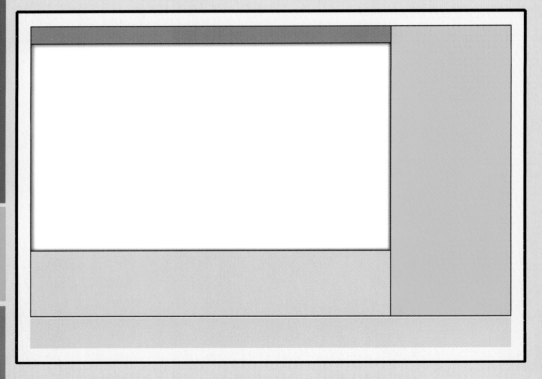

Vector Images

Recall from Session 1 that vector images are stored as a set of mathematical instructions. A vector graphic can be scaled to any size with no loss of quality.

A vector object retains its image quality no matter how big you stretch it, because it simply recalculates and redraws itself. Vectors give programs such as Flash their flexibility in resizing images on the fly.

TOOLS YOU'LL USE
Rectangle tool, Ellipse tool, Scale tool, Align command, Pen tool, Line tool, Property inspector, Layers panel, Optimize panel, Zoom tool, and the Text tool

MATERIALS NEEDED
colors.png, details.png, icons.png, sin.act, and stockimagenation.png. You'll also need to download a couple of fonts. The Amazone and Dragonwick fonts can be downloaded from http://www.fontmagic.com/cate/script1.html. Click the number 5 at the bottom of the page for Dragonwick. The Mac versions are at www.mastertech-home. com/The_Library/Font_Samples/Font_Indices/D.html.

TIME REQUIRED
90 minutes

Tutorial
» Saving and Loading a Custom Color Palette in Fireworks

In this tutorial you make a custom palette of swatches that contain only the site's colors. This prevents team members from using a wrong color by mistake. Because most of the graphics for this site are made in Fireworks, using this custom palette ensures that the colors are consistent throughout the site.

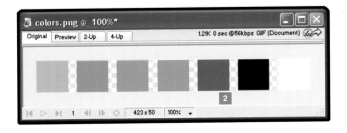

1. **Open Fireworks.**

2. **Choose File→Open and navigate to the session3 folder on the CD-ROM. Select the** colors.png **file and click Open.**
   You see the site's color plus white and gray are added.

3. **Click the white expander arrow to open the Optimize panel.**

4. **Select GIF from the Export File Format list.**

5. **Select Exact from the Indexed Palette list.**

<NOTE>
The color palettes are available only to formats, such as GIF, that use an indexed palette of colors (256 or fewer). You do not see these options for a JPEG image. You use this panel more in-depth in Session 7.

6. **Click the Optimize Options pop-up menu and select Save Palette.**

7. **Navigate to your site's root folder (stockimagenation/source_files/). Name the file** sin.act.

8. **Choose Window→Swatches.**
   The Swatches panel opens. This is the panel that you see whenever you click one of the color boxes in Fireworks. You are going to change the swatches so you only have access to the site's colors.

9. **Click the Swatches Options pop-up menu and select Replace Swatches.**

10. **Navigate to the siteimagenation/source_files folder. Select** `sin.act` **and open it.**

<TIP>

You can use the Replace Swatches method to open any .ACT or .GIF swatch files that you saved.

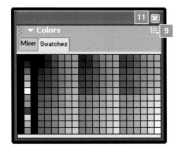

11. **Close the Swatches panel.**

12. **Click in the Fill color box in the Tools panel.**

13. **Click the right pointing arrow and select Swatches Panel.**

<TIP>

To restore the Cube swatches or whatever you were using, open the Swatches panel and select the one you want.

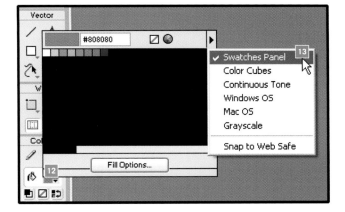

Tutorial
» Making the Site's Main Layout

In this tutorial, you make the framework for most of the site's pages. The homepage, the CD collections page, and others use the same general graphics. This site uses images for its entire layout so you make all the rectangles that hold various content for each page.

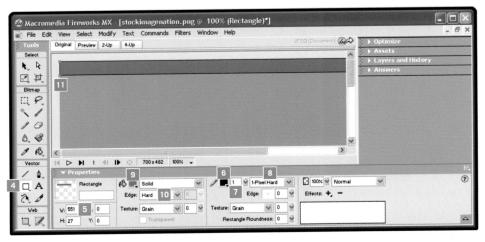

1. **Choose File→New. Enter a width of 700 and a height of 482.**

2. **Click in the color box of the Custom option and select the lightest blue.**
   When the dropper is over the color, you see the number #8CA2C1.

<NOTE>
If you want to specify a custom hex number, you can highlight the current color number and type your own. Be sure to press Enter to accept the change.

3. **Click OK.**

4. **Select the Rectangle tool and drag a rectangle any size in your document.**

5. **In the Property inspector, type 551 for the width (W) and 27 for the height (H).**
   Press the Enter key to activate changes, or click anywhere in the document.

6. **Click in the stroke color box and choose a black swatch.**

7. **Type 1 if the size is anything else.**

8. **From the Stroke Category drop-down menu, select Pencil→1-Pixel Hard.**

9. **Click the fill color box and select the medium blue color.**

10. **Set the Edge of the fill to hard if it's anything else.**
    Click the drop-down list and select Hard.

11. **Position the rectangle in the top-left corner.**

12. **Select the Rectangle tool and drag a rectangle any size in your document.**

13. **In the Property inspector, type** 525 **for the width (W) and** 312 **for the height (H).**
    Press the Enter key to activate changes, or click anywhere in the document.

14. **Your stroke settings should still be black and 1-Pixel Hard.**

15. **Click the fill color box and select white.**
    Place this white rectangle below the blue one at the top of the page.

16. **Set the Edge of the fill to Anti-Alias (default edge setting).**
    This edge blends the edge pixels with the background pixels surrounding it.

17. **Click the plus sign (+) near the word Effects in the Property inspector and pass your cursor over Shadow and Glow. Click Inner Shadow.**

18. **Use the following settings:**
    Distance: 6, Opacity: 65, Softness: 5, Angle: 321.
    To change the values, highlight what's there and type in new ones.

19. **Press Enter.**
    Notice the shadow effect on the left side only. The angle setting determined where it was placed. You have it on one side only because you can't get all the shading wanted in one step so it's broken into two effects.

20. **Choose Edit→Clone.**
    This puts a copy directly on top of the copied shape. You make some changes to this shape.

21. **Click the little i with a blue circle around it in the Effects list to edit the properties of the Inner Shadow.**

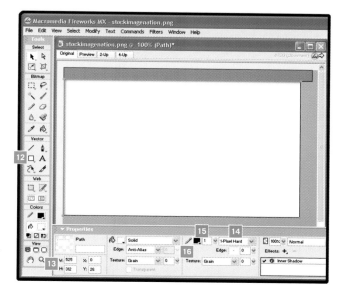

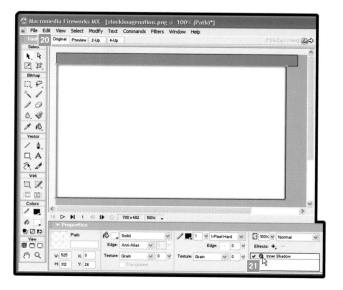

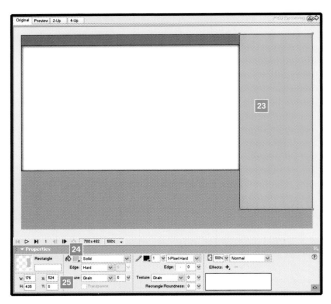

22. **Change the Distance to 4, the Softness to 3, and the Angle to 141. Press Enter.**

23. **Draw another rectangle. Set its size to a width of 176 and a height of 435 and a 1-Pixel Hard black stroke.**
Refer to steps 12 through 15.

24. **Click the fill color box and click the dark orange swatch.**

25. **Place the orange rectangle to the right of your document.**
To be sure it's in the correct place, check the Property inspector. The x and y coordinates should be x:524 and y:0. If they are different, simply type the correct value and press Enter. This rectangle is lined up against the white one and overlaps the blue one.

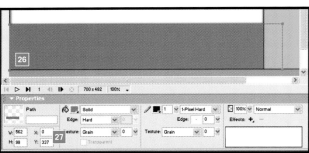

26. **Draw a light gray rectangle with a width of 562, a height of 98, and a black stroke.**
You've done this several times already, so the steps aren't repeated. If you need to review, refer to steps 12 through 18.

27. **Place this light gray rectangle directly below the white one and to the left. The coordinates should be x:0, y:337.**

28. **Choose Modify→Arrange→Send to Back.**
This puts the gray rectangle at the bottom of the stack so that the black stroke on the orange rectangle isn't covered.

<T I P>
You can also move the order of objects around in the Layers panel by dragging them above or below other objects.

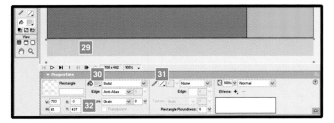

29. **Draw another rectangle with a width of 703 and a height of 61.**

30. **Click the fill color box and select the light gray.**

31. **Click the stroke color box and click the red slash for no stroke.**

32. **In the Property inspector, change the x and y coordinates to -x: 0 and y: 435.**
You've just laid out the background for the stockimagenation site.

33. **Double-click the layer in the Layers panel and change the name to background elements.**
Click on the expander arrow to open the Layers panel if it's closed.

34. **Save this image as** stockimagenation.png **in your source_files/pages/home folder.**

Tutorial

» Drawing the Home Icon

Drawing this icon primarily uses the Rectangle tool, but you do other new things in Fireworks such as transform, group, and change layer names as well as begin using the Text tool.

1. **Choose File→New. Enter a size of 200x200 and the same custom blue (#8CA2C1) canvas color you used before.**

2. **Select the Rectangle tool and draw a rectangle using these values:**
   Width: 100
   Height: 100
   Fill: None
   Stroke color: White
   Pencil→1-Pixel Soft

3. **Choose Modify→Transform→Numeric Transform. Select Rotate from the drop-down menu.**

4. **Enter** 45.

5. **Click OK.**
   This is the house's rooftop. The position isn't important, just place it in the center where you have room to work with it.

6. **Draw another rectangle, only change the stroke color to anything else. Change the width to 175 and the height to 80.**

7. **Use the Pointer tool to move the new rectangle to cover the bottom half of the first rotated rectangle.**

8. **Shift-select both rectangles.**
   Press the Shift key and select one object at a time.

9. **Choose Modify→Combine Paths→Punch.**
   You are now left with just the top rectangle.

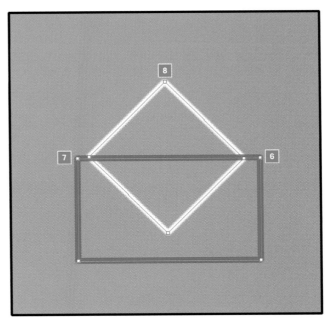

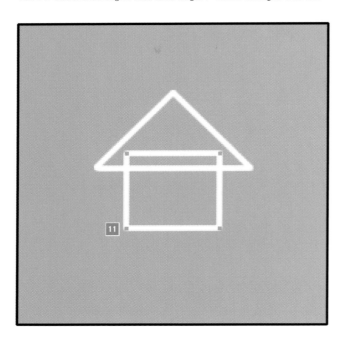

10. **Draw another rectangle with these properties:**
    Width: 80
    Height: 70
    Fill: None
    Stroke color: White
    Size: 1
    Hard Line (Basic category)

11. **Place the rectangle over the triangle.**

12. **Shift-select the rectangle and the triangle.**

13. **Choose Modify→Combine Paths→Union.**
    You now have a house shape. The roof peak is a bit tall for the icon so you adjust that next.

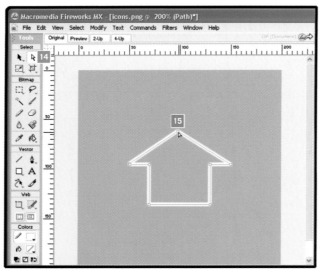

14. **Select the Subselect tool.**

15. **Click the top point and drag down a little to shorten the peak.**

16. **Draw a small rectangle with these properties:**
    Width: 30
    Height: 50
    Fill: Medium blue
    Stroke color: White
    Size: 1
    Hard Line (Basic category)

17. **Position this rectangle for the door. Line the bottom directly on top of the white stroke of the house.**
    You can also select both shapes and choose
    Modify→Align→Bottom then Modify→Align→Vertical Center to
    center the door.

18. **Select the line tool and change the stroke color to the medium blue, 1-Pixel Hard from the Pencil category.**

19. **Place your cursor over the white line at the bottom of the door and drag to the length of the door.**
    To get the exact length, you can change the width to 27 in the
    Property inspector and then use the arrow keys to line it up
    perfectly.

20. **Choose Select→Select All (Ctrl+A / ⌘+A).**

21. **Choose Modify→Group (Ctrl+G / ⌘+G).**
    You've just grouped all the pieces together; now they can be
    moved or manipulated as one object. You now need to make
    this icon smaller.

22. **Select the icon and change its width to 20 and the height to 14.**

23. **Double-click the Zoom tool.**
    You should now be able to see the tiny icon. But there is a
    problem with it so you need to zoom in close.

24. **With the Zoom tool still selected, drag around the icon.**
    This zooms in to the icon.

25. **Select the icon with the Pointer tool and choose
    Modify→Ungroup.**

26. **Click anywhere in the document to deselect, then click just on the little line you added.**
    Notice that the line is now into the white area beyond the blue
    part of the door. You need to make this smaller.

27. **Select the blue line at the bottom of the door and change the width to 2.**

28. **Shift-select the line, the door, and the house, and group (Ctrl+G / ⌘+G).**

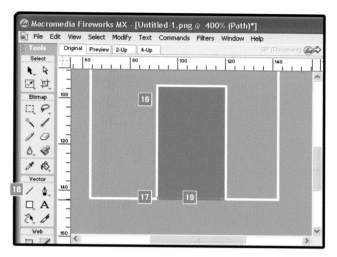

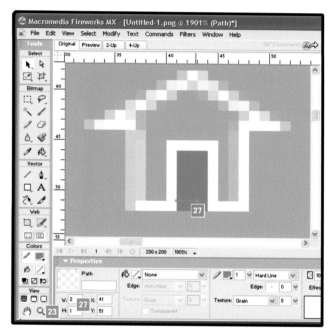

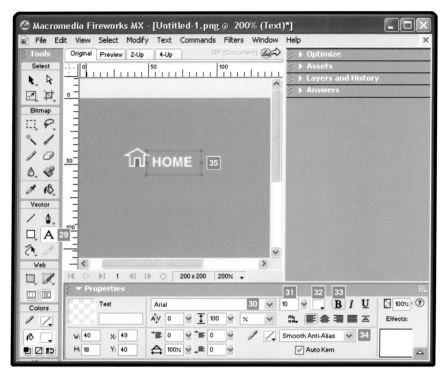

29. **Select the A icon in the Tools panel to add text.**

30. **In the Property inspector, click the arrow for the Font list and select Arial.**

31. **Type** 10 **for the Size (or use the slider).**

32. **Click in the color box and select white.**

33. **Click the Bold icon (B).**

34. **Click the arrow for the Anti-Aliasing Level and select Smooth Anti-Alias.**

35. **Click in the document and type** HOME **in all caps.**

36. **Position the text next to the icon.**

37. **Shift-select the icon and text and group it (Ctrl+G / ⌘+G).**

38. **Click the white expander arrow to open the Layers panel if it isn't open now.**

39. **Double-click the group name and type** home icon. **Press Enter.**

40. **Double-click the Layer 1 to rename it, and type** Icons.

41. **Choose File→Save As and navigate to your root folder. Save your work in the source_files/pages/home folder as** icons.png.
    A copy of all the source files is included in the stockimagenation_site folder. You use this file in the next tutorial.

Tutorial
» Building the Photo and Motion Icons

Next you make the icons for the photo and motion links. In this tutorial you continue working with the rectangle tool but you also learn how to edit a rectangle as well as align objects.

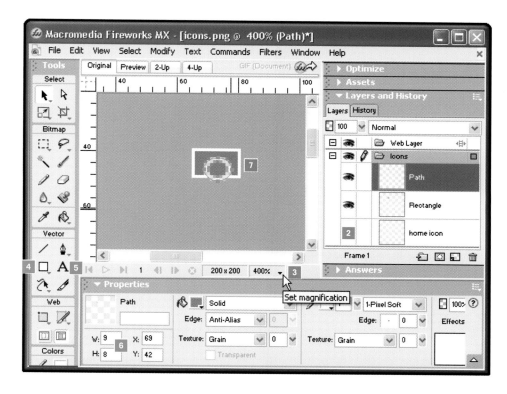

1. **If you've closed** icons.png, **open it again.**

2. **In the Layers panel, click the eye icon next to the object you named home icon.**
   This makes the home icon invisible.

3. **Click the Set Magnification drop-down menu and select 400%.**
   Because you are going to make a very small icon without resizing this time, you need to zoom to see what you are doing.

4. **Select the Rectangle tool and draw a rectangle with these properties:**
   Width: 16
   Height: 10
   Fill: Medium blue
   Stroke color: White
   Pencil➜1-Pixel hard

5. **Select the Ellipse tool and draw a circle in the document.**

6. **Change the size in the Property inspector to a width of 9 and a height of 8.**

7. **Position the circle in the center of the rectangle and down just a bit.**

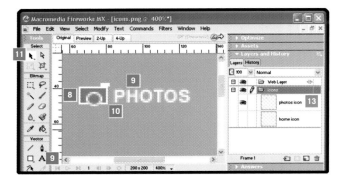

8. **Draw a little rectangle, 5x2, with a white fill and no stroke. Place this overlapping the top-right corner to look like a camera.**
   To set no stroke, click the stroke color box and then click the red slash on the top of the panel.

9. **Select the Text tool and type** PHOTOS **in all caps.**
   The settings you last used should still be active. Refer to steps 30 through 34 of the previous tutorial if you need to reset anything.

10. **Position the text next to the icon.**

11. **Select the Pointer tool and drag a selection around the icon and the text.**
    This selects everything.

12. **Press Ctrl+G (⌘+G) to group.**

13. **In the Layers panel, double-click the group name and name it** photos icon. **Press Enter.**

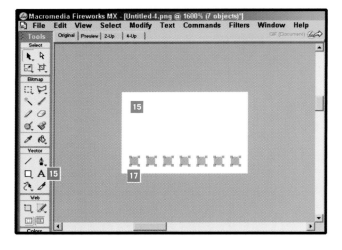

14. **Click the eye next to the photos icon to turn it off.**

15. **Select the Rectangle tool and draw a rectangle with these properties:**
    Width: 15
    Height: 10
    Fill: White
    Stroke color: None.

16. **Zoom in to 1600% and draw another rectangle that is 1x1. Change the fill to any other color.**

17. **Position the small rectangle in the bottom-left corner.**

18. **Press the Alt (Option) key, click the small rectangle and drag to the right.**
    This makes a duplicate copy of the rectangle.

19. **Repeat step 18 until you have a total of seven small rectangles.**

20. **Position the two corner rectangles but don't worry about the spacing of the others.**

21. **Select the left corner rectangle and note its y coordinate. Select each rectangle and be sure its y coordinate is the same.**

22. **Shift-select all the small rectangles and choose Modify→Align→Distribute Widths.**

23. **Choose Edit→Clone and press the up-arrow key until the set of rectangles is at the top.**

    They move as one unit because you have them all selected from step 22. Now you are going to use the small rectangles to punch a hole through the white rectangle, but you can only do one at a time.

24. **Shift-select a small rectangle and the large white rectangle.**

25. **Choose Modify→Combine Paths→Punch.**

26. **Repeat steps 24 and 25 for each rectangle.**

    The large rectangle stays selected so all you have to do after each punch is hold the Shift key and select another small rectangle and then punch.

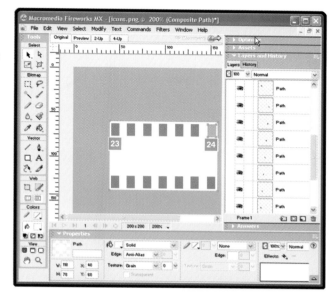

27. **Select the Text tool and type** MOTION.

28. **Place the text next to the icon and group.**

29. **Double-click the group name in the Layers panel and name it** motion icon.

30. **Save the file.**

31. **Click the eye next to motion icon to turn off the visibility.**

32. **Zoom in to at least 400% and draw a small rectangle 3x8 with no fill and a 1-Pixel Hard stroke.**

33. **Draw another rectangle 12x12 with a 1-Pixel Soft stroke, and position it near the first rectangle.**

34. **Select the Subselection tool and click the larger rectangle.**

35. **Click and drag on the lower-left point. A message opens saying that it needs to be ungrouped. Click OK and drag the point up.**

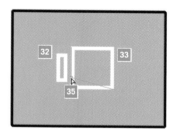

36. **Click and drag down on the upper-left point.**

37. **Place the shape next to the small rectangle.**

38. **Select the Text tool and type** AUDIO.

39. **Choose Select→Select All and Group.**

40. **Change the group's name in the Layers panel to** audio icon.

41. **Save the file.**

Tutorial
» Finishing the Fonts and Lightbox Icons

The next icon uses a free font that's included in the fonts/amazone folder on the CD-ROM. Be sure you install it prior to doing this tutorial. Copy the `amazone.ttf` file and paste it into the fonts directory of the Windows application folder.

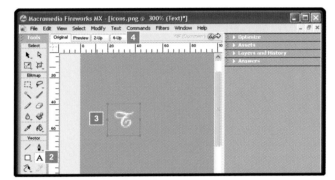

1. In the `icons.png` file, turn off the visibility of the audio object.

2. Select the Text tool and use the following properties:
   Font: Amazone BT, Size: 16, Bold, Color: White.

3. Type an uppercase T.

4. Select the T and choose Text→Convert to Paths.
   This ensures that the font style is maintained even if another user uses your source file and doesn't have the font. It has been changed into an image.

5. Click anywhere to deselect the text. Change the font to Arial and size 10 and type FONTS.

6. Place the word FONTS next to the icon.

7. Select the icon and the word and group them.

8. Rename the group font icon and click the eye to turn off visibility.

9. Draw a rectangle that is 6x6, with a white fill and no stroke.

10. Choose Edit→Clone.

11. Press the right arrow key seven times.

12. Choose Edit→Clone.

13. Press the down-arrow key seven times.

14. Choose Edit→Clone.

15. Press the left arrow key seven times.

16. Type the words MY LIGHTBOX and line them up next to the little rectangles.

17. Choose Select→Select All and Group (Ctrl+G / ⌘+G).

18. Name the group lightbox icons.

19. Save the file.

< NOTE >
Additional icon information can be found on this book's Web site at www.complete-course.com.

Tutorial
» Drawing the Sidebar Icons

There are only three more icons used on this site—the asset search and CD icon for the orange sidebar, and the shopping cart icon for the purchase pages. You learn how to edit a rectangle as well as use the Pen tool in this tutorial.

1. **Select the Ellipse tool and draw a circle with the following properties:**
   Size: 9x9
   Fill: None
   Stroke color: Black
   1-Pixel Soft

2. **Select the Rectangle tool and draw a small rectangle that is 4x10 with the same fill and stroke settings as the circle.**

3. **Select the Scale tool. When you pass your cursor over the edge of the small rectangle, you see a curved arrow. Click and drag to rotate the rectangle at an angle.**
   Because of the transform handles, it's difficult to see the rotation, so activate the change by pressing Enter. If the angle isn't right, click the Scale tool again and rotate some more. Press Enter again.

4. **Select the Subselection tool.**

5. **Click the top-left point of the rectangle and try to drag it.**
   The warning dialog box opens because a rectangle is automatically grouped.

6. **Click OK to close the dialog box.**

7. **Drag the top-left point near the top-right point.**

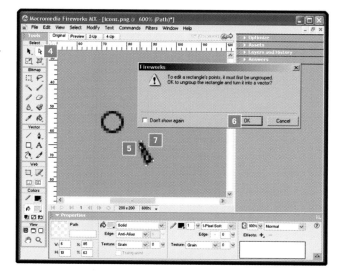

8. **Place the handle next to the circle.**

9. **Select the Text tool and change the color to black.**

10. **Type the words** ASSET SEARCH.

11. **Place the text near the icon.**

12. **Choose Select→Select All and Group.**

13. **Name the group** search icon.

14. **Save the file.**

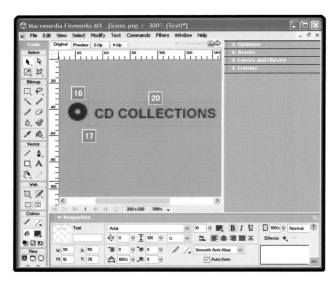

15. **Click the eye near the search icon to hide it.**

16. **Using the Ellipse tool draw a circle with these values:**
    Size: 14x14
    Fill: Black
    Stroke color: None

17. **Draw another circle, but change the color and make it 4x4.**

18. **Place the small circle in the center of the larger circle.**

19. **Shift-select both circles and choose Modify→Combine Paths→Punch.**
    You punched a hole through the larger circle, making a CD icon.

20. **Select the Text tool, use the same settings as the rest of the icon text, and type** CD COLLECTIONS.
    As a reminder, the text is Arial, size 10, bold, and black.

21. **Group the text and icon and change the name in the Layers panel to** cd icon.
    The last icon you make is for the shopping cart.

22. **Turn the visibility off for the CD collections icon.**

23. **Zoom into 400%.**

Notice the image that corresponds to this step. You see a drawing of the shape you make. You can use this as a guide when following the instructions.

<NOTE>

The points where you click are black so you can see them better.

24. **Select the Pen tool.**

25. **In the Property inspector, use a stroke of 1-Pixel Soft and white.**

26. **Click in the center of the document and release the mouse.**

27. **Press the Shift key and click again a short way from the first point you set.**

The Pen tool adds a line segment between each point. The first line should have a width of 13.

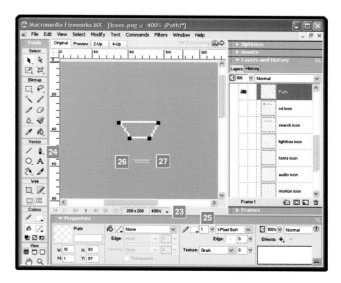

28. **Click again below the first line and at an angle.**

You don't want a perfect rectangle. You are drawing the side of the cart.

29. **Press the Shift key and click again for the bottom of the cart.**

The Shift key constrains your line and makes it straight.

30. **Click the very first point to connect the shape.**

Don't worry if the shape isn't perfect; you can edit it with the Subselection tool. This isn't a rectangle shape, so when you drag on a point you won't get the ungroup warning message.

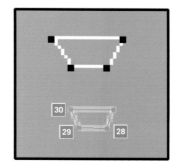

31. **Select the Ellipse tool and change the fill to white and the stroke to none.**

32. **Draw a small circle and change its size to 3x3 in the Property inspector.**

33. **Press the Alt (Option) key, select the circle, and then drag out to make a copy.**

34. **Place the wheels beneath the cart.**

35. **Select the Pen tool and click the top-right corner. Then, click up just a tiny bit and click to the right just a little.**

This is to make the handle, look at the illustration to know where to click.

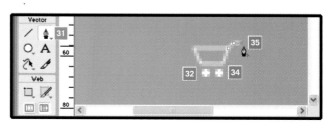

36. **Group the shapes and name it** shopping cart.

37. **Save the file.**

Tutorial
» Adding the Icons to the Background Layout

In this tutorial you add the icons to the navigation area of the main page background. You also learn how to work with layers as you transfer all the icons into folders of the main site page.

1. **Open the** stockimagenation.png **file from your stockimagenation/source_files/pages/home folder.**

2. **Open the Layers panel. Click the expander arrow to open it.**

3. **Click the area to the right of the eye icon.**
   You see a lock. This locks the layer so nothing can be moved or edited.

4. **Click the folder with a plus sign on it at the bottom of the Layers panel to add a new layer.**

5. **Choose File→Import and navigate to the** icons.png **file, which should be in the source_files/pages/home folder.**

6. **Click in the document to place the icons.**
   Notice that all the icons are placed in Layer 1.

7. **Double-click Layer 1 and rename the layer** icons for navigation buttons. **Also select the Share Across Frames option. Click OK when the warning appears because you have nothing in other frames yet.**

   By selecting this option, you ensure that the content is seen in other frames (this is frame 1).

8. **Unlock the background layer, double-click its name, and then select the Share Across Frames option. Lock the layer again.**

9. **Turn the visibility of the shopping cart off, but click the eye area for the home icon to turn it on.**

   You won't see the icon because it's white but you see the selection points (blue).

10. **Select the home icon and move it to the top of the navigation area.**

    You can set the x and y coordinates to 8 and 9, respectively, if you prefer.

11. **Turn on each navigation icon one at a time and place using the following coordinates:**

    Photo: x: 85, y: 9, Motion: x: 172, y: 9, Audio: x: 258, y: 9, Fonts: x: 335, y: 9, My Lightbox: x: 412, y: 9

12. **Click the New/Duplicate Layer icon three times to add three new layers.**

13. **In the navigation layer, select the search icon and drag it to the new Layer 1.**

14. **Double-click Layer 1 and name it** Asset Search. **Select the Share Across Frames option, and then click OK when the warning appears.**

15. **Click next to the search icon and turn off the visibility.**

16. **Click to the right of the eye for the Asset Search layer and lock it.**

17. **In the navigation layer, select the CD icon and drag it to the new Layer 2.**

18. **Double-click Layer 2 and name it** CD Collections (sidebar). **Check the Share Across Frames option (click OK on the warning).**

19. **Hide the visibility of the icon and lock the layer.**

20. **In the navigation layer, select the shopping cart icon and drag it to the new Layer 3.**

21. **Double-click Layer 3 and name it** Shopping Cart. **Check the Share Across Frames option (click OK on the warning).**

22. **Hide the visibility of the icon and lock the layer.**

Tutorial
» Adding the Logo Text

In this tutorial you make the logo using text. You also make an additional image from text to use on the Registration page of the site. You need the `dragonwick.ttf` font (in the fonts folder on the CD) installed prior to doing this tutorial.

1. **Open the** `stockimagenation.png` **file if you've closed it.**

2. **Click the lock next to the shopping cart icon to unlock it. Select the shopping cart layer and press the New/Duplicate Layer icon to add a new layer.**

<NOTE>
A new layer is added above the selected layer.

3. **Double-click the layer and name it** Logo.

4. **Select the Text tool and use these properties:**
   Font: Arial Black
   Color: Dark gray
   Size: 32
   Anti-Aliasing Level: Smooth Anti-Alias

5. **Click in the document and type** stockimagenation.

6. **Click and drag over the word image in the name to select it.**

7. **Click the fill color box and select black.**
   Just the word image is now black.

8. **Position it in the gray space below the white area. The coordinates are x: 14, y: 362.**

9. **Select the Text tool and change the font to Verdana, size 10 (it stays black).**
   Set the kerning to 2 (the A\V field just below the font field in the Property inspector).

10. **Type the phrase** GO AHEAD . SHAKE UP YOUR IMAGINATION!.

11. **Position the words below the logo text; the coordinates are X: 91, Y: 393**

12. **Lock the logo layer.**

13. **Save the file.**

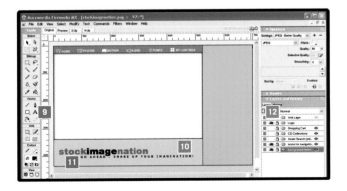

Tutorial

» Drawing the Custom Shape for the Details Page

The details page of the site is the one the users get when they click a specific item for sale that they want more details on. This page varies from the other pages, so you need to make a custom shape. The main reason the design varies is so you can learn how to make custom shapes; this page uses a masked image.

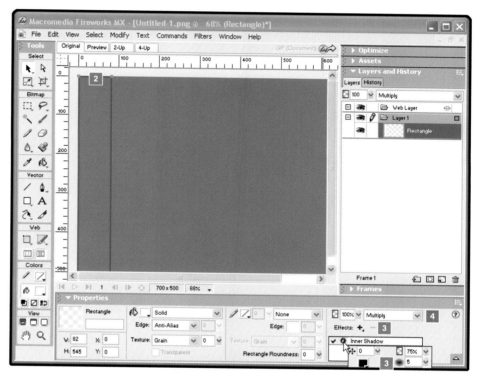

1. **Choose File→New and use a size of 700x500. Click the Custom option. Click in the color box and select the lighter blue. Click OK.**

2. **Draw a rectangle and change its size to 82 wide and 545 high, white, with no stroke. Position the rectangle on the left edge and top.**

3. **Click the Effects plus sign and select Shadow and Glow→Inner Shadow. Use these settings:**
   Distance: 0
   Opacity: 75%
   Softness: 5
   Angle: 305

4. **Set the Blend mode to Multiply.**
   The blend modes are in the Property inspector where you see the word Normal (top-right side). These blend options determine how your object interacts with the object below it. Multiply leaves only the shadow.

5. **Save the file as** details.png **into the source_files/pages/details folder.**

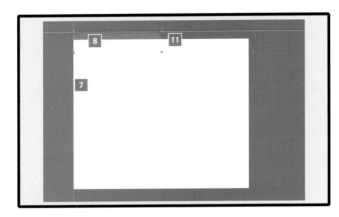

6. **Choose File→New and use a size of 600x600, the blue canvas is fine, and click OK.**

7. **Draw a rectangle, size 468x415, white, and no stroke. Position about a third of the way down from the top.**
   The position isn't vital at all.

8. **Draw another rectangle 235x60.**

9. **In the Property inspector change the Rectangle Roundness to 60.**
   You can click on the slider and drag it to the very top.

10. **Click the fill color box and change it to anything other than white so you can see it.**

11. **Position the small rectangle about half way into the large rectangle.**
    This is the tab.

12. **Shift-select both rectangles and choose Modify→Combine Paths→Union.**

13. **Draw a rectangle 43x414, any color (not white), and no stroke.**

14. **In the Property inspector, change the Roundness to 45.**

15. **Place the rectangle on the right edge of the white rectangle.**

16. **Shift-select the large rectangle and the new one.**

17. **Choose Modify→Combine Paths→Union.**
    You now have a custom shape. Next you cut a curve out of the the tab.

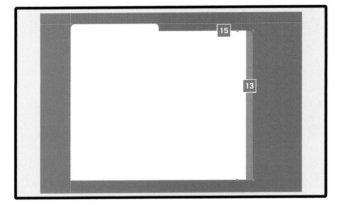

18. **Draw a rectangle 255x64 and change the roundness to 63.**

19. **Position the bottom-left corner over the end of the tab.**

20. **Shift-select the large shape and the new rectangle.**

21. **Choose Modify→Combine Paths→Punch.**
    The finished shape now has three rounded corners and a curved tab.

22. **Click the Effects plus sign and select Shadow and Glow→Drop Shadow with these settings:** Distance: 3, Opacity: 50, Softness: 3, and Angle: 55.

23. **Select the completed shape and copy it (Ctrl+C / ⌘+C).**

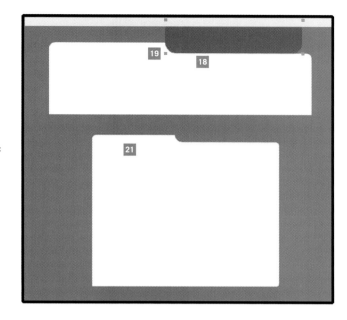

24. **Open your** details.png **page if you've closed it.**
    Remember you saved it in the source_files/pages/details folder.

25. **Paste into the details page (Ctrl+V / ⌘+V).**

26. **Line up the white shape using the coordinates of x: 82 and y: 31.**

27. **Save your file.**

<NOTE>
The starter file you have in another session has an orange table added to the layout. You don't make it now because it uses these same techniques. Look at the illustration and notice the two rounded corners. The pieces that aren't rounded are simply rectangles to represent what's in a table cell in Dreamweaver. They are in the Fireworks layout for comping (client sample) purposes only. But you would need to make the corner pieces of the top-left and bottom-right to use in the Dreamweaver layout.

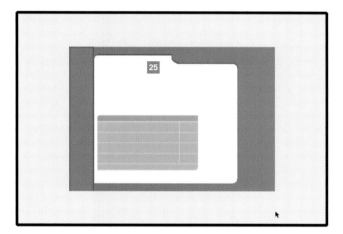

» Session Review

In this session you learned a lot about using the shape tools, including how to edit them and how to use the Text tool. You learned a bit about choosing colors and how to make a custom color palette to select site colors from, as well as working with layers and moving objects from one layer to another. Here are some questions to see how much you retained from this session's exercises. The answers to the questions can be found in the tutorial noted in parentheses.

1. What is the advantage to using vector images? (Session Introduction)

2. When a panel is closed, how do you open it? ("Tutorial: Saving and Loading a Custom Color Palette in Fireworks")

3. How do you change the width and height of an image? ("Tutorial: Making the Site's Main Layout")

4. How do you change colors of a fill or a stroke? ("Tutorial: Making the Site's Main Layout")

5. What is anti-alias? ("Tutorial: Making the Site's Main Layout")

6. How do you cut a hole in an image? ("Tutorial: Drawing the Home Icon")

7. How do you combine two images to make one? ("Tutorial: Drawing the Home Icon")

8. How do you deselect a selected object? ("Tutorial: Drawing the Home Icon")

9. How do you group objects? ("Tutorial: Building the Photo and Motion Icons")

10. How do you rename a layer? ("Tutorial: Adding the Icons to the Background Layout")

stock**image**nation

GO AHEAD , SHAKE UP YOUR IMAGINATION!

Session 4

Building the Site's Bitmap Images

Bitmap Images

Photographs are comprised of pixels, the smallest component part of a bitmapped image, also known as a raster image in some programs. Editing pixels involves adding, removing, or coloring individual pixels. Fireworks MX devotes a whole section of tools just for working with bitmap images.

Pixel images lose detail as they are scaled up because each image contains a set number of pixels. When you scale a bitmapped image up, Fireworks has to guess which pixels need to be resampled to "fake" the detail in the increased space. This stretching of pixels results in what is known as a "pixelated image."

TOOLS YOU'LL USE
Marquee tool, Magic Wand, Crop tool, Text tool, Mask command, Effects panel,
Batch Process, Pen tool

MATERIALS NEEDED
details.png, flower.png, LG_man.png, MD_man.jpg, shell.jpg,
SM_man.jpg, stockimagenation.png, water.jpg, water_detail.jpg.
You'll also need the details.png file you saved previously (a copy is in the
stockimagenation_site/source_files/pages/detail folder)

TIME REQUIRED
90 minutes

Tutorial
» Removing the Background from an Image

The site's main images all use the same technique to remove the background. In this example the background is white.

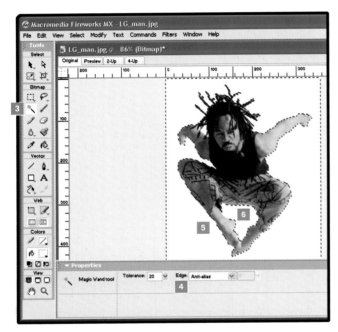

1. **Open Fireworks.**

2. **Choose File→Open and navigate to the session4 folder on the CD-ROM. Select the LG_man.jpg file and click Open.**
   This original image is stored in the stockimagenation_site/stockresources/photos folder. It's provided on the CD in the session4 folder for convenience only.

3. **Select the Magic Wand.**

4. **In the Property inspector, set the Tolerance to 20 and the Edge to Anti-Alias.**

5. **Click in the white part of the image.**
   Notice the moving dotted line (marching ants). Everything you see inside the lines is your selection.

<NOTE>
Selections are made when you want to work on only the part of the image within the selection. Your changes are constrained to the selected area.

6. **Press the Shift key and click in the white area between the legs.**
   All the white is now selected.

7. **Choose Select→Feather and type 1 for the Radius. Click OK.**
   The one-pixel feather achieves the desired softness.

8. **Choose Modify→Mask→Hide Selection.**

9. **Look at the Layers panel. The black and white image you see is the mask which covers the portion you don't want seen.**
   In this image it's the background, which is now transparent.

10. **Choose Modify→Canvas→Image Size.**
    The image is larger than needed so you make it smaller.

11. **Be sure the Constrain Proportions option is checked. Type 310 for the width and click OK.**
    The height automatically changes proportionately.

12. **Choose File→Save and navigate to the source_files/pages/home folder. Save the image as LG_man.png.**

13. **Repeat this tutorial for each of the people images on the home-page, using these sizes and filenames: sm_man.jpg: 160 wide (source_files/home/sm_man.png) and md_man.jpg: 217 wide (source_files/pages/home/md_man.png).**

<TIP>
If you want to select the man instead of the background, choose Select→Select Inverse. The selection is then just around what was previously unselected. This trick works particularly well when it's easier to select the background than it is the object.

Tutorial

» Cropping a Selection

In this tutorial you make one of the cover images for the CD Collections page. You use a larger than needed image that you crop by using a marquee selection. You then add the text to the CD cover.

1. **Choose File→Open and navigate to the session4 folder. Open** `shell.jpg`.
   This is a composition I made using masking techniques and layer blend modes which you experimented a bit with in Session 1 (the diver in the composition) and Session 2 (the rectangle in the details page).

2. **Select the Marquee tool.**

3. **In the Property inspector, select Fixed Size from the Style drop-down menu.**

4. **Change both the width and height to 300.**

5. **Click in the image and a selection that is 300x300 will automatically be placed.**

6. **Move the selection to the top-left corner.**
   Don't use the Pointer tool to move the selection or it cuts the area out of the image. Move the selection by clicking and dragging while the Marquee tool is still selected.

7. **Right-click (Control-click) in the selection and choose Crop Selected Bitmap.**
   The crop handles appear.

8. **Double-click to crop the document.**

9. **Choose Modify→Canvas→Trim Canvas.**
   This option crops the canvas to fit the content. If the content is outside your document, the canvas is cropped larger to fit the content.

10. **Choose Modify→Canvas→Image Size.**

<NOTE>
The next time you use the Marquee tool, the settings you made remain. Be sure to change it back to Normal before drawing a new marquee.

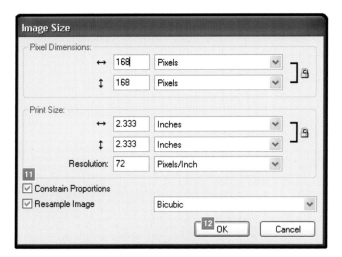

11. **Be sure the Constrain Proportions option is selected and type 310 pixels in the Pixel Dimensions area. Click OK.**
The height and width should both be 168.

12. **Click OK.**

13. **Select the Text tool and use these settings:**
Font: Dragonwick
Size: 20
Fill:Dark burgundy (sample from the left of the shell)
Stroke: Light pink (sample from the bottom shell area)
Alias: Smooth Anti-Alias

14. **Type** Shells Galore **and place the text near the bottom, centered.**

15. **Click the Effects plus sign and choose Shadow and Glow→Drop shadow. Change the Distance and Softness to 2.**

16. **Choose File→Save As and save as** shell.png **into your source_files/CD_covers/shell folder.**

Tutorial
» Adding a Border to a Bitmap Image

In this session, you add a one-pixel border to a bitmap image. With vector images, you add a border by adding a stroke. With bitmap images, you need to use a different technique.

1. **Choose File→New and use a canvas size of 200x200. Make it white.**

2. **Use the Rectangle tool to draw a rectangle and make it 168x168 with a fill color of medium blue.**

3. **Choose→File→Open. Navigate to the session4 folder and open** water.jpg.

4. **Select the image and choose Modify→Canvas→Image Size. Type 168 for the width. Click OK.**
   Be sure the Constrain Proportions option is checked.

5. **Copy the image (Ctrl+C / ⌘+C).**

6. **Close the water image and choose not to save the changes.**
   The image is still in memory.

7. **Paste (Ctrl+V / ⌘+V) into the CD image page (the one with the blue background).**

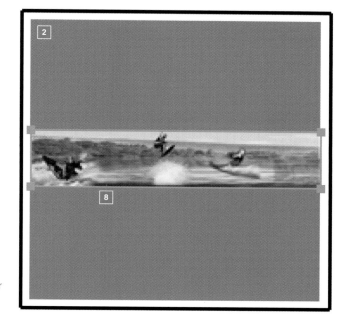

<TIP>
Instead of copying and pasting the image, you can drag the smaller water image into the CD cover document.

8. **Center the image in the center of the CD cover.**

9. **With the water image selected, click the plus sign near Effects in the Property inspector.**

10. **Select Shadow and Glow→Glow and use these settings:**
    Distance: 1
    Opacity: 100
    Softness: 0
    Offset: 0

11. **Click in the document to accept the effect.**
    This added a one-pixel border to the image.

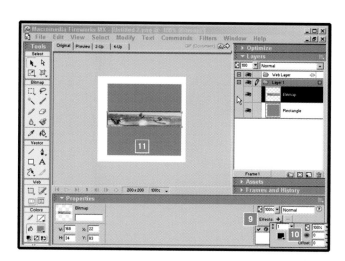

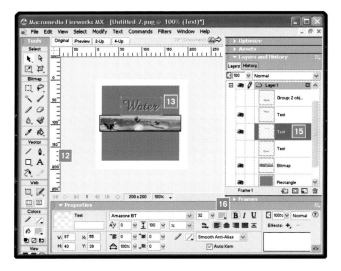

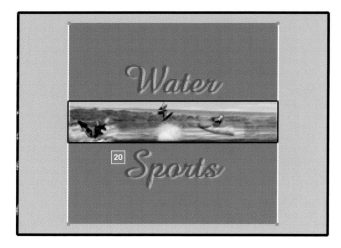

12. **Select the Text tool with these settings:**
    Font: Amazone BT, Size: 32, Color: Dark green (sample from the trees), Bold, and Alias: Smooth Anti-Alias.

13. **Type the word** Water **and center it over the image.**

< N O T E >
Select the size from the drop-down menu to the right of the font field.

14. **Choose Edit→Clone (or copy and paste).**

15. **In the Layers panel, select the first text object (below the clone).**

< T I P >
To see the field names for Distance, Softness, and so on, pass your mouse over the various fields. Distance is near the number in the top-left field and Softness is below the opacity.

16. **Click the fill color box, highlight the color number, and type** #99CCCC. **Press Enter.**

17. **Press the right arrow key two times and the down arrow one time.**
    By offsetting the bottom copy you are adding some dimension to the text.

18. **Shift-select both text objects and group them (Ctrl+G [⌘+G]).**
    The easiest way to select both text objects is to do it in the Layers panel.

19. **Center over the image.**

20. **Repeat steps 12 through19 for the word** Sports **and center it below the image.**

21. **Choose Modify→Fit Canvas.**

22. **Choose Select→Select All.**

23. **Choose Modify→Flatten Selection.**

24. **Choose File→Save As. Name the image** water.png **and save it into the source_files_CD_covers/water folder.**

Tutorial
» Placing Text on a Path

In this tutorial you place the text for one of the CD covers on a curved path.

1. **Choose File→Open and navigate to the session4 folder. Select** `flower.jpg` **and click Open.**
   This image was cropped out of a larger image using the crop from a selection technique you learned earlier in this session.

2. **Select the Ellipse tool and draw a circle that roughly covers the large flower in the center.**
   The sample uses a width of 131 and height of 111.

3. **Select the Text tool and use these settings:**
   Font: Arial
   Size: 16
   Color: Orange
   Stroke color: Black (click the stroke color box and click a black swatch)

4. **Type the words** Wild Flowers.

5. **Place the text above the circle and Shift-select the text and the circle.**

6. **Choose Text→Attach to Path.**
   Notice that the text isn't centered over the circle. You fix that next.

7. **The text should still be selected. In the Property inspector, type** 42 **into the Offset field and press Enter.**
   If you are using a different font or size, adjust the offset amount. You can also use negative values to move in the opposite direction.

8. **Choose Select→Select All and then choose Modify→Flatten Selection.**

9. **Choose File→Save As and navigate to the source_files/ CD_covers/flowers folder. Save your work as** `flower.png`.

<NOTE>
In the CD_covers folder in the session4 folder are some additional covers you didn't make here. The horses cover uses the same techniques as the water sports cover except it uses the Photoshop PSD image you imported in Session 1. The peoples CD cover uses the masking technique you used on the men for the home page.

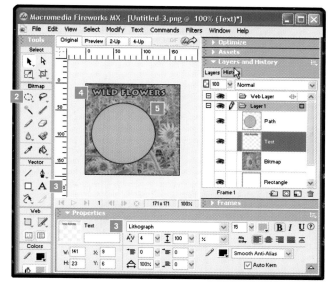

Tutorial
» Making a Command

In Fireworks, a command is a recording of actions you take. This command can then be replayed to automate a set of steps. In this tutorial, you add a 1-pixel border to an image and then record the command. The command is used in a batch process of the CD covers.

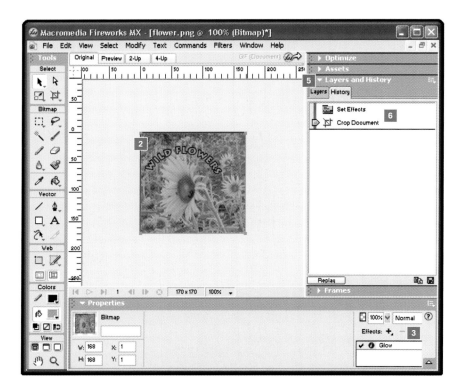

1. **Choose File→Open and navigate to the** flower.png **file you saved in the source_files/CD_covers/flowers folder.**
   You are using this image only to add a border to it. You save the action as a command.

2. **Select the flower image.**

3. **In the Property inspector, click the plus sign for Effects and select Shadow and Glow→Glow using these settings:**
   Distance: 1
   Color: Black
   Opacity: 100
   Softness: 0
   Offset: 0

4. **Choose Modify→Canvas→Fit Canvas.**
   You needed to do this because the one-pixel border was outside the canvas area. You can now see the border.

5. **Click the History panel expander arrow to open the panel group. Select the History tab.**

6. **Notice the entries there.**
   Set Effects and Crop Document are the two things you've done to the image.

7. **Shift-select both entries.**

8. **Open the History Options pop-up menu and select Save Command.**

<NOTE>

In the History panel there is a line visible dividing what records and what cannot record. If you see actions you take below a line, that action might not work properly. A warning dialog box alerts you of this. For example, the process of grouping objects isn't recordable.

9. **Name it** 1px_border **and click OK.**

10. **Close the flower image and don't save it.**

11. **Choose File→Open Recent and select** flower.png.

12. **Select the image and choose Commands→1px_border.**
The command adds to the Commands menu automatically. It is located at the bottom.

13. **Deselect the image.**
Notice that the border has been added and the image cropped automatically!

14. **Close the image without saving.**
This was just a test to show you how commands work and are applied.

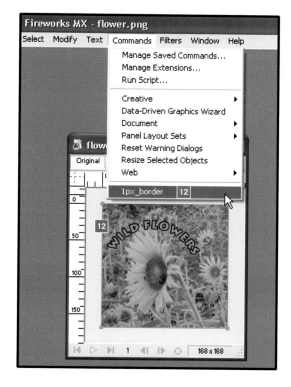

Tutorial
» Performing a Batch Process

In this tutorial, you learn how to automate tasks. You can add files from different folders into the process and automatically optimize, resize, and run the 1px_border command all at the same time.

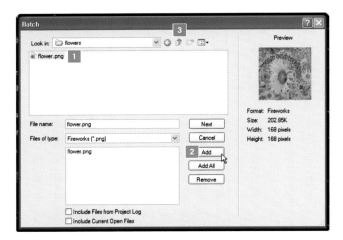

1. **Choose File→Batch Process. In the Batch dialog box, navigate to the source_files/CD_covers/flowers folder and select** `flower.png`**.**

2. **Click the Add button.**

3. **Click the Up One Level icon and navigate to the horses folder.**

4. **Select** `horses.jpg` **and click Add.**

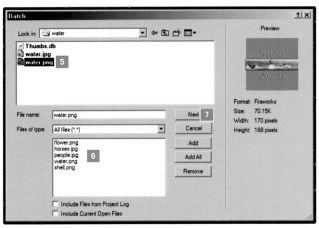

5. **Repeat steps 3 and 4 for the shell, people, and water folders.**

6. **Notice the files being added to the batch process.**

7. **Click the Next button.**

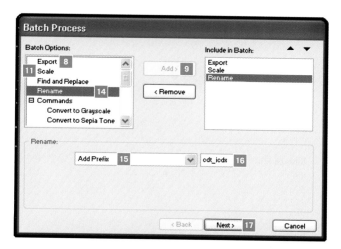

8. **Select the Export option.**

9. **Click the Add button.**

10. **In the Settings area, choose JPEG Better Quality from the drop-down list.**

11. **Select Scale and then click Add.**

12. **In the Scaling drop-down list box, choose Scale to Size.**

13. **Type 83x83.**

    The final thumbnail size you want is 85x85. Because there is a 1-pixel border you need to subtract one pixel for each side.

14. **Select Rename and click Add.**

15. **Select Add Prefix from the Rename drop-down list.**

16. **Type cdt_icdx.**

    This part of the name is added in front of the current name.

17. **Click the Next button.**

18. **Click Custom Location and navigate to the stockimagenation//html/images/cdts folder of your site's root folder.**

19. **Click Batch.**

    You may get a missing fonts warning. Just choose to Maintain Appearance.

20. **Check your cdts folder and you see the newly optimized images.**

21. **Choose File→Batch Process.**

22. **Navigate to the stockimagenation/html/images/cdts folder. Shift-select all the images except the macro image and click the Add button.**

23. **Click Next.**

24. **Click the arrow next to Commands. Scroll down and select 1px_border and click the Add button. Click the Next button.**

25. **Choose to save this in the same location as the original file. Click Batch.**

    You can open any of the images in the cdts folder and see that they have all been resized and a border added.

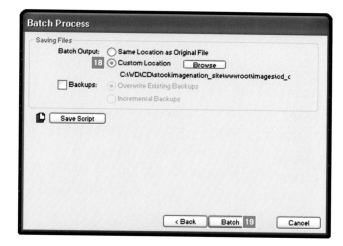

<TIP>
If you create a lot of thumbnails with the same settings, save the script to use again.

<NOTE>
You won't add the command in the batch process here because it currently doesn't work properly. You can do it separately if this bug is fixed.

Tutorial
» Fading an Image into the Background

In this tutorial, you blend images into the sidebar of the details page using a vector mask.

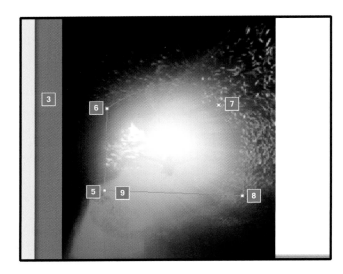

<NOTE>
If you are having a problem using the Pen tool, refer to the
Pen_tool.mov movie in the movies folder on the CD-ROM.

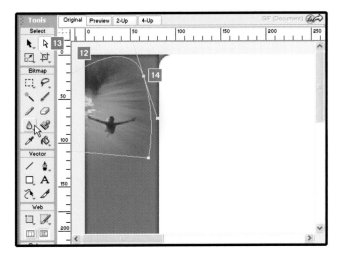

1. **Choose File→Open and navigate to the source_files/pages/ detail folder. Open** details.png.
   You can use the details.png file in the session4 folder if you'd prefer.

2. **Choose File→Import and navigate to the session4 folder. Open** swimmer_detail.jpg.

3. **Click in the** details.png **document to place the image.**
   You mask out all but the swimmer and add some water. The image is blended into the top of the left sidebar.

4. **Select the Pen tool and use these settings:**
   Fill: Solid
   Color: White
   Edge: Feather 50

5. **Click to place a point where you see the number 5 in the illustration (lower-left corner).**

6. **Click again straight up from the left corner point.**

7. **Click and drag to form the curve for the third point.**

8. **Click again for the bottom-right corner point.**

9. **Click the beginning point to close the shape.**

10. **Shift-select the vector shape and the image.**

11. **Choose Modify→Mask→Group As Mask.**
    All you see now is the swimmer and a bit of water.

12. **Place the image in the top-left corner.**
    If your shape is a bit too large and you see any of it overlapping the white, you can edit the mask.

13. **Select the Subselection tool and click the shape to select it.**

14. **Click and drag any point to move it or drag the handle of the curve to adjust the shape.**

15. Choose File→Import and open the water_detail.jpg image. Click in the details.png document to place the image.

16. Use the Pen tool to make a shape as seen in the illustration. You use only a small portion of this image.

17. Use a solid white fill and a feather of 80.

18. Shift-select both the shape and the image and choose Modify→Mask→Group As Mask.

19. Place the image in the lower portion of the left sidebar.

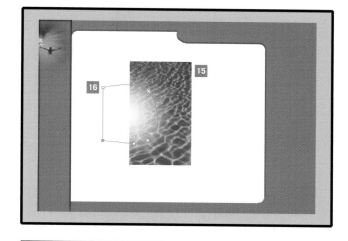

20. Draw a rectangle 82x69 with no stroke.

21. Select Linear from the Fill Category drop-down list in the Property inspector.

22. Click in the fill color box and click the left color marker. Use the eyedropper and click the blue in the document.

23. Change the right marker to the same color.

24. Click the right Transparency marker and change it to an opacity of 0.
    This setting will make the gradient go from invisible to 100% color.

25. Place the rectangle to cover the shadow in the lower-left part of the sidebar.

26. Click the small arrow in the corner of the Paint Bucket tool icon.
    From the flyout menu, select Gradient tool.

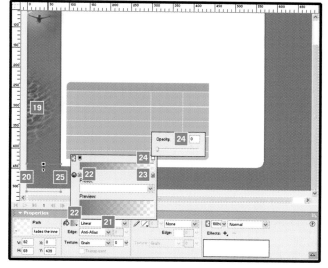

27. Select your small rectangle and hold the Gradient tool at the top center of the rectangle. Drag down.
    This changes the direction of the gradient from top to bottom instead of left to right.

28. Choose File→Save.

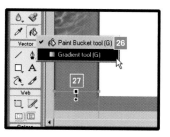

» Session Review

In this session you learned a lot about using the shape tools, including how to edit them and how to use the Text tool. Here are some questions to see how much you've retained from this session's exercises. The answers can be found in the tutorials listed in parentheses.

1. Which tool did you use to remove the white background from around the men on the homepage? ("Tutorial: Removing the Background from an Image")

2. How did you add more to the original selection? ("Tutorial: Removing the Background from an Image")

3. What color of the gradient can you see the image when the mask is applied? ("Tutorial: Removing the Background from an Image")

4. Do you have to select the Crop tool to make a selection? ("Tutorial: Cropping a Selection")

5. How did you get the marquee selection to be a specific size? ("Tutorial: Cropping a Selection")

6. Where do you find the Drop Shadow command? ("Tutorial: Cropping a Selection")

7. Which panel is used to save commands? ("Tutorial: Making a Command")

8. Where do you find a command you make and want to use? ("Tutorial: Making a Command")

9. Can you add files from more than one folder to a batch process? ("Tutorial: Performing a Batch Process")

10. How do you edit a mask that has already been applied to an image? ("Tutorial: Fading an Image into the Background")

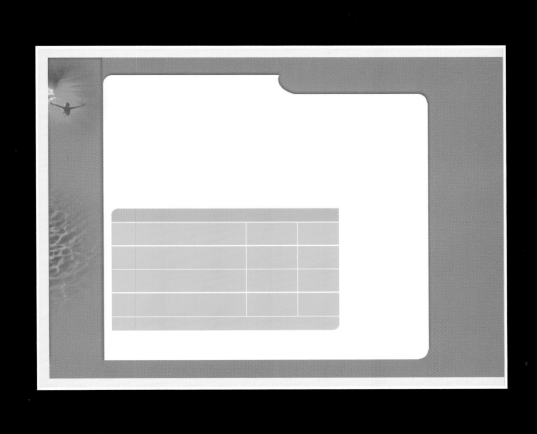

Session 5

Fireworks Animation

Tutorial: **Transforming Text to a Graphic and Scaling It**

Tutorial: **Finishing the Image Animation**

Tutorial: **Animating a Symbol**

Tutorial: **Editing a Symbol**

Working with Frames

What makes an animation different from other Fireworks objects is that the animation has multiple frames. Each frame contains different images to give the illusion of motion. Frames and layers are not the same. Layers are used to organize your content whereas frames are used to store images for animations or for rollover effects.

Fireworks frames are similar to the frames of a traditional filmstrip. One frame plays at a time. The more frames you add, the longer the movie and the larger the file size. You make two animations in this session. To learn advanced methods of using frames in Fireworks you might want to pick up one of the Fireworks reference books such as the *Fireworks MX Bible* or a project book such as the *Fireworks MX Zero to Hero* book.

<NOTE>

Because this session is not essential to the project you create in this book, it appears on the CD-ROM instead of in the book. If you want to learn all about Fireworks animation, try Session 5 on the CD before proceeding.

TOOLS YOU'LL USE
Text tool, Frames panel, Optimize panel, Library panel, Transform command

MATERIALS NEEDED
None

TIME REQUIRED
90 minutes

Part III
Finalizing the
Images for Export

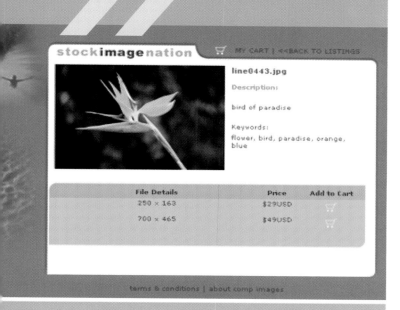

stockimagenation

MY CART | <<BACK TO LISTINGS

line0443.jpg

Description:

bird of paradise

Keywords:
flower, bird, paradise, orange,
blue

File Details	Price	Add to Cart
250 × 163	$29USD	
700 × 465	$49USD	

terms & conditions | about comp images

Preparing
the Mockups

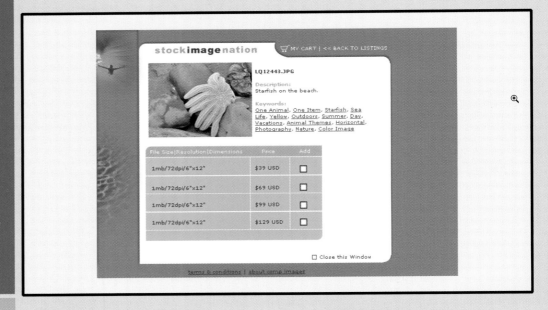

Tutorial: **Finishing the Home Page Layout**

Tutorial: **Preparing the Details Page Mockup**

Client Mockups

A mockup can be created in many ways. Some people simply create a preliminary sketch before making the design in Fireworks. The benefit of producing the mockup in Fireworks is that you can use it to present the site design idea to the client. Once your mockup is approved you can make any changes needed. Your Fireworks design or mockup can also be shared with others on a team so that everyone involved knows how the final page is supposed to look.

TOOLS YOU'LL USE
Rectangle tool, Text tool, Property inspector, Layers and Frames panels

MATERIALS NEEDED
cdt_icdxmacro.png, detail_image.png, details.png, LG_man.png, MD_man.png, register.png, SM_man.png, and stockimagenation.png

TIME REQUIRED
60 minutes

Tutorial
» Finishing the Home Page Layout

The home page needs some tweaking at this point. In this tutorial, you add the three men, move the sidebar icons, add mock content, and make the rollovers for the navigation buttons. The file is then be ready for slicing and optimizing in the next session.

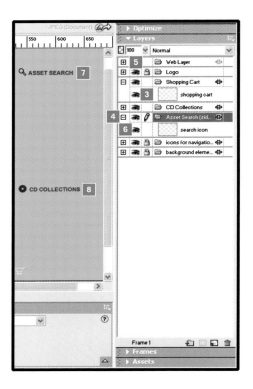

1. **Open Fireworks.**

2. **Choose File→Open and navigate to your** stockimagenation/ source_files/pages/home/ **folder. Select** stockimagenation.png **and open it.**
   There is also a copy on the CD-ROM in the session6 folder.

3. **Click the lock on the Asset Search layer to unlock it (the lock symbol is not visible).**

4. **Click the plus (+) symbol to open the layer.**

5. **Click the spot to the right of the minus sign to turn on the layer visibility (make the eye visible).**

6. **Click the visible area for the icon (underneath the layer's eye) to turn on its visibility.**

7. **You can see the icon in the main white area of the document. Click and drag it to the top of the orange sidebar.**

8. **Repeat steps 3 through 6 for CD Collections, and then move it toward the bottom third of the sidebar.**

9. **Repeat steps 3 through 6 for the Shopping cart icon. Just move it to the bottom corner of the sidebar, and then turn its visibility back off.**
   The cart is invisible. When you select it in the Layers panel it has four blue corners. Drag that to the sidebar area.

< N O T E >
You remove the shopping cart icon from this page and place it on the details page later in this session. You just needed to get it out from the white area so you didn't have to try and select it later when the photos of the men are in place.

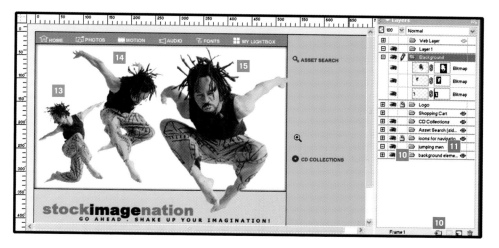

10. **Unlock the background elements layer and then select it. Click the New/Duplicate layer icon to add a new layer.**

11. **Double-click the new layer and name it** jumping men.

12. **Choose File→Import and navigate to the session6 folder on the CD-ROM. Select** SM_man.png **and open it.**
    You see a little corner shape cursor.

13. **Click to the left side of your document to place the image.**

14. **Import** MD_man.png **from the CD and click to place in the center.**
    Don't worry about alignment yet.

15. **Import** LG_man.png **from the CD and click to place on the right.**

16. **Now move the men around until they look good to you.**
    The coordinates used here are Small: x: -4, y: 134, Medium: x: 64, y: 18, and Large: x: 236, y: 17.

17. **Select the Text tool and use these settings:**
    Font: Verdana, Size: 10, Black, No Anti-Alias.

18. **At the top of the orange sidebar, type** Register | Sign In.

19. **Below the Asset Search icon, type the following:**
    Search our image, motion,
    audio, and font assets
    using keyword(s), image
    number(s), or collection
    title(s):

20. **Use the Pointer tool to place the text so it looks good.**

21. **Select the Rectangle tool and draw a rectangle. In the Property inspector, change the width (W) to 97 and the height (H) to 18.**

22. **In the Property inspector, click the color box for the stroke (pencil icon) and select the dark gray color. Change the fill color to white.**

NOTE
You are using No Anti-Alias on this text because it represents how the page is going to look. HTML text, which you enter in Dreamweaver, is not aliased text. This better represents how the end product will look. None of the sidebar text other than the icons will be exported from Fireworks. You are simply placing the text so clients and others can see how the page will look.

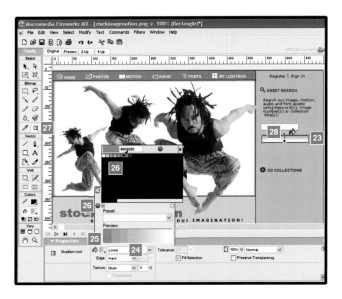

23. **Draw another rectangle and change the size to 121x20.**

24. **From the Fills category drop-down list, select Linear.**

25. **Click in the color box and choose Black/white from the preset drop-down list.**

26. **Click the left color tab and change the color to the dark gray.**
   The linear gradient is horizontal. You want it to be vertical, so you change that next.

27. **Next to the Paint Bucket tool is a little triangle. Click the triangle and hold and select the Gradient tool.**

28. **Press the Shift key and click and drag above the rectangle and down to make the vertical gradient.**
   You press the Shift key to keep the gradient straight.

29. **Select the Text tool and change the font to Arial, size 14, black (be sure the Fill type is set to Solid), and No anti-Alias. Type** Begin search. **Center the text on the button shape.**

30. **Change the font back to Verdana, size 10, black, Underlined (U). Type these three lines (the underline simulates a link):**
   Advanced Image Search
   Research Request
   Search Tips

31. **Use the Pointer tool to place the text under the Search button.**

32. **Choose File→Import and navigate to the session6 folder. Select** `cdt_icdxmacro.png` **and click Open. Place it below the CD collections icon.**

33. **Select the Text tool (Verdana should still be entered in the Property inspector) and type the following:**
    Check out the latest in our
    value-priced <u>CD collections</u>,
    from photographic essays to
    multi-asset discs.

<NOTE>
To underline just the CD collections part of the text, type all the text and then go back and highlight the words CD collections. Then click the Underline icon in the Property inspector.

34. **Place the text below the image.**

35. **You can lock all the layers except for the icons for navigation layer.**

36. **Open the Frames panel.**

37. **From the Frames Options pop-up menu select Duplicate Frame. Select the After Current Frame option and click OK.**
    Frame 2 is added.

38. **Select the Home icon at the top of the document and choose Modify→Ungroup. Repeat for the Photos and Audio icons.**
    You change the color of the text, which is a fill, and the color of the icons for the rollovers, which are coded in Dreamweaver.

<NOTE>
All the rollover icon images are on Frame 2. When you export in the next session, these images are exported as well and you use them in Dreamweaver for the rollovers. You can easily code rollovers in Fireworks but it's better to do so in Dreamweaver.

39. **Select the Home icon drawing (not the text). Click in the stroke color box and select black.**

40. **Select the Photos icon.**
    If you don't have the icon grouped, there are three pieces. Shift-select them all and change the stroke color to black. Repeat for the Audio icon.

41. **Shift-select the Home, Photos, Audio text as well as the Motion, Font, and Lightbox icons (which you didn't ungroup).**

42. **Click in the fill color box and select black.**
    When you are done, all your icons and text are black.

43. **Save your file in the source_files/pages/home folder.**

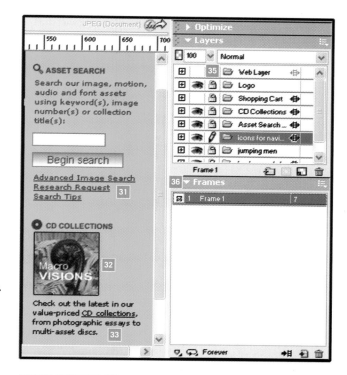

<NOTE>
Your home page is now ready to be optimized and sliced into smaller images for use in Dreamweaver. You can use the designs you make in Fireworks as your mockup for the client. If they approve the design, you are ready to optimize and export for use in Dreamweaver.

Tutorial
» Preparing the Details Page Mockup

In this tutorial, you prepare the Details page mockup.

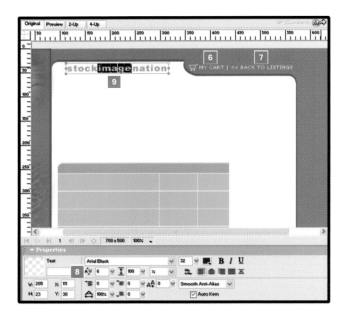

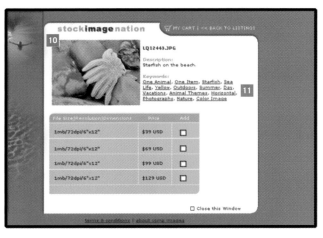

1. **Choose File→Open and navigate to your source_files/pages/home folder. Open the** `stockimagenation.png` **file.**

2. **Unlock the Shopping cart layer and turn on its visibility.**

3. **Select the shopping cart icon from the layout and choose Edit→Cut (Ctrl+X / ⌘+X).**

4. **Save and close the stockimagenation file.**

5. **Open** `details.png` **from the session6 folder and paste the shopping cart icon (Ctrl+V / ⌘+V).**

6. **Move the cart to the top-right side of the design in the blue area.**

7. **Select the Text tool. Use Verdana, Size 10, white, and No Anti-alias. Type** MY CART | <<BACK TO LISTINGS **and place the text next to the cart.**

8. **Change the text properties to Font: Arial Black, Size 20, dark gray, Smooth Anti-alias, and Kerning 6. Type** stockimagenation.

9. **Use the Text tool to highlight just the word** image. **Click in the fill color box and select black.**

10. **Choose File→import and navigate to the session6 folder. Select** `detail_image.png` **and click below the logo to place the image.**

11. **All that is left is to add the mock text. Because all of this text will be added in Dreamweaver, we won't take the time to fill it all in, but for a mockup you would.**

12. **Save your file in the source_files/pages/detail folder.**

» Session Review

Here are some questions to see how much you've retained from this session's exercises. The answers to the questions are located in the tutorial noted in parentheses.

1. How do you unlock a layer? ("Tutorial: Finishing the Home Page Layout")

2. How do you add an effect? ("Tutorial: Finishing the Home Page Layout")

3. Which tool do you use to make a vertical gradient? ("Tutorial: Finishing the Home Page Layout")

4. Where do you put images that you want to be rollovers? ("Tutorial: Finishing the Home Page Layout")

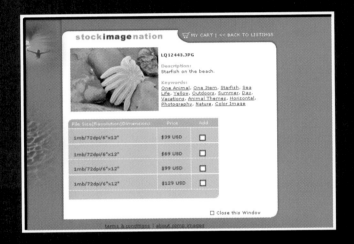

stock**image**nation   🛒 MY CART | << BACK TO LISTINGS

LQ12443.JPG

Description:
Starfish on the beach.

Keywords:
<u>One Animal</u>, <u>One Item</u>, <u>Starfish</u>, <u>Sea Life</u>, <u>Yellow</u>, <u>Outdoors</u>, <u>Summer</u>, <u>Day</u>, <u>Vacations</u>, <u>Animal Themes</u>, <u>Horizontal</u>, <u>Photography</u>, <u>Nature</u>, <u>Color Image</u>

File Size|Resolution|Dimensions	Price	Add
1mb/72dpi/6"x12"	$39 USD	☐
1mb/72dpi/6"x12"	$69 USD	☐
1mb/72dpi/6"x12"	$99 USD	☐
1mb/72dpi/6"x12"	$129 USD	☐

☐ Close this Window

terms & conditions | about comp images

Session 7

Optimizing and Exporting Images for Use in Dreamweaver Layouts

Slicing and Optimizing

This session explores how to intricately slice (divide) your designs and apply optimization settings. Slicing an image or document is one of the most important things you do in Fireworks. The decisions of whether to slice your document, as well as where and how to slice it all contribute to how, and sometimes whether, users view your Web pages. Slicing, when needed, allows for better and specialized optimization to decrease the file size. Using slicing techniques ultimately reduces the file size of your project.

Once your slices are defined, you learn how to optimize them. *Optimization*, the process of shrinking a file or image to its smallest possible size while retaining acceptable quality, is one of the most important factors in how fast your Web page loads. Once the images are sliced and optimized, you learn how to export your images.

TOOLS YOU'LL USE
Slice tool, Optimize panel, Preview, Export dialog box

MATERIALS NEEDED
details_table.png, image_animation.png, nation4animation.png, shake.png, stock4animation.png, stockimagenation.png, and submenu_graphics.png

TIME REQUIRED
90 minutes

Tutorial
» Slicing the Home Page Layout

The home page created in this book is almost entirely images, so you slice most of it up to use in a Dreamweaver layout. You then optimize each slice to get the smallest file sizes possible.

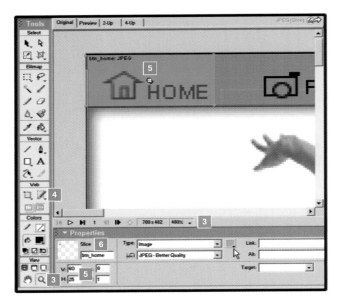

1. **Open Fireworks.**

2. **Choose File→Open and navigate to the session7 folder on the CD. Select** stockimagenation.png **and open it.**

3. **Select the Zoom tool and click the document a few times. Zoom in to about 400%.**
   Look at the status bar on the bottom of the document to see the zoom amount.

4. **Select the Slice tool.**

5. **Click and drag a rectangle around the word** *Home*. **Place your cursor inside the black lines.**
   The slice size should be 60x25 (check and/or change it in the Property inspector). Use the keyboard arrow keys to position the slice exactly. The coordinates are x: 1, y: 1. This places the slice just under and to the right of the black border.

<TIP>
Some parts of a design can be done in Dreamweaver without an image. Whenever you can add color or design elements without using images, you can reduce the file size of your page.

<NOTE>
Before you slice a Fireworks document, it helps to understand how the images are used. For example, the navigation area uses rollovers, so you need a separate slice for each image. If you are new to using Dreamweaver, you won't understand which slices to make or where to make them. When you are more comfortable with Dreamweaver, you will be able to make these decisions. For teaching purposes you are given the dimensions so that your slices fit properly when you get to Dreamweaver. Don't despair! You'll understand the reasoning more when you learn to do your own Dreamweaver layout.

6. **In the Property inspector, type** btn_home **for the slice name. Enter it in the Slice field.**
   I use btn in front of the name so that all the buttons list together alphabetically in the Assets panel in Dreamweaver. Also, this is the name Fireworks uses when exporting the image. Don't worry about the extension you see in Fireworks after the slice name such as GIF or JPEG. You change these settings in the next tutorial.

<NOTE>
Notice the red lines. These are slice lines that Fireworks generates to slice the rest of the document based on the slice you defined. You can export the document right now and Fireworks would automatically slice where the red lines are. However, I don't show you how to do this because I don't recommend this technique. It always produces far too many images. It's better to define only the slices you need.

To Slice or Not to Slice

Before beginning to slice your images, you need to understand why an image might need to be sliced. Many people mistakenly believe that slicing always increases the loading speed. This usually isn't so; in most cases, the page actually takes longer to load. This is because there are more requests for files from the server. Each request then requires the server to find, access, and send the file out. However, slicing does make the page *appear* to load faster, because the users can see parts of the image before the whole thing loads. This is an important perception to present—it beats staring at a blank page.

Many reasons exist to slice an image:

» If an image is over 20KB, it needs to be sliced.

» If you need to export some slices as JPEGs and some as GIFs, or GIF animations within the same image, slicing is best way to go; that way some of the slices can be a different format to suit your needs.

» If you want to attach behaviors such as rollovers to an area, it has to be a slice or hotspot object.

» Slices ease page loading when you have a logo or other repeating elements in the Web site because you can place the same slice on every page using the repeating element.

When you have a logo or element that is repeated often within your site, be sure that the element or slice is linked to the same image file. That way, after the server retrieves it one time, it is in the browser's cache on the local machine. If you use the same image and give it different names or put it in different folders, the server has to fetch it each time.

Another wonderful advantage of slices is that if you need to update one section or slice, you don't have to redo the whole image. For instance, suppose you have a complicated sliced image that you have optimized, sliced, exported, and incorporated into every page on a large site. You then discover that one of the major slices contains a misspelled word. You can simply fix a copy of the one sliced image, optimize it, export it, and upload it to replace the image with the error.

7. **Select the Slice tool again. This time, draw another slice next to the first slice in the blank area.**
   The slice size needs to be 21x25. Be sure it has the same y coordinate of 1.

8. **Name this slice** spacer1 **in the Slice field of the Property inspector.**

9. **Repeat these same steps for the remaining icons and spacers. Refer to Table 2.1 for the sizes and names of each slice.**
   You won't actually be exporting the spacers, but they are there to help you get the correct slice for the buttons. Fireworks requires that you name each slice differently.

Table 2.1: Slice Instructions

Slice Area	Slice Size	Slice Name
Photos icon	65x25	btn_photos
Next spacer	21x25	spacer2
Motion icon	65x25	btn_motion
Next spacer	21x25	spacer3
Audio icon	56x25	btn_audio
Next spacer	21x25	spacer4
Fonts icon	56x25	btn_fonts
Next spacer	21x25	spacer5
Lightbox icon	95x25	btn_mybox
Next spacer	21x25	spacer6

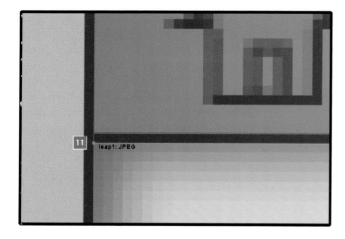

10. **Select the Slice tool and draw a slice around the entire white box with the shadow and men.**
    Stay within the black outline. The slice size needs to be 523x310. After the slice is made and sized, use your keyboard arrows to position it exactly. The feet of the large man and his hand won't be included in the slice. The coordinates are x: 1, y: 27.

11. **Name the slice leap1.**

12. **Draw another slice right below the white area to cover most of the bottom. It'll go over the man's feet.**
    The size should be 523x97. Position it against the bottom of the leap1 slice and to the right of the black line. The coordinates are x: 1, y: 338.

13. **Name the slice leap_logo.**

14. **In the Layers panel, unlock the Logo layer and turn the visibility off for both text objects. You don't want to see any of the logo.**
    Recall that you made an animation for the logo, which you export separately. In this layout the logo was for the mockup only, but you don't want to export it. By turning off the visibility, you won't export it.

Understanding the Web Layer

In the Layers panel you see the Web Layer. The Web Layer contains all the hotspot coordinates and slices that you make in your document. Everything on this layer is shared across all layers, meaning that if a slice or hotspot encloses elements that are actually on different layers, the slice or hotspot is active on each layer. The slice or hotspot activates whatever behavior you have assigned to it. You can't delete the Web layer and you can't add another one.

15. **Zoom 600% into the top area by the black border and the orange sidebar.**

16. **Draw a slice that is 6x25 and name it** sbcol1.
    The name stands for sidebar column 1, which is where it is placed in Dreamweaver.

17. **Use the arrow keys to position the slice directly over the black line and into the orange area.**
    The coordinates should be x: 525, y: 1.

18. **Draw another slice that is 6x1 and name it** sbcol2. **Place it directly beneath the first slice.**

19. **Draw one more slice for this area and make it 6x310. Name it** sbcol3. **Place it directly below the sbcol2.**

20. **Draw one more slice that is 6x1 and place it below the third column slice. Name it** sbcol4.
    These four slices are used for spaces in a column in Dreamweaver. This extra small column is necessary because of the hand that overlaps into the orange area.

21. **Draw a slice over the Asset Search icon and text. It should be 168x17 and be placed against the column slice. Name it** sbbtn_assets.

22. **Draw the last slice over the CD Collections text and icon. Make it 168x16 and name it** sbbtn_cds.

23. **Save your file.**

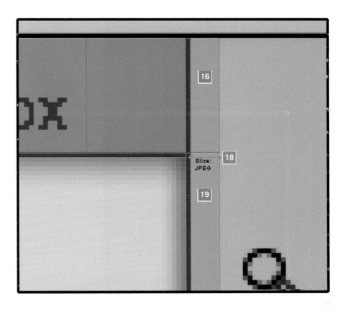

<N O T E>
Images that go beyond their rectangle boundaries create more work, but make this site look better. Such images give the site that extra WOW appeal.

Discussion
Optimizing Your Images

The technology of high-speed Internet connections is improving every day, but the majority of users in the world—the Internet is global—still use modem connections. Users in most U.S. urban areas enjoy all kinds of options for high-speed connections, but many rural areas don't have that option, nor do a lot of other countries. When you get used to using high-speed connections, it can be easy to forget that you are privileged and that many users don't have such access.

Optimization, the process of shrinking a file or image to its smallest possible size while retaining acceptable quality, is one of the most important factors determining how fast your Web page loads. Not only can you export with GIF and JPEG images in the same document, but you can also actually apply different settings to specific areas of a JPEG image. The file types currently available for the Web include the PNG format, but not all browsers support it.

Previewing an image's optimization settings is vital and Fireworks makes it easy. You can view one setting or up to four optimization settings, including different file formats. The Preview tab in your document window shows the selected slice/slices without the slice overlay, with the current optimization settings applied.

Optimizing GIF Images

There are quite a few settings you can alter for optimizing a GIF image. You can select which indexed palette and how many colors you want to use. This image shows the Optimize panel with a GIF file format. The bottom row of icons is used to change or lock specific color swatches you choose to alter.

The Indexed Palette

GIF images are limited to 256 colors; the indexed palette you choose determines which 256 colors are included. You can lock a specific color in before you reduce colors if you want to be sure that that color isn't removed. There are nine preset indexed palettes in the Indexed Palette drop-down menu, plus custom (this is how you access a custom setting). Each palette makes available a different set of colors. With each palette you can customize it so that a site uses a specific set of colors. Then you save the new custom palette with a unique name.

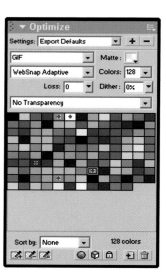

Table 7.1: Color Palettes in Fireworks

Palette Type	Purpose
Adaptive	A custom palette derived from the actual colors in the open document. You normally get the best looking image using this palette.
WebSnap Adaptive	This palette is derived from the actual colors in the document but any non-Web-safe colors are converted to the closest Web-safe color.
Web 216	216 of the colors common to both Windows and Macintosh computers.
Exact	The exact colors used in an image. This can be used only on images with 256 or fewer colors.
Macintosh	The 256 colors defined by the Macintosh platform standards.
Windows	The 256 colors defined by the Windows platform standards.
Grayscale	Up to 256 shades of gray. This palette converts your image to grayscale.
Black and White	A two-color palette of only black and white.
Uniform	A mathematical palette based on RGB pixel values.
Custom	A palette that has been modified or has been loaded from an external palette file.

Matte

The Matte option is available in all the file formats. On the right side of the Optimize panel, you see the label *Matte*. Notice the color box; gray and white checks indicate that the image is transparent. The Matte option allows you to export your image/slice as if it had a background color—without changing the canvas background color. This option is particularly important when you want to use the exported image in an environment different than the one it was designed in or if the image is going to be used on a variety of different colored backgrounds.

There is no transparency in a JPEG image so there is always be a background color. For GIF images that have transparent backgrounds, you want to use a Matte color that closely matches the background the image appears on. Images that have an anti-alias edge (most do) blend in with the background color.

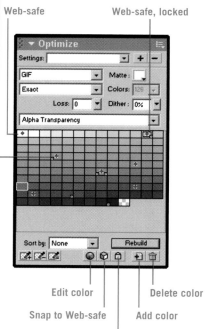

Snap to Web-safe

Web-safe

Web-safe, locked

Edit color

Delete color

Snap to Web-safe

Add color

Lock color

Reducing Colors

You can reduce the size of your image file by reducing the amount of colors used. You simply choose a number from the Maximum Number of Colors pop-up menu or reduce colors from the Color Table. If you choose a color amount from the Maximum Number of Colors pop-up and the number is less than the colors that are actually present in your image, Fireworks deletes colors based on the least used colors in the image.

The Color Table is the area where you see color swatches in the Optimize panel. If you don't see the swatches or if you make a change to the optimizations settings, just click the Rebuild button in the lower-right corner. An updated table of colors displays. The Rebuild button is only visible if the colors in the color table don't reflect the most current settings you chose as shown in the figure.

Setting Transparency

Transparency is available for GIF and PNG files. Your choices are Index and Alpha transparency. The difference is often confusing. To experience the difference first-hand, follow these steps:

1. Open a new document that's 300x300 and has a white background.

2. Select the Rectangle drawing tool and draw a square filled with black.

3. Draw another square in the center of the white one and fill it with white.

4. From the Optimize panel, be sure Matte is set to none and choose Index Transparency.

5. Click the Preview tab so you can see the results. The Index Transparency setting removes the background color, as well as any other areas that contain this color. Notice that the white box in the center is also gone.

6. Because removing color from other areas usually isn't acceptable, Alpha transparency, which removes only the background colors, is more frequently used.

< T I P >
When choosing Alpha Transparency, the view might not always show properly. Try clicking *No Transparency* first and then reselecting Alpha Transparency.

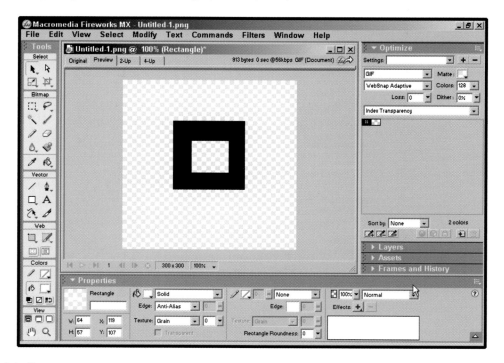

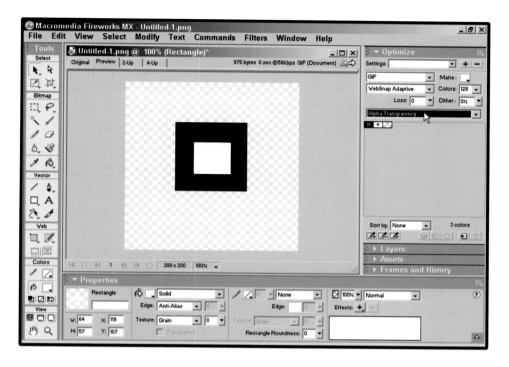

Optimizing JPEG Images

There aren't as many choices to make when optimizing JPEG images, but you still have some flexibility. Selective JPEG compression is used to set higher optimization to selected areas of an image.

Quality

The quality setting determines how much compression is applied to the image. Be sure you check in the Preview mode. It's a good idea to zoom in a bit to see the artifact effect on your image.

Smoothing

When you lower the quality setting, you may see visible artifacts. The Smooth option adds a bit of blur to blend the image a bit. You lose some image sharpness, of course, but it may be a compromise you are willing to make when a small file size is a must.

<TIP>
You have greater control over which colors are eliminated by using the color table. To make changes to colors, click the color (or use Shift-click to select multiple colors) and then make the change.

Tutorial
» Optimizing the Sliced Images

In this tutorial, you learn how to optimize each slice on the stockimagenation home page.

1. **Open your saved** stockimagenation.png **file if you've closed it.**

2. **You should still be able to see the slices. If not, click the Show slices and hotspots icon.**

3. **If you ever want to turn the slice view off, click the Hide slices and hotspots icon.**

4. **Select the home icon slice (btn_home).**

5. **Click the expander arrow of the Optimize panel to open it.**

6. **From the File Format drop-down menu, select GIF.**
   Gif is being used because the image has only a few colors and no gradients.

7. **Click the Preview tab in the document window to see how the image looks on the Web.**

8. **Set the indexed Palette to Adaptive.**

9. **Set the color to 32. Now look carefully at the preview and change it to 16.**
   You won't see any difference. Change it to 8 and colors drop out and the text is more jagged. Reset the colors to 16.
   This is a good way to test to get the lowest number of colors without losing quality. Even though there are only a few colors you still need to use 16 because of the anti-aliasing. If you use fewer colors you get jagged edges.

10. **Leave Transparency set to No Transparency.**

11. **Repeat the same settings for each of the navigation icons but not for the spacers.**

12. **Select the first spacer image (spacer1).**

13. **In the Optimize panel use these settings:**
   File Format: GIF
   Indexed Palette: Adaptive
   Colors: 2
   Transparency: No Transparency

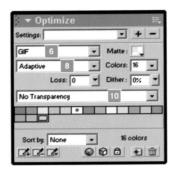

< N O T E >
When you are more experienced using the Optimize panel you can also eliminate specific colors by selecting them in the Optimize panel and clicking the trash can. You can remove colors that are very close to each other this way and not see a noticible difference in quality.

< N O T E >
The optimization settings you apply to the slice are also used for the rollover images in frame 2. You see after you export, that everything in the slice (including other frames) is exported.

14. **Select the large slice with the jumping men.**

15. **In the Optimize panel, change the Export File Format to JPEG.**
    Because this slice contains photos, it looks best as a JPEG.

16. **Set the Quality to 50 percent.**
    This setting is rather low, but if you check the Preview, it's quite acceptable. The file size is around 16KB, which is excellent for such a large image.

17. **Select the slice with the feet in it and zoom in so you can see the feet better.**

18. **Click the Preview tab. Now keep an eye on the feet and change the Export File Format to GIF and 128 colors.**
    Switch back to JPEG and then to GIF again to see the difference. There is some loss of color.

<NOTE>

The image of just the feet is an optional image if you want to add the animated logo (a bonus tutorial on the CD). You build the home page with the slice including the logo (non-animated).

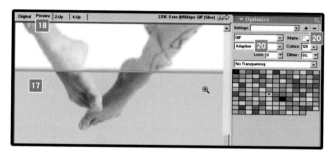

19. **Change the colors to 256.**
    This is a time that you have to make a judgment call. You might find that using 256 colors instead of 128 affords no improvement.

20. **Change the colors back to 128 and the Indexed Palette to Adaptive.**

<NOTE>

Although JPEG is the best format to use for the feet, you use GIF because the majority of this slice contains text eventually. You turn the text back on in the next tutorial to export it.

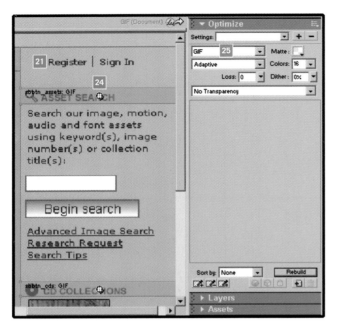

21. **Zoom in to the column slices.**

    You have to zoom in quite a bit to be able to select the slices.

22. **Shift-select all four column slices.**

23. **Change the Export File Format to GIF and select 2 colors.**

24. **Shift-select the two sidebar icon slices (Assets Search and CD Collections).**

    As you saw in step 22, you can change the optimization settings for multiple slices by selecting them all at once.

25. **Set the Export File Format to GIF, Adaptive, and 16 colors.**

< N O T E >

You can open the details.png file from the stockimagenation_site/source_files/pages/details folder on the CD-ROM. Be sure you have the view set to see slices. You can check this file over to see what areas were sliced. If you click each slice, you see the settings used in the Optimize panel.

Tutorial
» Exporting the Navigation Images

There are many ways to export images from Fireworks. If you plan on designing Web pages for a living, you will most frequently use the method taught in this tutorial. With this method, you can export images into specific site folders for use in a Dreamweaver layout.

1. **Open the** `stockimagenation.png` **file you optimized if you've closed it.**

2. **Shift-select all the top navigation icon slices only, not the spacer images.**

3. **Choose File→Export. The Export dialog box opens.**

4. **In the Save In field, click the down arrow and navigate to the stockimagenation/html/images/main_navs folder.**

5. **Type** nav **for the filename.**

6. **Click the Selected Slices Only option to select it.**
   None of the other options should be selected.

7. **Click Save.**

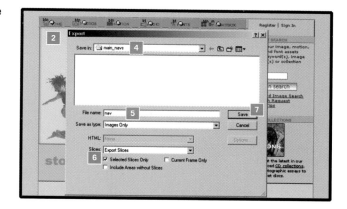

<NOTE>
Check your main_navs folder and you see each of your slices plus another one with _f2 added to the end of the name. This is for the rollover in Frame 2.

8. **Shift-select the navigation spacer images.**

9. **Choose File→Export.**

10. **Navigate to the main_navs folder.**
    You see the filenames of the slices you already exported. Notice the Notes folder. This folder is added automatically and is used by Fireworks and Dreamweaver to locate the original PNG file you used to export these images. This becomes important when you want to edit from within Dreamweaver.

11. **Select the Selected Slices Only option.**

12. **Select the Current Frame Only option.**
    The spacers are also on Frame 2 but you don't need the second image, so you check this option.

13. **Click Save.**

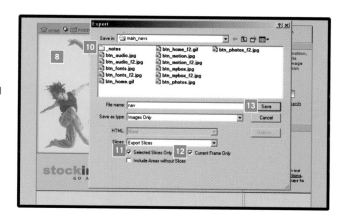

Tutorial
» Exporting the Submenus

In Dreamweaver, the menu icons show a drop-down menu when clicked. For this to work you need a couple of images in Dreamweaver. The menu is simply comprised of a rectangle and an arrow. Because you already know how to make these objects, you can simply use the submenu_graphics.png file in the session7 folder on the CD-ROM.

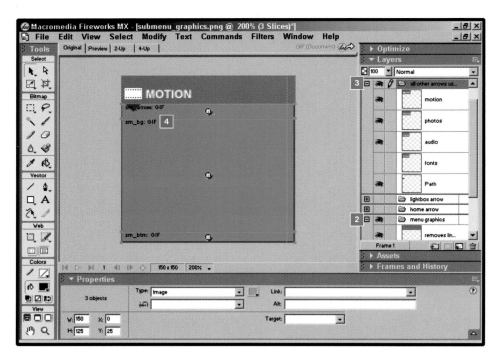

1. **Choose File→Open and navigate to the session7 folder. Select** submenu_graphics.png **and open it.**

<NOTE>

The submenu_graphics.png file contains graphics for each of the menus with the arrow in a different location. All but one is hidden until you are ready to export them. The motion icon is there simply so you can see how the menu relates to the menu icons; it isn't exported.

2. **In the Layers panel, click the plus sign (turns into a minus when clicked) in the menu graphics layer so you can see what it contains. Click the center text object to see sample menu text.**
Be sure to turn the visibility back off; you don't want to export it.

3. **Click the plus sign next to all the other layers so you can see what is in each layer. Notice that the motion icon is visible (the eye icon is present).**
This is the first one you are going to export. This arrow is used for all the menus except home and lightbox, which you export separately.

4. **Shift-select all three slices (the one with the arrow, the large one below it, and thin one on the bottom).**

5. **Choose File→Export. Select Images Only and select Export Selected Slices Only.**

6. **Navigate to the stockimagenation/html/images/submenus folder.**

7. **Name the file** submenus.

8. **Click Save.**

9. Hide all the other arrow layers and the lightbox layer.

10. Turn the visibility on for the home arrow layer.

11. Select the slice over the arrow and choose File→Export.

12. Navigate to the submenus folder.

13. In the Name field, type sm_arrow_home and click the Selected Slices Only option.

14. Click Save.

15. Turn the visibility off for the home arrow layer and turn it on for the lightbox arrow layer.

16. Repeat steps 11 through 14, except change the filename to sm_arrow_lightbox.

17. You can close the submenu_graphics file without saving.

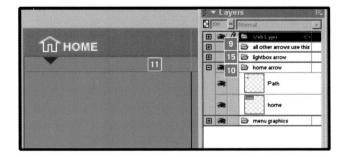

Tutorial
» Exporting the Rest of the Home Page

In this tutorial, you export the remaining images of the home page into their respective folders.

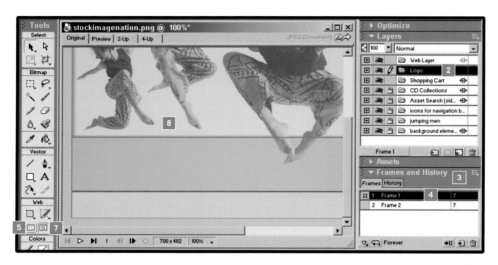

1. **Open** stockimagenation.png **if you've closed it.**

2. **In the Layers panel, turn the visibility on for the Logo layer.**

3. **Open the Frames panel. From the Frames Options pop-up menu, select Duplicate Layer. Accept the default and click OK.**

4. **Click Frame 1.**

5. **Click the Hide slices and hotspots icon to turn off the slices.**

6. **Delete the logo from frame 1.**
   You need to export the logo as a static image (without the animation you made), but you also need the slice with just the feet, which is why you do this. By having it both ways on different frames, you only have to perform one export to get both images.

7. **Click the Show slices and hotspots icon.**

8. **Select the leap1 and leap_logo slices (jumping men and logo/feet area).**

9. **Choose File→Export and navigate to the html/images/homeimages folder.**

10. **Name the file** leap **and select Selected Slices Only option and click Save.**

11. **Zoom in close enough to select the sidebar slices. Shift-select the four sidebar column slices as well as the two icon slices.**

12. **Choose File→Export and navigate to the html/images/sidebar-images folder.**

13. **Name the file** sidebar. **Select the Selected Slices only and Current Frame Only options and click Save.**

14. **Save the file and close.**

Tutorial

» Exporting the Animated Logo

The animated logo has portions that are animated and portions that are static. You slice it so you can export the different types of file formats separately.

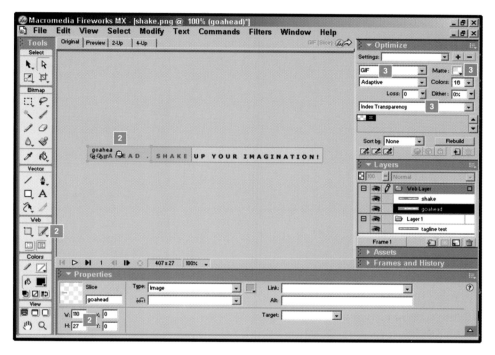

1. **Choose File→Open. From the session7 folder, open** shake.png. You saved this file in the source_files/logo_ani folder.

2. **Select the Slice tool and draw a slice over GO AHEAD. In the Property inspector, make the size 110x27 and name it** goahead. **Place the slice at the left of the image.**

3. **In the Optimize panel set the Export File Format to GIF, 16 colors, and Index Transparency.**

   Index Transparency makes the background color transparent.

<NOTE>

If the image happens to contain the same color as the background, you should use Alpha Transparency so that only the background color becomes transparent.

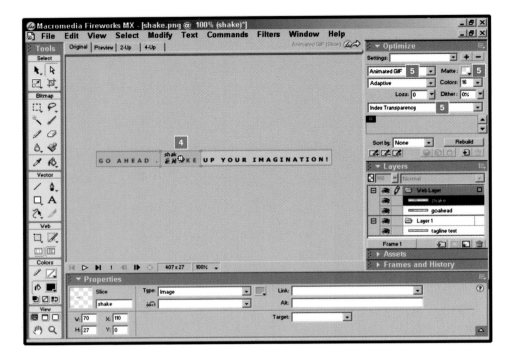

4. **Draw a slice over *Shake* and make it 70x27. Name it** shake.

5. **In the Optimize panel, change the Export File Format to Animated GIF. Leave the colors at 16 and Index Transparency.**

6. **Draw a slice over the remainder of the image and make it 227x27. Name it** imagenation **and use the same settings as in step 5.**

7. **Shift-select all three slices and choose File→Export. Select Selected Slices Only, name the file** imagination, **and save.**

8. **Navigate to the html/images/homeimages folder.**

9. **Choose File→Open. Navigate to the session7 folder and open** image_animation.png.

10. **Draw a slice over the entire image. The size will be 115x46. Name it** image.

11. **In the Optimize panel, change the Export File Format to Animated GIF, colors to 16, and choose Index Transparency.**

12. **Choose File→Export.**
    A window might open saying that the slice will be ignored. Just click OK.

13. **In the Slices drop-down menu, select Export Slices.**

14. **In the Export dialog box, be sure that the Save As Type field has Images Only selected.**

15. **Uncheck the Include Areas without Slices option and select the Selected Slices Only option. Save the file as** image.

16. **Choose File→Open and select** stock4animation.gif. **Press the Ctrl (⌘) key and select the** nation4animation.gif **file. Click Open.**
    Both files open.

17. **Draw a slice over each image and repeat steps 11 through 15 for each image. This time, use the GIF Export File Format. Name the stock4animation slice** stock **and the nation4animation slice** nation.
    These are exported as GIF only because they are not animations.

18. **Close all files and save them.**

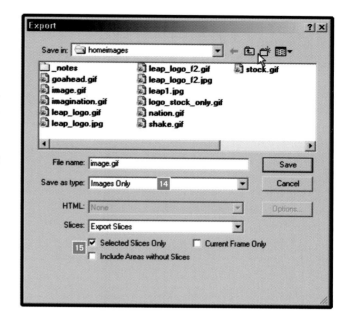

Tutorial
» Exporting the HTML and Images Directly

You can also export images and all the code to automatically produce an entire Web page from Fireworks. This technique is fine if you plan on making a site or two. But for serious designers, the previous method is the way to go. In this tutorial, you export the orange table with two rounded corners used in the details page as HTML and images. The file is then inserted with all the code into a Dreamweaver layout.

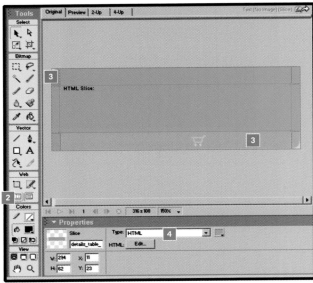

1. **Choose File→Open and navigate to the session7 folder. Open** `details_table.png`.

2. **Click the Hide slices or hotspots icon to see the table. Click the Show slices or hotspots icon again.**

3. **Notice that the top-right corner and the bottom-right corner images are a different color.**
   They are a different color because they are image slices like you already made.

4. **Click the large center bright green slice. Check the Property inspector. Notice that the Type field says HTML instead of images.**
   This slice and the other bright green slices are HTML slices. This means that you can either enter HTML text here in Fireworks or in Dreamweaver. In this case it's going to be done in Dreamweaver.

5. **Choose File→Export.**
   HTML and Images appear automatically in the Save as type field.

6. **Check the Put Images in Subfolder option and click Save.**

<TIP>

When you use the export HTML and Images option, all the code is exported to put the table together in a Web page. You can also upload the HTML file and all the images and have a working Web page.

» Session Review

In this session you learned how to slice images. You also learned how to set the optimization settings for GIFs, GIF animations, and JPEGs. Now is the time to test yourself to see how much you remember. The answers to the questions can be found in the tutorials noted in parentheses.

1. Does slicing its images make a page load faster? ("Tutorial: Slicing the Home Page Layout")

2. How are rollover images exported? ("Tutorial: Slicing the Home Page Layout")

3. What is the name of the layer that holds the slices you've made? ("Tutorial: Slicing the Home Page Layout")

4. How can you tell what your image will look like on the Web? ("Tutorial: Optimizing the Sliced Images")

5. Can you export more than one slice at a time? ("Tutorial: Exporting the Navigation Images")

6. What is the advantage to exporting slices only? ("Tutorial: Exporting the Navigation Images")

7. If an object or image is not visible, does it export with the slice? ("Tutorial: Exporting the Submenus")

8. Which Export File format do you use for an animation? ("Tutorial: Exporting the Animated Logo")

9. Where do you determine which slice is used? ("Tutorial: Exporting the HTML and Images Directly")

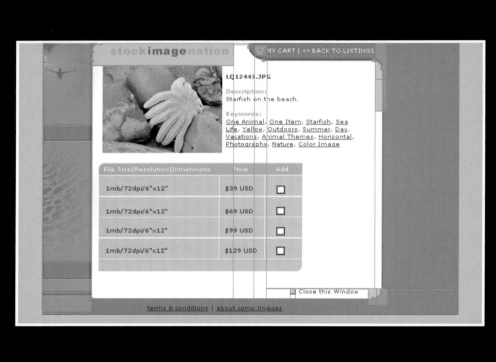

LQ12443.JPG

Description:
Starfish on the beach.

Keywords:
One Animal, One Item, Starfish, Sea Life, Yellow, Outdoors, Summer, Day, Vacations, Animal Themes, Horizontal, Photography, Nature, Color Image

File Size|Resolution|Dimensions	Price	Add
1mb/72dpi/6"x12"	$39 USD	☐
1mb/72dpi/6"x12"	$69 USD	☐
1mb/72dpi/6"x12"	$99 USD	☐
1mb/72dpi/6"x12"	$129 USD	☐

☐ Close this Window

terms & conditions | about comp images

Part IV
Laying Out the Site Using Dreamweaver MX

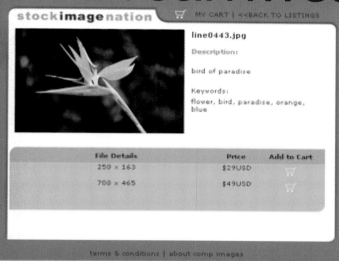

Setting Up the Site in Dreamweaver

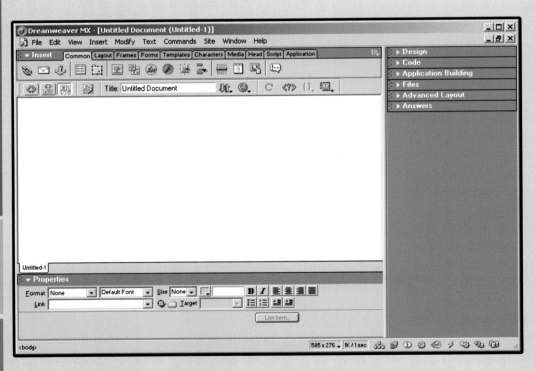

Laying the Foundation

Getting comfortable with a design tool such as Dreamweaver increases your productivity and shortens the learning curve. In this session, you explore the major menu and panel areas in the Dreamweaver workspace and learn how to customize them for the way you work best. You won't look at every panel and every tool in this session — that would be tedious. The manual that ships with Dreamweaver and the help files are more than efficient for tool recognition. What you do is explore the major areas you'll likely use the most.

You set up a local root folder in which to develop your site. Later in the book, you set up a remote folder and learn how to upload your Web site to a server. You learn how to set preferences as well as how to set up different browsers in which to test your site.

TOOLS YOU'LL USE
Site window, Property inspector, Code View, Design and Code View,
Design View, Page Properties dialog box, Insert menu, and Preferences

MATERIALS NEEDED
Copy the stockimagenation_site_start folder to your hard drive. Then
rename it stockimagenation.

TIME REQUIRED
90 minutes

Tutorial
» Setting Up and Viewing the Workspace

Your work environment is an important one. You set it up in this tutorial, as well as get a feel for where all the tools in your workspace that you use are located.

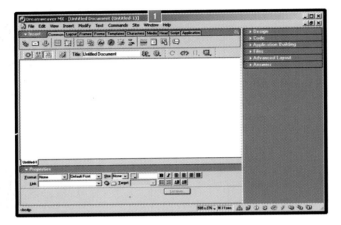

1. **Open the Dreamweaver application.**
   A. From Windows, click the Start button. Choose Programs→Macromedia→Macromedia Dreamweaver MX.
   The path from your start folder might vary depending on your operating system. This is the path for Windows XP. A new untitled document opens by default.

   B. Mac users should double-click the hard drive icon, and then the Macromedia Dreamweaver MX folder. Finally, double-click the Dreamweaver MX program icon.
   A new untitled document opens by default.

2. **First-time users with Windows need to click to select the Dreamweaver MX workspace option in the dialog box that opens.**
   This book assumes you are using the Dreamweaver MX workspace.

3. **Look at the Title bar.**
   The program and document names are displayed in the Title bar. Untitled_1 is the default name until you save it.

<NOTE>

The integrated workspace using MDI (Multiple Document Interface) isn't supported on the Mac, so the windows and panels float.

Changing Workspaces

Dreamweaver MX offers optional workspaces for Windows users. If you're familiar and comfortable in Dreamweaver 4 or HomeSite, you can opt to use those workspaces. Choose Edit→Preferences. Click General, and then click the Change Workspace button. Click the Dreamweaver MX workspace option. You can always change back to Dreamweaver 4 when you finish this book. The changes take effect the next time you start Dreamweaver.

Title Bar
Menu Bar
Insert Bar

4. **Look at the Menu bar.**

    The Menu bar contains menus with various commands. Many of the menu items can be accessed using shortcut keys or by using various panels.

5. **Look at the Insert bar. You can close the Insert bar by clicking the expander arrow.**

    The Common tab, selected by default, shows the most commonly used functions.

6. **Look at the Document toolbar.**

    The Document toolbar has buttons and pop-up menus with options for different views of the Document window, as listed in Table 8.1.

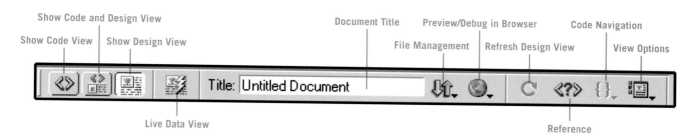

Show Code and Design View
Show Code View   Show Design View
Document Title   Preview/Debug in Browser   Code Navigation
File Management   Refresh Design View   View Options
Title: Untitled Document
Live Data View
Reference

Table 8.1: Functions Accessed from the Dreamweaver Document Toolbar

Name	Function
Design View	Provides a visual working environment.
Code View	Provides a code view for those who want to hand-code or edit any other type of code such as JavaScript or ColdFusion.
Code and Design View	Provides a split working environment with the code on top and your visual work area below.
View Live Data	Provides a live preview of dynamic content in pages that use server-side scripting.
Title	Where you type the title of your page.
File Management	Displays file-management options.
Preview/Debug in Browser	Gives you the choice of browser to use for a preview.
Refresh Design View	Forces the browser to reread the page to view any changes you made.
Reference	Activates the Reference panel.
Code Navigation	Allows you to navigate through the source code.
View Options	Offers a range of visual display aids for both Design and Code Views.

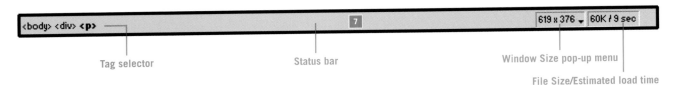

Tag selector   Status bar   Window Size pop-up menu

File Size/Estimated load time

7. **Look at the Status bar.**

   The status bar is at the bottom of the Document window and provides information about your document, including:

   >> Tag selector. The Tag selector reveals the document structure of the current location of your cursor.

   >> Window Size pop-up menu. If your document window is maximized, the window sizes will be grayed out. In the menu bar, click the Restore Down icon (it looks like the Windows Minimize/Maximize icons) and then choose the window size from the pop-up menu.

   >> Document size and estimated download time for the page.

8. **Note that the Property inspector is context-sensitive.**

   The options displayed depend on which element you have selected. To see all of the properties of a selected element, click the expander arrow in the lower-right corner.

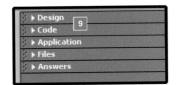

9. **Look at the Panel groups.**

   To access grouped panels, you click the expander arrows and then click the specific panel tab. If a panel isn't open by default, you can open it by choosing Window→*Panel Name*. You can also customize the panel area for the way you work, which is explained in the next tutorial.

   < T I P >

   You can click the tab with an arrow on it that sits between the document and the panel sets to open and close all the panels. This is great when you need more space to view your page.

Tutorial
» Customizing Your Workspace

Every site has different requirements and, depending on your site, you may not need all the panels or panel groups. In this tutorial, you learn how to choose and arrange the panels you use in the tutorials to follow.

1. **To expand or collapse the Design panel group (or any panel group), click the expander arrow in the Design panel group.**
   Tabs for the CSS Styles, HTML Styles, and Behavior panels are visible.

<TIP>
If you want to temporarily undock a panel and then redock it, you can do so by clicking and dragging the grabber and releasing when you see the solid black line. Drag to the location you want to dock it in. The solid line indicates where the panel docks. Release the mouse when you have it where you want.

2. **Right-click (Control-click) the HTML Styles panel name. From the contextual menu, choose Group HTML Styles With→New Panel Group.**
   The panel is now undocked and floating. You can move it anywhere you want. You can move any panel using this method.

3. **Click the X in the top-right corner of the now floating HTML Styles panel to close it.**
   This panel has now been removed from the panel group sets.

4. **Click the Expander arrow of the Answers panel. Click the Options pop-up menu and select Close Panel Group.**
   This removes a panel group that you won't be using in this book. You can close any group in the same manner.

5. **Choose Window→Others→Layers (F2).**
   The Advanced Layout panel group opens in the panel set area with the Layout panel activated.

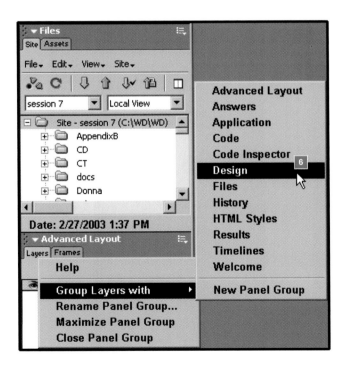

<NOTE>
There are quite a few panels that don't open by default in Dreamweaver. To access additional panels, select them from the Window menu.

6. **Right-click (Control-click) the Layers panel tab and select Group Layers With→Design.**
   Look in the Design panel group and you can see the Layers panel.

<TIP>
The Property inspector can be undocked by dragging its Gripper and moving it to wherever you prefer it to be.

Tutorial
» Setting Accessibility Preferences

Making a site accessible to as many people as possible is not only the best approach to take, but is also a legal requirement for some types of organizations, such as government, educational, and non-profit groups. Dreamweaver has a built-in feature to help you add the appropriate tags and labels to various elements.

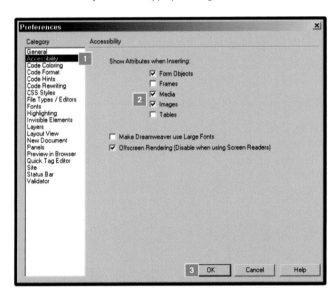

1. **Click Edit→Preferences. When the Preferences dialog box opens, select Accessibility from the Category window.**

2. **Check Form Objects, Media, and Images.**
   You won't be adding any frames in this design so you don't need to select that option.

3. **Click OK.**
   Now whenever you insert one of the elements that you checked, a dialog box opens to enter data into. Each dialog box is discussed as it appears in the workflow.

< N O T E >

The Accessibiltiy standards are set by the World Wide Consortium (W3C). For an extensive study of the standards, check out the Web site at www.w3c.org. It's pretty heavy reading, but very informative. For more information on accessibility issues, you can also refer to the Dreamweaver Help files (Help→Using Dreamweaver). Type **Accessibility** into the Search area and you get a list of additional subjects.

Tutorial
» Setting Browser Preferences

As a Web designer, your biggest challenge when developing Web pages is getting your work to display correctly in target browsers. For this project, the targets are Netscape 4x, 7x, and Internet Explorer 5+ or 6. Although most modern browsers follow the standards set by the World Wide Web Consortium, every browser has its quirks. When working in Dreamweaver MX, you see your page as it might appear in a browser, but Dreamweaver cannot take into account how each browser renders a page. In this tutorial, you set up your target browsers to easily view the state of a page at any time by using preset keyboard shortcuts or by choosing a target browser from several menu options. A good designer/developer tests early and often!

1. **Click the Preview/Debug in Browser icon in the Toolbar and click Edit Browser List.**
   The Preview in Browser category of the Preferences dialog box is selected. Your default browser will most likely be shown in the browser window area.

2. **Click the plus sign next to the word Browsers.**

3. **Click the Browse button to find the browser you want to add.**

4. **Locate the browser application's executable (application) file and open it.**
   The executable file is usually in the applications root folder and has an icon next to it. Netscape often has an icon with an *N* in it.

5. **Type a name for the browser you are adding in the Add Browser dialog box.**
   I like to name my browsers with actual browser names. In this case I'm adding Netscape 7 so I typed **NN7**.

6. **Click Secondary Browser to select it, or check Primary Browser if you are adding a primary browser.**
   If you see a check mark, the option is selected.

7. **Click OK to close the Add Browser dialog box.**

8. **Repeat steps 1 through 7 to add other browsers.**
   The third browser being used to test in this book is Netscape 4 (NN4).

9. **Click OK to close the Browser Preferences dialog box.**

10. **You can preview your work in a browser by choosing one of these options:**
    » Choose a target browser from the Preview/Debug menu in the Document bar.
    » Press F12 to access the primary browser.
    » Press Ctrl+F12 (⌘+F12) to access the secondary browser.
    » Choose File→Preview in Browser. From the pop-up menu, select the appropriate browser.
    » Right-click a page in the Site panel and select the desired browser from the Preview in Browser→options.

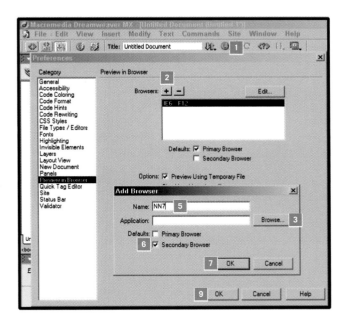

<NOTE>
You can install multiple versions of Netscape easily, but if you install multiple versions of Internet Explorer, they overwrite each other. The only way to have multiple versions of Internet Explorer is to use multiple operating systems and install a different version in each or have more than one testing machine.

<NOTE>
Dreamweaver generates a temporary file whenever you preview a file. This can cause your system to slow down depending on your resources. To prevent this slow down, set your disk cleanup utility to automatically delete temp files. See Windows help for more information on how to do this on your particular operating system. Optionally you can uncheck the "Preview Using Temporary File" option in the Edit Preferences dialog box.

Tutorial
» Defining the Local Root Folder

In Dreamweaver, defining your site is extremely important. By defining every site you work with, Dreamweaver can track your assets and links and a lot of other functions as well. Defining a site allows Dreamweaver to manage the file paths and keep the linking accurate.

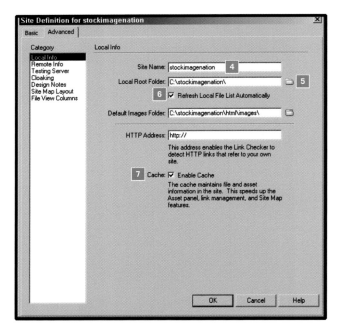

<TIP>
In the Site Definition dialog box, you can also use the Basic tab. It contains a wizard to help you define your site.

<NOTE>
When starting a site from scratch, you can create a new folder for the site root in the Site Definition process. First, navigate to the desired location and then click the New Folder icon. Name the folder and then select it as the site root, as described in step 5.

<NOTE>
The Remote Info category relates to the remote root folder — a folder on a Web server that serves up Web pages to site visitors. When developing a site that uses server-side scripting to display dynamic content, you use the Testing Server category to indicate the server model and location of special application server software. You use both of these categories later in the project.

1. **Copy the stockimagenation_site_start folder from the book's CD-ROM to your hard drive.**

<NOTE>
Copy the stockimagenation_site_start folder and paste it into the C drive. You can choose any drive you like, but the book's instructions use the path C:/stockimagenation. Otherwise you need to substitute your drive letter for C. After the folder is copied to your hard drive, right-click (Control-click) the folder and choose Properties. Uncheck the Read Only option and click OK. This unlocks all the files in the folder.

2. **Rename the folder** stockimagenation.

3. **Choose Site→New Site from the Site Menu bar in the Site panel.**
   In the Site Definition dialog box that opens, the Advanced tab is open and the Category of Local Info is selected.

4. **In the Site Name field, highlight the default name and type** stockimagenation.
   You don't have to be concerned about long names here; this is just a name for you and in no way affects any of your files.

5. **Click the yellow folder icon in the Local Root Folder area. Navigate to the stockimagenation folder. Select the folder, click the Open button, and then click the Select button. Macintosh users should simply select the folder and click the Choose button.**
   The local root folder is your working directory for all your Web site's files. You need to make a local root folder for every Web site you develop.

6. **Select the Refresh Local File List Automatically check box.**
   This option shows you any current changes made to your site structure and files in the Site and Assets panels.

7. **Leave the Enable Cache check box checked if you want quick access to your links and site assets. It's up to you.**
   Leaving the Enable Cache option checked allows Dreamweaver to make comparisons faster. But if you are low on computer memory, you might want to uncheck this option.

8. **Click OK to complete the site definition.**
   You use the Remote Info category and Testing Server categories later in the development of the site.

Tutorial

» Managing Files and Folders with the Site Panel (Window)

The Site panel is one that many beginners avoid or never use. You begin using it right away because it is a great timesaver and it isn't nearly as intimidating as it appears. The Site panel is in the Files panel group. From the Site panel, you can view a list of files, rename files, add files and folders, and refresh the view when changes have been made. It keeps all the files and links on your site coordinated. (On the Mac, it's called the Site window and is a floating panel.)

1. **If the Site panel is closed, press F8 to make it active.**
   The Site panel is used to add, open, and delete files and folders. When you move files or folders within a defined site using the Site panel, Dreamweaver can maintain any paths used by images or links that might otherwise be broken. The icons at the top of the Site panel are used (from left to right) for:
   Connecting to a remote root folder
   Refreshing the current site list
   Moving files and folders to and from a Web server
   Check in/out during the file transfer process, used when working in teams
   Expanding/collapsing the Site panel to view local and remote site files and/or site maps

2. **Click the Expand/Collapse icon to expand the Site panel.**
   For Windows, this icon is located at the top of the Site panel; for Macintosh, click the small white arrow at the bottom-left of the panel. To collapse the panel, click the icon or arrow again.

3. **Click the plus sign (+) next to the Site name to open the folder.**

4. **Click the plus sign next to html to open that folder.**

5. **Click the plus sign next to the stockimagenation folder. Right-click (Control-click) and choose New File.**

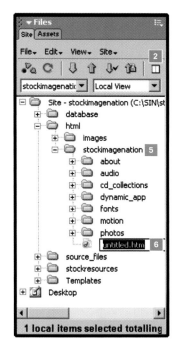

<TIP>
If you click any folder that you want to add a file or folder to, the new file or folder is added to the folder you have selected. You can also use the File menu within the Site panel to add a new file.

6. **A new file called** untitled.htm **appears in the stockimagenation folder. While the name is still highlighted, change it to** legal.htm.
   The default file extension for Windows is .HTM and for Macintosh it's .HTML.

<NOTE>
You can rename any file or folder by choosing File menu in the Site panel and selecting Rename. You can also right-click and choose Rename from the menu. On a Mac, you choose Site➔Rename or Control-click for the menu and choose Rename.

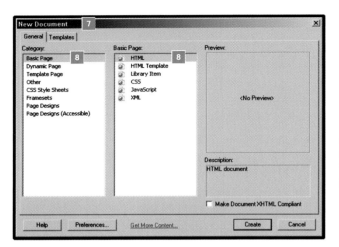

7. **Choose File→New from the main menu to open Dreamweaver's Document Gallery.**

   This opens the New Document dialog box. Notice the Basic Page category is selected and HTML is the extension for a basic page. The gallery offers many types of documents and can be used to add an alternate type of page to your site.

8. **With Basic Page and HTML selected, click the Create button.**

   < N O T E >

   Click various categories and options and see what is available. There are some pre-made CSS and templates that you may find interesting for your own projects.

9. **Choose File→Save As. Navigate to the stockimagenation/html/ stockimagenation/about folder. Name the file** index.htm **and click Save.**

   Whenever you open a new file using the File menu, you need to save before it becomes part of the site. When you add files in the Site panel, they are automatically saved as part of the site.

Tutorial

» Choosing a Design View

Dreamweaver MX gives you many options for developing pages. Visual designers may prefer to work in Design view to see the page as it would be displayed in a browser; HTML developers may prefer to work entirely in Code view, seeing only the tags used. Or, you can opt to work in Split view, which splits the screen to show both Design and Code views. You can even change which view is placed where via the View menu. Whichever view you work in, do check out the other views occasionally—you learn a lot in the process.

1. **Click the Show Code View icon in the toolbar.**
   You can now see the code in the document window. Right now it's only HTML code; that changes later.

2. **Choose View→Code View Options→Word Wrap.**

3. **Choose View→Code View Options→Line Numbers.**

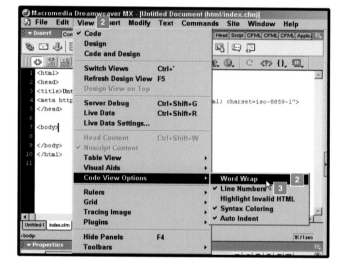

4. **Click the Show Design View icon in the Toolbar.**
   The document window shows only the working area.

5. **Click the Show Code and Design View icon.**
   Notice how there is both code and the visual design area. You can adjust how much code you see by dragging the code display up or down.

6. **Close Dreamweaver.**
   There is nothing to save. The changes you made in the Site panel were actually made to your folder structure on your hard drive.

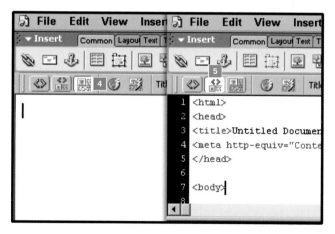

» Session Review

In this session, you set up your Dreamweaver workspace and learned how to set a few preferences. You defined a local root folder for the stockimagenation project and explored the Site panel's management features. Now it's time to see how much you remember. The answers to the questions can be found in the tutorial noted in parentheses.

1. Which three workspaces are available in Dreamweaver? ("Tutorial: Setting Up and Viewing the Workspace")

2. How do you open a panel group to display the panels within it? ("Tutorial: Setting Up and Viewing the Workspace")

3. How do you expand or contract the Site panel (Window)? ("Tutorial: Customizing Your Workspace")

4. How do you undock a panel group? ("Tutorial: Customizing Your Workspace")

5. How do you move panels to different groups? ("Tutorial: Customizing Your Workspace")

6. How many copies of Internet Explorer can you set up? ("Tutorial: Setting Browser Preferences")

7. What is the keyboard shortcut to preview in your primary browser? ("Tutorial: Setting Browser Preferences")

8. Where did you save your root folder? ("Tutorial: Defining the Local Root Folder")

9. Can you preview a ColdFusion page in a local browser? ("Tutorial: Managing Files and Folders with the Site Panel (Window)")

10. Name Dreamweaver's three view options. ("Tutorial: Choosing a Design View")

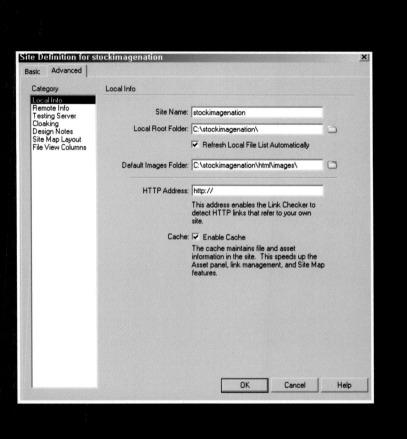

Session 9

HTML Page Structure

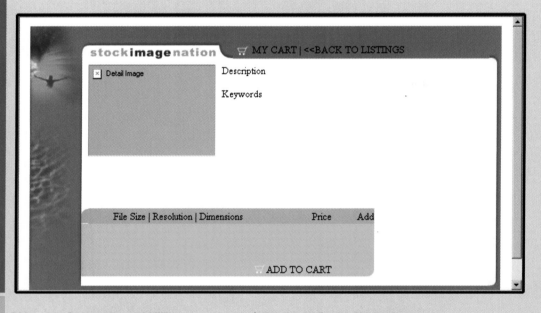

Working with Tables

In this session, you learn the ins and outs of building HTML tables. A table is a container, meaning it is used to hold various elements such as text and images. Like a spreadsheet, an HTML table contains rows, columns, and cells. Dreamweaver makes building a table easy by automating the process, as you see in the next tutorial. Tables were originally made to hold data, but Web designers discovered they were great containers to aid in the placement of images. Not only can you use them to hold content but also you can place tables inside of tables, ad infinitum.

Tables come in three varieties. A *fixed table* is a specific size no matter what size a browser window is, an *autostretch table* (also called fluid or stretchy table) expands to fill the browser window, and a *hybrid* table contains fixed and autostretch columns. In this session you build all three types of tables. There are several sidebars throughout that show you some of the different table options available that aren't used in the building of this site.

TOOLS YOU'LL USE
Site window, Property inspector, Assets panel, Insert panel, Forms panel, and Character panel, Point to File

MATERIALS NEEDED
Images folder in the session9 folder. Copy the images folder into your stockimagenation/html folder, overwriting any files you have there now

TIME REQUIRED
90 minutes

Discussion

Dreamweaver and HTML

HTML (HyperText Markup Language) is a markup language containing a series of tags that define the structure of a Web page. This markup tells a browser how to present the content of your page. All you need to write HTML is a text editor, even Notepad suffices. Because many developers want to save time, they use visual editors such as Dreamweaver to help speed up the process of marking up a Web page. In this course you use Dreamweaver MX.

Dreamweaver is a deceptively easy tool, but it's also an industrial strength application, making it a favorite among Web design professionals. With Dreamweaver you can develop one page or a huge site. You can also open pages from co-workers or code produced in other editors, just to edit and clean up the code. You can add JavaScript, forms, tables, and more without writing or viewing a piece of code. As your skills develop, you might want more access to the code, and Dreamweaver has this built-in functionality. It is as easy or as complex as you desire.

Dreamweaver utilizes Web technologies and HTML standards and also provides backward compatibility for older browsers. It was designed for the professional Web developer so it can accommodate a designer's workflow. There are basically two kinds of Web developers, the coders and the designers. The designers typically want to design in a visual environment so Dreamweaver provides the "Design View" or the WYSIWYG (or almost) environment. For the coders Dreamweaver provides the Code View. Then there is the Design and Code View for those who want it all. The illustrations here show the three design view types of the home page you are developing.

Design view

Code and Design view

Code view

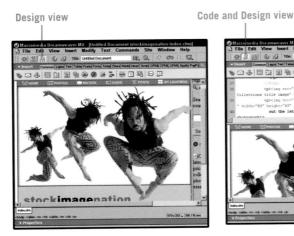  

Basic HTML

You can actually get by designing in Dreamweaver without knowing any HTML code. But you are better off learning at least the basics. HTML isn't nearly as intimidating as it looks. It's very easy to learn the basics. You are introduced to a bit of code here and there throughout this book. Before you know it, you'll be recognizing HTML code and understanding it.

The World Wide Web Consortium (W3C) is a standards body that oversees and promulgates the standards for HTML code. Although compliance is voluntary, most Web browsers (especially the newer ones) support the standards consistently. Find out more about this organization at www.w3c.org.

HTML Tags

HTML markup language uses tags to indicate how things should appear in a browser. There are certain tags required in every HTML page for a Web page to display properly. In order for a browser to know a file contains HTML, the document has to declare itself with an `<html>` opening tag and end with a closing tag of `</html>`. An opening tag declares what type of content follows. The ending tag declares the end of that particular type of content. Opening and closing tags act as a container for the content they surround. Every HTML document requires a `<head>` `<body>` and `<title>` tag. Dreamweaver generates all these tags automatically whenever you open or add a new document. The complete code Dreamweaver generates when you choose File→New and a Basic page contains the required code and tags as seen in this illustration. You learn in this session how to change the title from Untitled Document to a meaningful name.

```
1  <!DOCTYPE HTML PUBLIC "-//W3C//DTD HTML 4.01 Transitional//EN">
2  <html>
3  <head>
4  <title>Untitled Document</title>
5  <meta http-equiv="Content-Type" content="text/html; charset=iso-8859-1">
6  </head>
7
8  <body>
9
10 </body>
11 </html>
12
```

Other Basic Tags

There are a handful of other tags that appear in the `<body>` section of a Web page that you use every time you build a Web page, whether you see the code or not. You briefly take a look at some of them. Don't worry if you don't remember them; you see and use these tags throughout this course.

Paragraph tags are extremely common; they appear as `<p>` and close with `</p>`. This tag places an empty line of white space around each block of text contained within the tag container; the container consists of the opening and closing paragraph tags.

Anchor tags are used for linking from one page to another or to another spot within a page. A typical anchor tag would look like this:

```
<a href="linknamehere.htm"> Click on this text </a>
```

When the user clicks the text, they are taken to the page referenced in the anchor tag container.

Image tags are included with every image you insert into your document. Dreamweaver automatically adds the height and width dimensions of the image into the tag and the alt text if you entered it into the Property inspector. An image tag appears like this:

```
<img src="images/logo.gif" width="300" height="100"
alt="Palmetto Design Group">
```

There are no ending tags for the image tag.

You also frequently see the table tags. Within the `<table></table>` container tags, you'll see `<tr>`, the tag for a specific row, and `<td>`, the tag for a specific cell.

Table 9.1: Reserved Characters

Character	Function
:	Used for some command scripts.
!	Used for comments.
/ or \	Forward slash is used in a file path name indicating files are nested in a folder. The backward slash is not allowed on Windows servers.
" "	Used to denote a value of tags and attributes. In the example `<body BGCOLOR="#FFFFFF">` the attribute is background color and its value is white.
.	Dots are used for the filename extension.

There are a few characters in HTML that are reserved for HTML code and can't be used in filenames; they are listed in Table 9.1.

New Standards

The final version of HTML is HTML 4.01 transitional. The new standard, set by the W3C is XHTML. Although XHTML is officially the new standard, we are still waiting for better browser support. Don't worry. You don't have to jump into it just yet but you should start thinking about it, and do some reading on it when you get a chance. Because this book continues supporting Netscape 4, no XHTML coding is included.

HTML Learning Resources

There are many places on the Internet to learn about HTML and about design in general. Listed here are a few to get you going.

World Wide Consortium — www.w3c.org/

Webmonkey — www.hotwired.lycos.com/webmonkey/teachingtool/index.html

Web Reference — www.webreference.com

Builder.com — www.builder.com

Tutorial

» Building a Relative Table for the Legal Page

In this tutorial you add the table to hold the content of the legal.htm page, which becomes a pop-up window later. You need to copy the images folder inside the session9 folder on the CD-ROM. Navigate to your stockimagenation/html/ folder and paste. This overwrites your current images folder. This is okay; the new images folder contains additional exported images from Fireworks. After you paste it into your root folder, Windows users need to right-click the folder and select Properties. Uncheck the Read Only option and click OK. This unlocks the files.

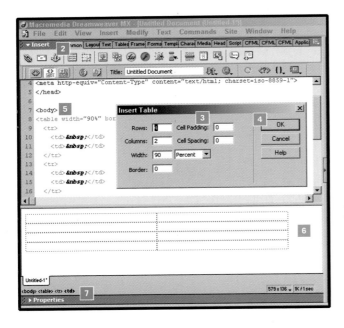

1. **Double-click the** legal.htm **page name in the Site panel to open it. Remember it is in the stockimagenation folder.**

2. **Click the Insert Table icon.**

3. **In the Insert Table dialog box, enter the following settings:**
   Rows: 4
   Columns: 2
   Percent: 90
   Border: 0
   Cell Padding: 0
   Cell Spacing: 0

4. **Click OK to close the Insert Table dialog box.**

<NOTE>
You need to specifically enter zero for the border, cell padding, and spacing. Blank does not mean zero. There is default spacing applied if you don't type a zero.

5. **Click the Code and Design View icon to see the code. Notice the table code added.**
   You see the opening table tag <table> and then the <tr> tag which is the row and <td> tags for each cell. The next <tr> tag is the next row; then it's <td> tags for each cell and so on. It ends with the closing table tag of </table>.

<NOTE>
Between the opening and closing <td> tags, you see the special character . This stands for *non-breaking space*. Here Dreamweaver is using it to provide minimum content in the cell to avoid leaving the cell empty. (Dreamweaver frequently collapses empty cells when you add content to another.) When you add content into the cell, the character will be removed automatically.

6. **Notice the table is added to the document.**
   The dotted outline does not appear in a browser. It's just a visual aid for you while working in Dreamweaver.

7. **Look at the Status bar; you see the** <table>, <tr>, **and** <td> **tags.**

Table Tips

» **Avoid** *nesting* **too many tables.**

» **Build modular tables to avoid overly complex row and column spanning.**

» **Don't attempt to build one big table that holds everything.**

» **If you can position elements without a table, you can put the same elements in a single table cell.**

» **Be sure that column widths add up to match the table's width.**

» **In the Property inspector be sure to type the width of every column. This gets Netscape 4x browsers to work property.**

8. **Select the `<body>` tag.**
   You center the table by wrapping a `<div>` tag around it. You center the contents of the `<div>` tag rather than the table.

9. **Click the center alignment icon.**

10. **Look at the code.**
    You see `<div align="center">` before the table code and a `</div>` after the ending table tag. This is a container that contains all of the HTML elements between the tags. You also see the `<div>` tag next to the `<body>` tag in the Tag Selector of the Status bar.

Do not select the table tag and center the table itself. If you do, the code align=center will be added to the <table> tag, giving `<table align="center">`. This is *deprecated* code (code that is being phased out).

11. **Choose File→Save.**

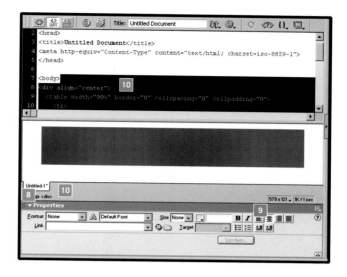

Tutorial
» Adding Images to the Legal Page

In this tutorial, you add the logo and the two corner images that round the top-left and lower-right corners.

1. **Open the Files panel group if it's closed and click the Assets tab to activate it.**

   The Assets panel is where you manage your assets for the site. The icons reference the Asset categories available in Dreamweaver, as shown in the illustration.

2. **Click the Images icon if you don't see a list of images in the window.**

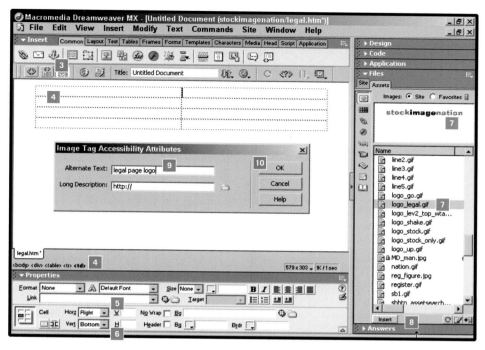

3. **Click the Design View icon in the Document bar.**

4. **Click inside the left cell of the first row of the table.**
   In the Tag Selector you see `<body><div> <table> <tr> <td>`. `<td>` is highlighted because it is the cell you currently have selected.

5. **In the Property inspector, click the down arrow next to the Horz field and select Right.**

6. **Click the down arrow next to the Vert field and select Bottom.**
   You have just set the properties of this cell only. Any content now added to this cell is aligned to the right and to the bottom.

7. **In the Assets panel, scroll down the list of images until you find** `logo_legal.gif`. **Select it.**
   Notice the preview pane; you can see the selected image.

8. **Click the Insert button to add the image to the cell.**

9. **Type** legal page logo **into the Alternate Text field of the Image Tag Accessibility Attributes dialog box.**

10. **Click OK to close this box.**
    Notice your second column has collapsed. I show you how to easily select it next. It collapsed because there is no content yet to hold it open.

<NOTE>

The Image Tag Accessibility Attributes dialog box opens because you set the accessibilty preferences in the last session for images. The Alternate Text field holds the text that users read. It also shows in the browser before the image loads; in some browsers it's the tooltip when you pass your cursor over it.

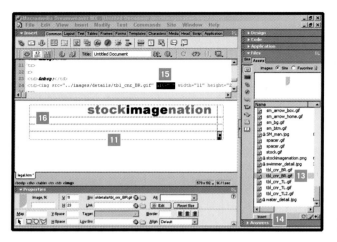

11. **Click in the left large cell of the bottom row.**

12. **Press the Tab key on your keyboard.**
This automatically moves you to the next cell.

13. **In the Assets panel, scroll down and select** tbl_cnr_BR.gif.

14. **Click the Insert button to add the image.**

15. **When the Image Accessibility dialog box opens, press Enter
(Return) from the keyboard.**
Because this image is design oriented, pressing Enter adds an
empty alt tag. If you look at the code you'll see alt= "".
Later when you test your site for accessibility it does not return
an error message stating that you have an empty alt tag.

< N O T E >
You can also insert images by using the Insert Image icon in the
Insert panel and navigating to the image you want to select.

16. **Click to place your cursor in the left cell of the second row (just
below the row with the logo).**

17. **In the Assets panel, select** tbl_cnr_TL2.gif **and click Insert.**

18. **Press the Enter key for Alternate text and click OK.**
I won't keep repeating this step. From now on when you insert
a layout image repeat this step. When you add an important
image add the Alternative text.

19. **Save your document by choosing File➔Save or by clicking the
Save icon.**
If you don't see the Save icon and you want to use then
choose View➔Toolbars and select Standard.

Tutorial
» Setting Table Cell Properties

In the previous tutorial you set the properties for cell alignment to one cell. In this tutorial you finish adding the properties to the rest of the cells. You see how to do it even if there is already an image in the cell. You also add a background color. This color is added for now but you change it in the next session using CSS.

1. **Click to place your cursor in the right cell of the first row.**

2. **In the Property inspector, change the Horz field to Right and the Vert to Bottom.**

3. **Click in the left cell of the second row; don't click the image.**

4. **In the Property inspector, type** 95% **into the Width (W) field.**
   This sets this cell to 95% of the available space instead of to a set amount of pixels. You must type the percent sign.

5. **In the Tag Selector, select the** <tr> **tag.**
   You see a black line around both cells of the second row.

6. **In the Property inspector, click the Bg (background) color box.**

7. **Move your cursor (it's an eyedropper now) to the dark blue corner image (it looks nearly black but isn't) and click.**
   You can choose colors by either selecting a color swatch or take a sample of a color from an image.

8. **Click into the right cell of the second row and type** 5% **for the width.**

9. **For the third row, type these values:**
   Left cell: Vert: Top, Height: 400
   Right cell: Vert: Top

<NOTE>
Remember to place your cursor into the appropriate cell before changing the properties in the Property inspector.

10. **Select the** <tr> **tag from the Tag Selector.**

11. **Click the bg color box and sample the orange color from the corner image.**

<NOTE>
Be sure to type a percentage sign in the width field only when instructed to. If you only type a number, the cell is set to the specific number of pixels you typed.

12. **For the fourth row, select these values:**
    Left cell: Horz: Right, Vert: Middle
    Right cell: Horz: Right, Vert: Bottom

13. **Select the** <tr> **tag and change the background color of the fourth row (bg) to orange.**

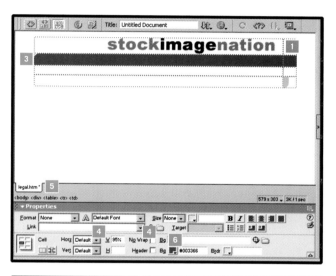

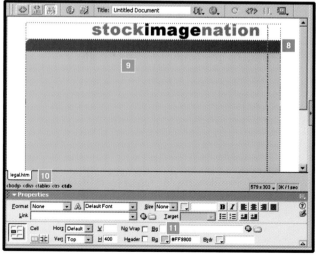

<NOTE>
If you have trouble getting the cursor into the right cell and not the image, select the image and use your keyboard right- or left-arrow key to select the cell. The other alternative is to select the image and click the <td> tag from the Tag Selector.

Tutorial
» Adding Placeholder Text

In this tutorial, you add *lorem ipsum* text, which acts as placeholder text until the client gives you the real content. The first thing you need to do is get the *lorem ipsum* text.

1. **Go to Google (www.google.com). Type** lorem ipsum **into the Search field and press Enter.**

2. **Locate the site for the ipsum generator.**
   At the time of this writing the first entry was a site for a generator at www.lpsum.com.

3. **You can read what the site has to say and then scroll down to the Generate Lorem Ipsum button.**

4. **Select four paragraphs and check the Start with 'Lorem ipsum dolor sit amet...' option (notice the other options you have available). Click the Generate button.**

5. **Copy the paragraphs and paste them into the large orange cell (left cell third row).**

6. **Click the Back button on your Web browser to return to the generator. This time, select list, type in the number** 1**, and click the Generate button.**

7. **Copy just the first four lines. In the** legal.htm **page place your cursor at the end of the text and Press the Enter (Return) key. Now paste the copied bulleted text below the paragraphs.**
   The bullets are removed but that's OK, you add them back in.

8. **Click to place your cursor in the left cell of the bottom row.**

9. **Type the words** Close this window.
   Notice how it automatically lines up to the right of the cell. This is because you set the cells property to a vertical alignment of right.

10. **Select the four lines of what used to be a bulleted list.**

11. **In the Property inspector, click the Unordered List icon.**
Only one bullet is added. This is because there is only a space
(a <br> tag) between each line. The bullets want a paragraph
tag. You see an easy way to fix this next.

12. **Click to place your cursor at the end of the first line in the list.**

13. **Press Enter (Return) and then press Delete to get the next line of
text next to the bullet. Repeat for the next two lines.**
If you check the code, you see that <p> tags have been
added. You now have a bullet next to each line of text.

<NOTE>
To check the code, click the Show Code and Design Views icon in
the Document bar.

14. **Save the file.**

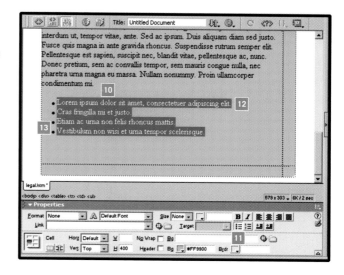

Tutorial
» Building the Home Page

In the next series of tutorials, you construct the home page of the stockimagenation site. In this tutorial, you add a table that simply adds a thin black line around the entire design, giving it a nice clean look.

Dreamweaver supports many types of server applications. These applications allow you to interact with a database and provide dynamic data. The server technology you learn to use in this book is ColdFusion. You haven't been instructed to install it yet but you can still use ColdFusion pages. ColdFusion pages have a .CFM extension.

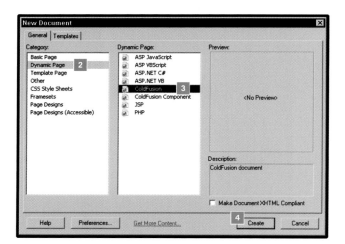

1. **Choose File→New.**

2. **Select Dynamic Page in the Category area.**

3. **Select ColdFusion in the Dynamic Page area.**

4. **Click Create.**

5. **Choose File→Save As and navigate to the stockimagenation/html/stockimagenation folder. Name the file** index.cfm **and save.**

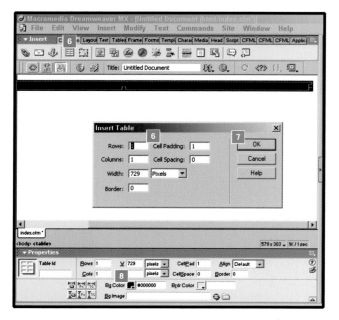

6. **Click the Insert Table icon and use these parameters:**
   Rows: 1
   Columns: 1
   729 Pixels
   Border: 0
   Cell Padding: 1
   Cell Spacing: 0

< N O T E >

The large one-row one column table is being used to add the border around the design. The one-pixel Cell Pad forms the line after you nest another table inside of it. This particular table has a fixed width of 729 pixels.

7. **Click OK.**

8. **In the Property inspector, click the Bg color box and select black.**

9. **Click to place your cursor inside the black table.**

10. **Click the Insert Table icon and use these parameters:**
    Rows: 3
    Columns: 4
    Width: 100 Percent
    Border, Cell Padding, and Cell Spacing: 0

11. **Click OK.**

12. **Click to place your cursor inside the first cell first row (top-left cell).**

13. **In the Property inspector, change the Vert to Top and type** 25 **for the Height.**

14. **Save the page, but keep it open.**

<NOTE>
You can't specify a maximum height but you can specify a minimum. Both the height and width can be altered by the size of the image/s you insert. If they are larger than the size you specified, the table/cell stretches to fit it.

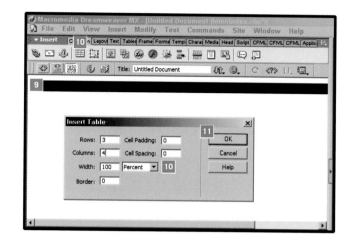

Tutorial
» Adding Navigational Icons to the Home Page

In this tutorial, you add the navigational icons to your home page.

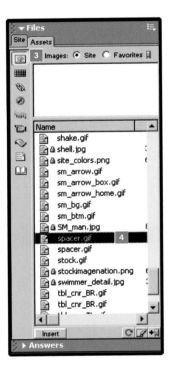

1. **Open the** `index.cfm` **file if you've closed it.**

2. **Place your cursor in the first cell of the first row (top left).**

3. **In the Files panel, click the Assets tab to make it active.**
   If you don't see the list of images, click the images icon.

4. **Select the** `spacer.gif` **file and click the Insert button.**

<NOTE>
Your table cells collapse because there isn't any content in them, but don't worry about it. I show you how to navigate to them when you need to.

5. **Press the space bar for the Alternative text and click OK.**
   You add another image soon but you won't need to move your cursor. When you insert multiple images you don't need to move your cursor. The image you insert is selected. When you insert another it goes next to the one you just inserted.

6. **In the Property inspector, highlight the number one of the Width (W) and type** 6. **Change the Height (W) to 25.**
   The spacer image is a transparent 1x1 image that is used simply to add space where needed. Because it's transparent, you can alter the size in Dreamweaver to anything. Once you change the width and height, the numbers are bolded. This indicates that you changed it from the original size.

<NOTE>
Never resize a picture or other images with content in Dreamweaver using the height and width fields. The viewing size changes but the content is still all in the file size. You can change the size of a transparent image because there is no content.

7. **In the Assets panel, select btn_home and click the Insert button. Type** Home **in the Alt Text field and click OK.**

8. **Select** spacer.gif **again from the Assets panel. Click Insert. Press the spacebar and press OK for the Alt text.**

9. **Set the size of the spacer to 23x25.**

10. **Select** btn_photos.gif **and click the Insert button.**

11. **Type** Click for Photographic Stock Resources **in the Alt Text field and click OK.**
    You can see the Alt text in the Property inspector.

12. **Select the** spacer.gif **in the Assets panel and insert it. Press the spacebar and click OK for the Alt text. Change the size to 23x25.**

13. **Select btn_motion and insert it. Type** Click for Video Stock Resources **for the Alt text and click OK.**

14. **Select** spacer.gif **and insert it. Press Enter (Return) and click OK for Alt text. Change the spacer size to 23x25.**

15. **Select btn_audio and insert it. Type** Click for Audio Stock Resources **for the Alt text and click OK.**
    The Audio button is added next to all the others.

16. **Select** spacer.gif **and insert it. Press Enter (Return) and click OK for Alt text. Change the spacer size to 23x25.**

17. **Select btn_fonts and insert it. Type** Click for Typographic Resources **for the Alt text and click OK.**

18. **Select** spacer.gif **and insert it. Press Enter (Return) and click OK for Alt text. Change the size of the spacer to 23x25.**

19. **Select btn_mybox and insert it. Type** LightBox **for the Alt text and click OK.**

20. **Select** spacer.gif **and insert it. Press Enter and click OK for the Alt text. Change the size of the spacer to 7x25.**

21. **Select the last spacer. Press the right-arrow key.**

22. **In the Property inspector, click the Bg color box.**

23. **Click the Options pop-up menu. If you see a check mark by the Snap to Web Safe Colors, click it to turn it off.**
    If you ever notice that a color is different from what you selected, check the Snap to Web Safe option. This changes the selected color to the closest Web Safe color.

24. **Use the eyedropper to sample the color of the icon images.**

25. **Save the file, but leave it open.**

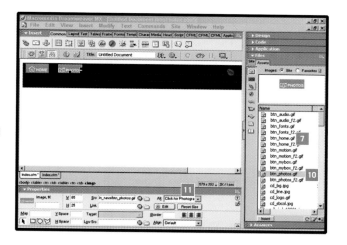

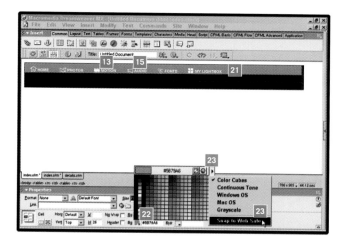

<NOTE>
You don't need a separate cell for each image. You can insert them side-by-side like you are doing for this navigation bar.

Tutorial
» Moving Between Columns

When empty cells have collapsed, it's difficult to select them. If you place your cursor in the cell before the collapsed one, you can use the Tab key to place the cursor in the collapsed cell. If you need to get your cursor into a cell that has an image in it (and it fills the cell so you can't click next to it), you can still get to the cell by using a keyboard arrow key or clicking the <td> tag in the Tag Selector that precedes the <img> tag. To see how to move between columns, you can view tables.mov in the Movies folder on the CD.

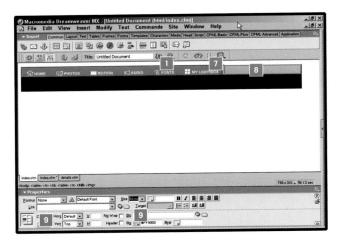

<NOTE>

If at any time you lose focus (or are not sure if a column is actually selected), put your cursor back into a cell that you can select easily and tab over to the correct cell. Remember that you can select an image and then use the keyboard arrow key to get into a cell.

1. **Your cursor should still be in the first row where the navigation is. If it isn't, select any image.**

2. **Press the Tab key.**
   You can see your cursor blink. It's difficult to see anything since your cursor is now in the collapsed cell. But now you can adjust that cell.

3. **In the Property inspector, change the vertical (Vert) to Top.**

4. **In the Assets panel, select** spacer.gif **and change its size to 1x25.**
   The space holds the cell open at 1 pixel by 25 pixels (the height of the cell containing the icons. This cell is going to be a thin black line between the columns.

5. **Press the Tab key again.**
   Now you are in the third cell or column.

6. **In the Property inspector, change the vertical of this cell to Top.**

7. **In the Assets panel, select the** sbcol1.gif **image and insert it. You can press Enter and OK for the Alternative text. Press the right-arrow key to get the cell properties. In the Property inspector change the background color to the same orange as the image.**

8. **Press the Tab key to get into the fourth column.**

9. **In the Property inspector, change the vertical to Top and the background to orange.**
   You can sample the orange image you added into column 3.

10. **Insert a spacer and make it 23x25.**

11. **Press F12 to preview in your primary browser.**
    Notice that you can see the navigation buttons, a thin vertical black line, and then an orange column. This completes the first row of the table.

Tutorial

» Adding the Main Content

In this tutorial, you add the large main image as well as the part of the hand that appears outside of the cell. It's a bit more difficult when you design "outside of the box," but not impossible. You simply add an extra column to accommodate the slice with the hand.

1. **Click to place your cursor in the left cell of the second row.**

2. **In the Property inspector, change the vertical to Top.**

3. **Insert a spacer image.**
   This cell is black because you can see through the spacer image to the black table that surrounds the inside table.

4. **Tab over to the next column/cell and change its vertical to Top. Add a spacer image as well.**
   Use the default spacer of 1x1 unless given other dimensions.

5. **Tab over to the next column and change its vertical to Top.**

6. **In the Assets panel, select** sbcol2.gif **and insert it. Press the right-arrow key and make the background color orange.**
   This image is 6x1 and orange.

7. **Tab over to the fourth column and change the vertical to Top and the background color to orange. Add a spacer image.**
   You added a thin black line below the navigation and kept the orange columns orange by using 1x1 spacers and an orange background color.

<NOTE>

Sometimes it's difficult to tab between these small columns. When you tab, check the Property inspector to see whether your cursor is actually in the cell. If you still see the spacer image information, you aren't. When this happens I place my cursor back in the left cell and then tab to the correct column. I don't know why the tab doesn't always work but I suspect it has to do with the focus. For instance, when the spacer image is selected, that's where the focus is—in the Assets panel instead of the document.

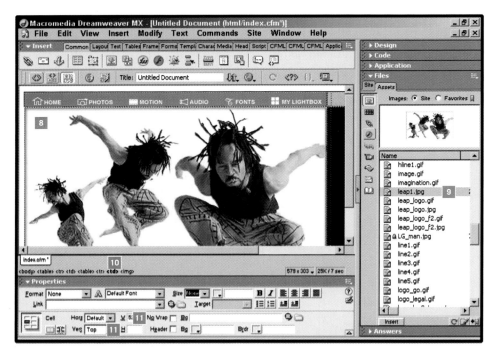

8. **Click to place your cursor in the left cell of the third row.**

9. **In the Assets panel, select** `leap1.jpg` **and insert it. Type** Shake
   it Up! **for the Alternative text.**

10. **The image is selected. Press your keyboard right-arrow key one
    time to get into the cell.**
    Or you can select the `<td>` tag from the Tag inspector.

11. **Change the vertical to Top and type** 523 **for the width.**
    523 is the width of the image. By adding the width in the
    Property inspector, the cell is forced to close around it.

12. **Preview your work in a browser. Press F12 for your default
    browser.**

13. **Press the Tab key to get into the second column. Change the vertical to Top.**

14. **From the Assets panel, insert `line3.gif`.**
    This is a 1x310 black line with a bit of the hand color right where the hand crosses over the box.

15. **Tab over to the next column and change the vertical to Top.**

16. **From the Assets panel, insert sbcol3. Press the right-arrow key on the keyboard and change the background color to orange.**

17. **Tab over or click into the right column. Change the vertical to Top and the background color to orange.**

18. **Select the large image with the men.**

19. **In the Assets panel, select `leap_logo.gif`. Type** Logo image for the Alternative text and click OK.
    The image stacks below the large one because the cell is set to the same size as the large image. Because the next one won't fit next to it, it automatically goes below it.

20. **Save your file (choose File→Save).**

21. **Preview your work in all of your target browsers.**

Tutorial
» Adding the Sidebar Content

In this tutorial, you add the content for the sidebar. You insert your first simple form field for the search function.

1. **Click the spacer image in the top-right cell. Press the left-arrow key to place the cursor in front of the spacer image.**

2. **Type** register I sign in **and then preview in your browsers.**
   Don't worry about how the text looks just yet; you format it and make it look nice in Session 11.

3. **Click in the large orange area of the third row (to the right of the men image) and click the Assets panel to activate it. Select sbbtn_assetsearch. Insert it. Type** Asset Search **for the Alternative text.**

4. **Press the keyboard right-arrow key to place the cursor to the right of the image. Add a paragraph space by pressing the Enter (Return) key.**

5. **Type** Search our photos, movies, sounds and fonts using keyword:.

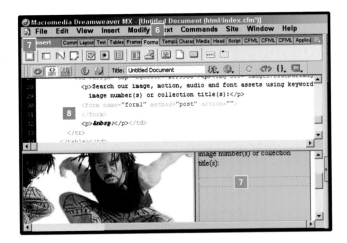

6. **Press the Enter (Return) key. In the Insert panel (top of the document), click the Forms tab.**

7. **Click the Form icon.**
   This inserts a form element (container) only. Next you add a specific type of form that goes inside the form element.

8. **Click the Design and Code View icon. Check the code and notice the form tags.**
   Notice that the FORM has a name attribute assigned; it is form1.

9. **In the Property inspector in the Form Name field, type** Keyword.

10. **Click inside the red dotted lines of the form in the sidebar. In the Forms panel (on the Insert bar), click the Text Field icon.**

11. **In the Input Tag Accessibility Attributes dialog box, select the No Label Tag option and click OK.**

12. **In the TextField box of the Property inspector, type** Keyword.

13. **In the Char Width field, type** 12.
    This makes the search field smaller, but if a word is longer than 12 characters they can still enter it and the word scrolls.

<NOTE>
If you want to limit the amount of characters in a field, you specify that in the Max Width field.

14. **Click to the right of the text field and type** (Single Keyword) **and then Press Shift-Enter (Shift-Return).**

15. **In the Forms panel, click the Button icon.**

16. **Select No Label Tag and click OK for the Accessibility dialog box.**

17. **In the Property inspector, change the Button Name to Search. Type** Search **into the Label field.**

18. **Click below and outside of the form to place your cursor.**

19. **In the Assets panel, select the sbbtn_cds image and insert it. Type** CD covers title image.

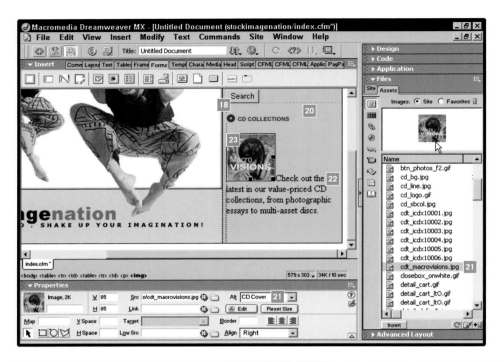

Table 9.2: Alignment Attributes

Property	Function
Default	The browser default; usually bottom alignment.
Baseline	Aligns the image's bottom with the baseline of the first line of text.
Top	Aligns image's top with the first line of text.
Middle	Aligns the image's middle with the baseline of the first line of text.
Bottom	Aligns the bottom of the image with the baseline of the first line of text.
Text Top	Aligns the image's top with the top of the first line of text.
Absolute Middle	Aligns the image's middle with the middle of the first line of text.
Absolute Bottom	Aligns the image's bottom with the bottom of the first line of text.
Left	Aligns the image flush left on the page or cell; text is to the right.
Right	Aligns the image flush right on the page or cell; text is to the left.

20. **Click to the right of the CD Collections icon and press Enter (Return).**

21. **In the Assets panel, select** cdt_macrovisions.jpg **and insert it. Type** CD Cover **for the Alternative text.**

22. **Type** Check out the latest in our value-priced CD collections, from photographic essays to multi-asset discs. The text is next to the bottom of the image.

23. **Select the Macro Visions image. In the Property inspector, change the Align field to Right.**
    The image is too close to the edge.

24. **In the H Space field, enter** 5.
    This adds five pixels to the horizontal edge of the image. See Table 9.2 for other image alignment options.

< N O T E >
You see black below the logo part of the image but don't worry about it. When you change the size of the font, the sidebar area shrinks and the black goes away.

25. **At the top of your document is a Title field, which currently says Untitled Document. Highlight the name and type**
    stockimagenation : royalty-free images, motion graphics and more! This is the title of the page that displays in a browser. Many search engines place a higher listing rating based on the words found in the title so it's good to make it descriptive.

Tutorial

» Adding Content Outside the Table

In this tutorial, you add links to the bottom of the page outside of the table. When your main navigation uses images, it's always a good idea to include text links as well for those who cannot see images. A screen reader can read the text links, and anyone browsing without images can still navigate your site.

1. **Click to place your cursor to the right of the table and press Enter (Return) to add a paragraph space.**
   Your cursor is below the table.

2. **Type** Home | Photos | Motion | Audio | Fonts | My Lightbox **and then press Enter (Return).**

3. **In the Insert panel, click the Characters tab.**

4. **Click the Copyright symbol. Click next to the symbol and type** copyright 2003 all rights reserved.

5. **Press the Shift-Enter (Shift-Return) keys again and type** terms & conditions | about us.

6. **Save your file but keep it open.**

Tutorial
» Building Links

In this tutorial, you add the links to the home page, some to actual pages, and some to placeholder links.

1. **Choose File→New and select Dynamic Page and ColdFusion. Click Create.**

2. **Choose File→Save As and navigate to your stockimagenation/html/stockimagenation/about folder. Name the file** index.cfm **and save.**
   Don't worry that it's the same filename as the home page. It's okay because it's in a different folder.

3. **In the File Name field, type** index.cfm **and save.**

4. **Repeat steps 2 and 3 to add the** index.cfm **file to the following folders: audio, cd_collections, fonts, motion, photos, and lightbox.**
   Close the new page when you are done.

5. **In the Site panel, be sure each folder is open that you added a file to.**
   This is so you can see each index page. You point to each file in the following steps.

6. **Select the Home icon.**

7. **In the Property inspector, click and drag on the Point to File icon. Drag it to the** index.cfm, **which is the home page.**
   This file is in the stockimagenation folder. Notice in the Property inspector the link of index.cfm has been added.

8. **Select the photos icon. Drag the Point to File icon to the** index.cfm **that is inside the photos folder.**
   Notice the link name changed to photos/index.cfm. It points to the folder path. This is a relative path, in that it points to a file in the same root folder. An absolute path is when you include the entire path such as http://www.whatever.com/whatever.htm.

9. **Repeat this process for each of the icons.**

<NOTE>
In step 4, the index pages you are adding are placeholders for the real pages. But when you use these files to add links, the links remain accurate.

<NOTE>
In step 4, to quickly save the same blank page with the same name, you can use the same new document you saved in the About folder. You can simply save it into different folders.

10. Highlight the word *Home* in the row of navigation text at the bottom of the site design.

11. Use the Point to File icon and drag to `index.cfm` to link to the home page.

12. Repeat for the other words, highlighting the link words only and not the pipe characters.

13. Highlight *terms and conditions* and link it to `legal.htm`. `legal.htm` is in the stockimagenation folder with the site `index.cfm` page.

14. Highlight *about us* and link it to the `index.cfm` page inside the about folder.

15. Select the Register text and add `javascript;:` in the link field in the Property inspector. Repeat for the words sign in.

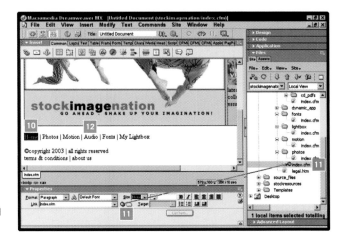

< N O T E >

Be careful not to select the spacer image that is next to the words *sign in*, otherwise they will be linked as well.

16. Highlight the words CD Collections in the descriptive text under the CD Collections icon. Use the Point to File icon and drag it to the `index.cfm` page in the cd_collections folder.

17. Save the file and close it.

Tutorial
» Building a Hybrid Table for the Details Page

In this tutorial, you build tables that stretch with the page. The main table is 98%, which means it fills 98% of the browser window. The nested tables (a table inside a table) have certain columns set to 100%, which stretch to fill 100% of the available space in that column. A hybrid table has fixed cells as well as autostretch or percentage cells.

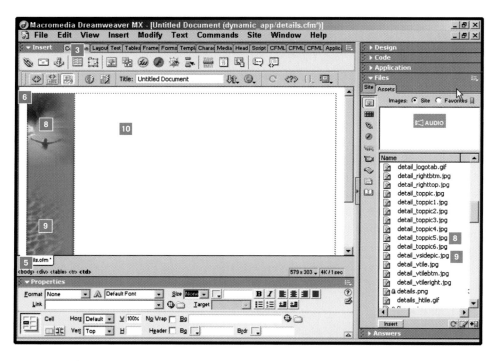

1. **Choose File→New and select Dynamic Page and ColdFusion. Click the Create button.**

2. **Choose File→Save As. Navigate to the stockimagenation/html/stockimagenation/dynamic_app folder and name the file** details.cfm. **Leave the page open.**

3. **From the Insert panel, click the Insert Table icon and use these parameters:**
   Rows: 3   Width: 98 percent
   Columns: 3   Border, Cell Padding, Cell Spacing: 0

4. **Click OK to close the Insert Table dialog box.**

5. **Select the** <body> **tag and click the Center icon (to the right of the bold icon in the Property inspector) to add the** <div> **tags around the table.**

6. **Click to place your cursor in the top-left cell of the first row.**

7. **In the Property inspector, set the cell width to 82 and vertical to Top.**

8. **In the Assets panel, select** detail_toppic5.jpg **and insert it. Type** Swimmer Image **for the Alt text.**

9. **Select the** detail_vsidepic.jpg **and insert it. Type** Water Image **for the Alt text.**
   The image stacks under the first one you added because you set the maximum width to 82.

10. **Tab over to the second column of the first row. Set the vertical to Top, width to 100%, and background color to white.**
    Don't forget to actually type the percent sign. This also collapses the last column (cell), but you can tab to select it.

11. **Save the file, but keep it open.**

Tutorial
» Nesting Tables

In this tutorial, you nest a table inside the second cell of the first table. Then you nest another small table into the second table you just nested. Only nest tables when it's absolutely necessary. Nesting makes the table more complex.

1. **Click the Insert Table icon and use these parameters:**
   Rows: 1
   Columns: 2
   Width: 100 percent
   Border, Cell Padding, Cell Spacing: 0

2. **Click OK to close the Insert Table dialog box.**
   You just nested a table inside the second column of the first table.

3. **Click to place your cursor in the left cell of the nested table.**

4. **In the Assets panel, select** detail_logotab.gif **and insert it. Type** stockimagenation logo **for the Alt text.**

5. **Take note of the width of the image. It's 238 pixels wide.**

6. **Press the right arrow on your keyboard to access the cell and make the width 238. Change the vertical to Bottom.**

7. **Either tab over to the next cell/column of the nested table or just click into it.**

8. **Set the vertical to bottom and width to 100% and make the background color blue (sample from the top of the logo).**
   You are now going to nest another small table into this table.

9. **Click the Insert Table icon and use these parameters:**
   Rows: 1
   Columns: 2
   Width: 100 percent
   Border, Cell Padding: 0
   Cell Spacing: 5

10. **Click OK to close the Insert Table dialog box.**
    Take a look at the table you inserted. Notice the extra space around each cell indicated by the dotted lines. This is the cell spacing of five pixels you added.

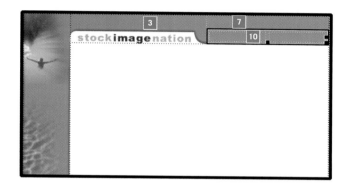

\<NOTE\>
If you don't see the appropriate attribute fields in the Property inspector, then you may have lost focus on the selected item. In Dreamweaver if you do something else (even if the item is still selected), you lose focus. If this happens, just reselect the item to gain focus.

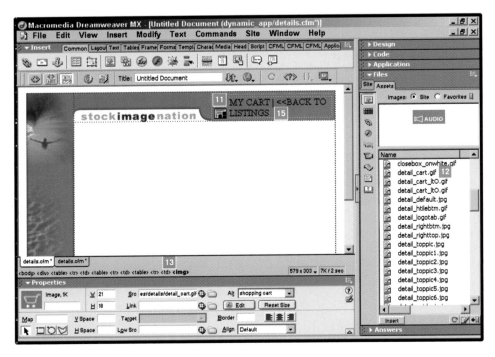

11. **Click to place your cursor in the left cell of the new nested table. Change the vertical to Bottom.**

12. **In the Assets panel, select** detail_cart.gif **and type** Shopping Cart **for the Alt text.**
    Note the width of the image. In the Tag selector, you now see three <table> tags and the last <img> tag is bold because that is what is selected.

13. **Click the** <td> **in front of the bold** <img> **tag to select the cell. Change the width to 21 and press Enter (Return).**
    Notice how the cell collapsed around the cart icon.

< N O T E >
To accept parameters you enter in the Property inspector, you can press Enter (Return) or click anywhere in the document. Be careful using Enter (Return), though; you don't want to be adding paragraph spaces.

14. **Click to place your cursor in the right cell of the icon table.**

15. **Type** MY CART I <<BACK TO LISTINGS.
    This text distorts your table, but you fix this in Session 11 when you apply CSS styles to the text.

16. **Save the file but keep it open.**

< N O T E >
You notice that you are instructed to save frequently. If you ever work for hours without saving and an application crashes, you'll appreciate why you are told to save so frequently.

Tutorial

» Adding Background Images and Table Corners

In this tutorial, you add the background images and table corners to the home page.

1. Select the swimmer image and tab two times to get into the third column of the main table.

2. Set the vertical to Top. In the assets panel, select `detail_right-top.jpg` and press Enter (Return) for the Alt text.
   Notice the corner image added at the right side of the page.

3. Select the `<td>` tag in front of the `<img>` tag. In the Property inspector, click the folder icon next to the bg (background) image field. Navigate to your html/images/details folder and select `detail_vtileright.jpg`. Click OK. Press Enter (Return) for the Alt text.
   You just added a background image. This image tiles to fill the space of this last column.

4. Place your cursor and click into the second cell of the second row of the large table.

5. Click the folder for the background image and navigate to the html/images/details folder. Select `detail_htilebtm.gif` and click OK. Set the vertical to Bottom.
   Just Press Enter (Return) for the alternative text.

6. In the Assets panel, add a spacer.
   Whenever you have a background image and no real content such as an image or text, you need to add a spacer. If you don't, the background won't show up in Netscape 4.

7. Tab over to the third column and set the vertical to Bottom.

8. In the Assets panel, select `detail_rightbtn.jpg` and insert it. Press Enter (Return) for the Alt text.

9. Click into the first cell of the second row of the main table. In the Assets panel, select `detail_vtilebtm.jpg` and insert it. Press Enter (Return) for the Alt text.

10. Click into the first cell of the third row, set the vertical to Bottom, and change the background color to blue.

11. Insert a spacer.

12. Click into the second cell of the third row and change the vertical to Bottom, horizontal to Center, and the background color to blue.
    Type terms & conditions I about comp images.

13. Tab into the third cell of the third column and set the vertical to Bottom and the background color to blue. Insert a spacer.

14. Save your file but keep it open.

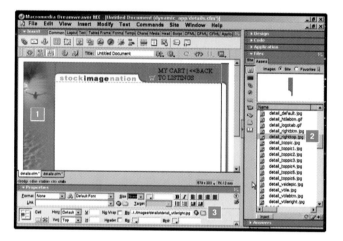

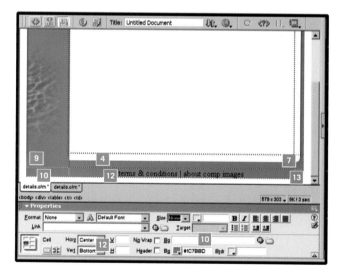

Tutorial
» Using a Placeholder Image

In this tutorial, you add another nested table. In that table, you add a placeholder image that is replaced dynamically from the database.

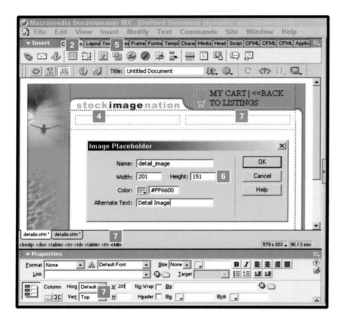

1. **Click inside the second cell of the main table. Click in the large white area.**
   The cursor is behind the nested tables you added. It looks like it's in the wrong column but it isn't, as you see as soon as you add the table.

2. **Click the Insert Table icon and use these parameters:**
   Rows: 1
   Columns: 2
   Width: 100 percent
   Border, Cell Padding: 0
   Cell Spacing: 10

3. **Click OK to close the Insert Table dialog box.**
   Notice how the table stacked below the nested tables and now sits just below the table with the logo in it.

4. **Click inside the first cell of the new table.**

5. **In the Insert panel, click the Image Placeholder icon.**

6. **Type** detail_image **for the Name. Choose a size of 201x151, the color orange, and Alternative text of Detail Image. Click OK.**

7. **Click the <td> tag before the <img> tag and set the Vertical to Top and the Width to 201.**
   You won't see the <img> tag in the illustration because once you selected the <td> tag the <img> tag doesn't show.

8. **Click in the second cell and type Title (press Enter) Description: (press Enter), Keywords.**
   This information fills in dynamically from the database.

9. **Save the file, but leave it open.**

Tutorial

» Inserting Fireworks HTML and Images

In Fireworks you exported the table with rounded corners, including the images, and the HTML code that placed the images into a table. In this tutorial, you learn how you can use that file and images in Dreamweaver.

1. **Click in the large white area below the placeholder image table (cursor is on the right side of the placeholder image table) and press the Enter (Return) key.**
   The cursor is now below the placeholder image table.

2. **Choose Insert→Interactive Images→Fireworks HTML.**

3. **Click the Browse button and navigate to the html/images/details folder. Select** details_table.htm.

4. **Click to select the Delete File after Insertion option and click OK.**

5. **Click into the second cell next to the orange corner. Set the background to orange (sample from the top-left corner) and Horz to Center. Type** File Size | Resolution | Dimensions.

6. **Tab to the next column, set the background color to the same orange as the rest of the row, set Horz to Center, and insert a spacer image. Make it 60x1.**

7. **Type** Price.

8. **Tab over to the last column.**

9. **Tab over to the new column and make the background orange and Horz Center. Add a 40x1 spacer and type** Add.

10. **Delete the image with the cart in it.**
    You aren't going to use this because it needs to have text with it. You insert the cart instead.

11. **Delete the bottom corner image as well.**

12. **Click into each of the remaining cells on the bottom and change the background color to the lighter orange.**

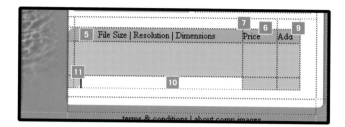

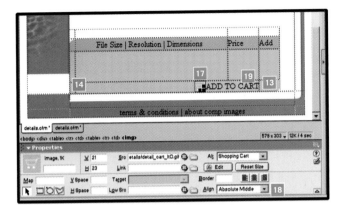

<NOTE>

There are times when you want one image or paragraph to span multiple columns or rows or both. You can do this by merging two or more cells into one. Dreamweaver makes it easy by supplying an icon to click. But take a look at the HTML; you see that the attribute rowspan or colspan has been added to the row <tr> or column <td> tag. You can also do the reverse; split a cell into two or more rows or columns. Again, Dreamweaver generates the additional code for you.

<NOTE>

You just saw how you can import text and formatting from Fireworks into Dreamweaver. Once it's imported, text remains fully editable.

13. **Click into the bottom corner cell and, in the Property inspector, set the Horz to Right. From the Assets panel, select** tbl_cnr_BR.gif **and insert it. Press Enter (Return) for the Alternative text.**

14. **Place your cursor into the two center cells and drag to the right until both cells are selected.**

15. **Right-click (Control-click) and select Table→Merge Cells.**

16. **Set the Horz to right-aligned.**

17. **Click inside the newly merged cell. In the Assets panel, select** detail_cart_lt0.gif **and insert it. Type** Shopping Cart **for the Alternative text.**

18. **With the cart still selected, select Absolute Middle from the Align list.**

19. **Press the keyboard right-arrow key and type** ADD TO CART.
    This extends the cell a bit and messes up the corner graphic but you make the text smaller in Session 11, which fixes the problem.

20. **Click the water image in the first column. Click the** <td> **tag before the** <img> **tag.**
    There is white showing below the images because the background image doesn't appear in this area.

21. **Click the folder for the background image in the Properties inspector. Navigate to the html/images/details folder and select** detail_vtile.jpg. **Click OK.**

22. **Save the file and close it.**

» Session Review

In this session, you became familiar with the Dreamweaver environment. You also learned how to set a few preferences and to define your local root folder. Now it's time to see how much you remember. Answers to the questions can be found in the sections noted in parentheses.

1. What is a block element? ("Discussion: Dreamweaver and HTML")

2. What is a fixed width table? ("Tutorial: Building a Relative Table for the Legal Page")

3. What do the `<tr>` and `<td>` tags do? ("Tutorial: Building a Relative Table for the Legal Page")

4. What is the easiest way to select a specific tag? ("Tutorial: Building a Relative Table for the Legal Page")

5. Name two ways to insert images. ("Tutorial: Adding Images to the Legal Page")

6. What is a `spacer.gif`? ("Tutorial: Adding Navigational Icons to the Home Page")

7. How do you change the background color of a cell? ("Tutorial: Setting Table Cell Properties")

8. Do you need to place each image in its own cell? ("Tutorial: Adding Navigation Icons to the Home Page")

9. Do you need to add a `<br>` tag (Shift-Enter [Shift-Return]) between images in a cell? ("Tutorial: Adding the Main Content")

10. How do you make a cell fit the image perfectly? ("Tutorial: Adding the Main Content")

11. How do you make a null link? ("Tutorial: Building Links")

12. Can you have an image and a background image in the same cell? ("Tutorial: Adding Background Images and Table Corners")

register | sign in

🔍 ASSET SEARCH

Search our image, motion, audio and font assets using keyword (s), image number(s) or collection title(s):

[Search]

Advanced Image Search
Research Request
Search Tips

⬤ CD COLLECTIONS

Check out the latest in our value-priced CD collections, from photographic essays to multi-asset discs.

Home | Photos | Motion | Audio | Fonts | My Lightbox
©copyright 2002 | all rights reserved.
terms & conditions | about this design

Session 10

Behaviors, Snippets, and Client-Side Scripting

Today is June 12, 2003

⌂ HOME   PHOTOS   MOTION   AUDIO   FONTS   MY LIGHTBOX

register | sign in

ASSET SEARCH

Search our photos, movies, sounds and fonts using keyword:

(Single Keyword)

Search

CD COLLECTIONS

Check out the latest in our value-priced CD collections, from photographic essays to multi-asset discs.

Macro VISIONS

stockimagenation
GO AHEAD . SHAKE UP YOUR IMAGINATION!

Home | Photos | Motion | Audio | Fonts | My Lightbox

©copyright 2003 | all rights reserved
terms & conditions | about us

The Power of Client-Side Scripting

From interactive rollover buttons to pop-up windows to writing the current day and date on your pages, the power of client-side JavaScript provides a level of interactivity that is both functional and fun. JavaScript runs in the client browser and requires no other program, plug-in, or helper application to function. You simply need a browser that understands the events and functions used by the script. An *event* is something that happens, like clicking an object (onClick), moving the cursor over a link or object (onMouseOver), or clicking to load a new page in the browser window (onLoad). When the event occurs, an *action*, pre-defined in a *function*, occurs. Typically, such functions are written in the head of the HTML page or even in a separate .JS page. Dreamweaver MX calls the combination of an event and an action a behavior. You can add all sorts of interactivity to your page through the use of the Behaviors panel.

Along with the pre-built behaviors in Dreamweaver MX, you also have other options. You can use custom scripts in your page and even save such scripts in the Snippets panel to keep them handy for all your sites. And perhaps the most wonderful feature in Dreamweaver is its *extensibility* — there are all sorts of free and commercial extensions that you can download and install into Dreamweaver to add even more behaviors and other great tools to the program.

In this session, you use some of Dreamweaver's most popular behaviors to build interactive rollover buttons that open a new browser window on demand. You also learn how to insert a dynamic date in your pages through the use of a custom script. Finally, you take a look at how the Snippets panel can be used to store code, scripts, and other content for use throughout all your sites.

TOOLS YOU'LL USE
Behaviors panel, Snippets panel, Swap Image behavior, Open Browser Window behavior, Script Assets, Code view, Invisible Elements, Extension Manager

MATERIALS NEEDED
None unless you want to use the session10_starter files

TIME REQUIRED
60 minutes

Tutorial
» Swapping Images for Rollover Buttons

They're everywhere! Move your cursor over the button and it changes color or even looks like a button being pressed — how do they do it? Using JavaScript, of course! In this tutorial, you learn how to build "rollovers" by applying Dreamweaver's Swap Image behavior to the links that surround the home page's navigation buttons. When using JavaScript to apply a function to an object in the Web page, you must reference the object. Dreamweaver's Property inspector includes a field that enables you to give your object a *reference name.* Each name must be unique and can't start with numbers or special characters.

Table 10.1: Button Image Names

Button	JavaScript Name
Home	btnHome
Photos	btnPhoto
Motion	btnMotion
Audio	btnAudio
Fonts	btnFonts
LightBox	btnBox

< N O T E >

To apply a script to a graphic button, you should first make it a link, even if you have to make it a null link. The code that calls a JavaScript function is written in the anchor tag `<a href="">button here</a>`. In Session 9, you added links to all the page buttons.

1. **Double-click the** `index.cfm` **page in the stockimagenation directory in the Site panel to open it.**

2. **Select the Home button.**

3. **Click into the image field in the top-left corner of the Property inspector and name this image** btnHome.

4. **Repeat this process for each button image using the names shown in Table 10.1.**

< N O T E >

When using JavaScript to apply a function to an object in the Web page, you must reference that object somehow. Typically, you don't directly reference the object's filename; in fact, some objects won't have a filename. When you plan to reference an object, you should give it a reference name. You cannot start reference names with a number or use special characters or spaces in the name. Each name must, of course, be unique.

5. **Re-select the Home button.**

6. **Press Shift+F3 to open the Behaviors panel.**

7. **Press the Add (+) button in the Behaviors panel and choose Swap Image.**

   In the Swap Image dialog box, you see a list of images and the btnHome image is highlighted. The button is the *trigger* for the JavaScript behavior. Typically (but not always), you want the trigger selected in the Images list because that is the object that the JavaScript acts on. Dreamweaver tries to make your job easier by pre-selecting the name of the object that you selected in the page.

8. **Click the Browse button.**

   You'll locate the over state for this button in the main_navs folder.

<N O T E>

The pre-checked `PreloadImages` and `ImageRestore` functions at the bottom of the dialog box automatically add scripts to allow the hidden state(s) of the button graphics to be loaded as the page loads and also to restore the starting state as the cursor moves off the button. You'll almost always leave these checked as you build rollover buttons — unless one or more of the button states is an animated GIF. In that case, you don't want the image to be pre-loaded (because it will start playing before it is shown) so you uncheck the Preload function.

What's a Rollover?

A *rollover* generally refers to the technique that applies changes to images as you move your cursor over them. A JavaScript function manipulates the source (the filename) of the image, which serves as the trigger. A call to the JavaScript function is placed in a link that surrounds the image and an event is selected, such as onMouseOver or onClick. The event calls the script function and the image source file is changed to the new source, which is generally referred to as the button's "over" state. Other functions can also be used to track which button is clicked, giving a button a "down" state that occurs onClick.

Dreamweaver contains several behaviors and tools used to create both rollovers and navigation bars. Navigation bars are sets of buttons that are tracked for the down state and are typically used when developing sites that use framesets.

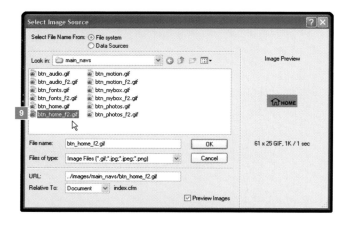

9. **Navigate to the stockimagenation/html/images/main_navs folder and select** `btn_home_f2.gif`. **Click OK to return to the Swap Image dialog box.**

When you exported the graphics from Fireworks, the graphics on frame 2 used the slice name appended with _f2 (for frame 2). All the "over" states for the buttons have _f2 after the button's name.

10. **Close the Swap Image dialog box.**

In the Behaviors panel, you see the new behaviors listed as an Event and Action. In this case, the event listed is `onMouseOver` and the action is Swap Image. Another event (`onMouseOut`) is used for the RestoreImage action that returns the rollover image to its original state. Remember, the Restore function was added automatically because the option was checked in the Swap Image dialog box.

11. **Repeat steps 5 through 10 for each button. In each case, you select the _f2 version of the graphic from the html/images/main_navs folder. Use Table 10.2 for reference.**

12. **Save your page and then preview it by pressing F12.**

Move your cursor over the buttons to see the rollovers in action! If any of the over button states are incorrect, return to the page, select the button, and double-click the existing Swap Image behavior to re-open it and choose the correct over state.

13. **Leave this page open for the next tutorial.**

Table 10.2: Button Names for Over States

Button Name	Over State Graphic
Home	btn_home_f2.gif
Photos	btn_photos_f2.gif
Motion	btn_motion_f2.gif
Audio	btn_audio_f2.gif
Fonts	btn_fonts_f2.gif
LightBox	btn_mybox_f2.gif

Events and Behaviors in the Behavior Panel

To change the listed event, you click the current event and a pull-down menu is available to select a new event. The available events depend upon which Show Events For option you've chosen. You can change the events option in the Add Behavior menu—the same place where you add a behavior. Earlier versions of browsers don't understand as many events as later ones. Typically, you want to have Show Events For Version 4.0 and Later. Choosing a different event option doesn't change which behaviors are available. In fact, it depends on what kind of page element is selected as to which behaviors are available. When a behavior is unavailable, it is grayed out in the menu.

Tutorial
» Opening a Pop-Up Browser Window

Another commonly seen (if somewhat abused) Web element is the pop-up window. Pop-up windows aren't anything especially new because HTML also has the capability to call a new document window. To use HTML to do this, you set a target in a link `<a href="page.html" target="_blank">open a new window</a>`. With JavaScript, you can call a window and control the presentation of both the window and the document within. You can control the width and height of the window and the features provided to the users, such as scrollbars, buttons, and the option to resize the window.

In this tutorial, you use Dreamweaver's Open Browser Window behavior to pop up a window that displays the legal notice of the site. The terms and conditions link at the bottom of the page is the link to open the legal page in a pop-up window. The action that they take to trigger this link is the event for opening the new browser window — `onClick`.

1. **Open the home page by double-clicking on the** `index.cfm` **page in the stockimagenation folder of the Site panel.**

2. **Select the text** *terms and conditions* **in the link area at the bottom of the page. Add a null link by typing** javascript:; **into the link field in the Property inspector.**
This is the preferred method of building a "fake" link because it is more compatible with different browsers.

3. **Click into the** *terms and conditions* **link to place your cursor. In the Behaviors panel click the plus sign and select Open Browser Window.**

4. **In the Open Browser Window dialog box, click the Browse button and navigate to the** legal.htm **page. Select it and click OK.**

5. **Set the width and height of the new window to 400.**

6. **Click Scrollbars as Needed and Resize Handles to select these options.**
It's always a good idea to let the user control these options because varying text default sizes can require a larger or smaller window size.

7. **Name the new window** LegalWin, **and then OK the settings to close the Open Browser Window dialog box.**
You are not required to name a window, but in this case, you do. Naming a window gives you the option to control the window through more JavaScript or other server-side scripting.

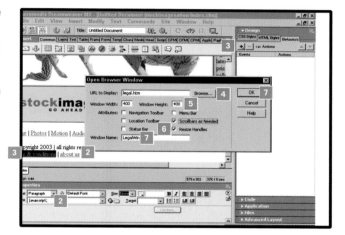

8. **Check the Behaviors panel to verify that your event is** `onClick`. **If it is not, click the arrow for the event listed and change it to** `onClick`.

<NOTE>

If `onClick` is not available, select Show Events For and select 4.0 and Later Browsers.

9. **Save your home page and preview it in your browsers.**

Click the *terms and conditions* link to pop up your new window and page. Drag the sides larger and smaller and notice how the content resizes. This is because you used an autostretch table in the legal page. You can close this page after testing.

Tutorial

» Closing a Pop-Up Window with JavaScript

Now that you opened a browser window, you should know how to close one. It's considered good form to give the user a "close this window" button or link. Oddly, although Dreamweaver includes a behavior to open a browser window, it doesn't have one to close it. But that is okay because you use a simple bit of JavaScript to close the window.

1. **Double-click the `legal.htm` page in the Site panel to open it.**

2. **Scroll down to the bottom of the page and select *Close this window*.**

3. **In the link field for the selected text, type the following:**
   javascript:window.self.close();

4. **Save this page.**
   Because you call this page from another page, it's important that this be saved—if it is not, you get the previous page rendition instead of the new one.

5. **In the Site panel (window, for Macintosh users), highlight the home page (`index.cfm`), and press F12 to preview it in a browser.**
   If you get an error, then go back and check your link code. It has to be exact including the punctuation.

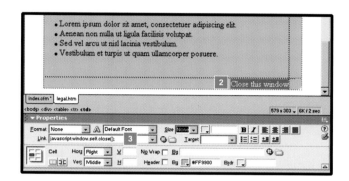

<TIP>
You don't have to have a page open to preview it. Simply selecting a page in the site panel allows you to use F12 for your primary browser and Ctrl+F12 (⌘+F12) for the secondary browser. Alternatively, you can right-click (Ctrl+click) the selected page and choose Preview in Browser to select any listed browser.

6. **Open the pop-up window by clicking the link.**

7. **Test the *close this window* link.**

8. **Keep the legal page open for the next tutorial.**

Tutorial
» Building Snippets

If you haven't discovered this new feature of Dreamweaver MX, you're in for a treat! A snippet is stored code, content, well . . . just about anything! The Snippets panel is designed to let you save code, from HTML structures to complex JavaScript and more, in your Dreamweaver program. Dreamweaver ships with pre-built snippets but you can build your own snippets, too. In fact, you can organize and store just about anything in the Snippets panel, including client or site content. In this tutorial, you make a snippet out of the "close this window" link you created. You also build a couple of snippets to use later in this book.

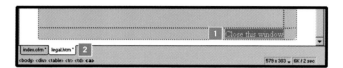

1. **Insert your cursor (or select) into the** `legal.htm` **page's** *close this window* **link.**

2. **Use the Tag selector to select the last** `<a>` **tag in the Status bar.**

<NOTE>

Using the Tag selector speeds up the development process. It acts like a "tree" view of the objects in the page. Every object in a page is in a box or container. The entire document is a box or container. The Tag selector lets you see all the boxes for the object where your cursor is currently located. It's kind of like one of those sets of ever-smaller boxes inside each other, except the Tag selector makes it possible to select any box that contains the currently-selected object.

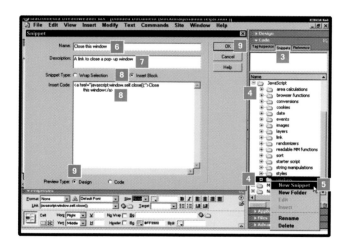

3. **Press Shift+F9 to open the Snippets panel.**

4. **Expand the JavaScript folder within the panel and right-click (Control-click) the windows folder at the bottom of the list of folders.**

5. **Choose New Snippet.**
   The Snippet dialog box opens.

6. **Name the new snippet** Close this window.

7. **In the Snippet Description field, type** A link to close a pop-up window.

8. **Select the Insert Block option.**
   Because the code was actively selected in the document, Dreamweaver added it to the snippet code. If it wasn't selected you would need to copy the code from Code view and paste it into the Insert Code area.

9. **Leave the Preview Type as Design view and click OK to close the dialog box.**
   Some snippets are better inserted in Code view. In this case, you will probably be in the body of the page, so either mode works. If you make a snippet to use in the head of a page (such as meta information), you have to insert that snippet in Code view.

10. **Close the `legal.htm` page.**

    To see how to build a snippet without a selection, you create two more snippets—for DOCTYPE. DOCTYPE is a declaration that is placed at the beginning of the page before the opening `<html>` tag and controls how pages are rendered by a browser. In this case, the DOCTYPES you build as snippets are for CSS (Cascading Style Sheets) rendering.

11. **Close any open folders (such as the JavaScript folder) in the Snippets panel.**

12. **Click Name (the heading in the gray area of the panel) to see how this organizes the folders alphabetically.**

13. **Right-click (Control-click) Name and select New Folder.**

14. **Name the new folder CSS.**

    The new folder is open and selected.

15. **Click the New Folder icon to add a new folder to the CSS folder.**

    When you select this icon with a folder selected, it places a folder inside the open folder.

16. **Select and name the new folder DocTypes.**

17. **Click the New Snippet (+) icon to add a blank snippet to the DocTypes folder.**

    The Snippet dialog box opens.

18. **Enter the following information into the Snippet dialog box for two snippets listed in Table 10.3.**

    In Session 11, which covers Cascading Style Sheets, you insert the DOCTYPE snippet into your pages.

Table 10.3: Snippet Dialog Box Code Details

Name	Description	Type	Code (All on One Line)	View
`transitional doctype`	Causes the browser to render the CSS of the page in quirks mode.	Block	`<!DOCTYPE HTML PUBLIC "-//W3C//DTD HTML 4.01 Transitional//EN" "">`	Code
`strict doctype`	Causes the browser to adhere to CSS standards, rendering the page more strictly.	Block	`<!DOCTYPE HTML PUBLIC "-//W3C//DTD HTML 4.01//EN" "">`	Code

Tutorial
» Using Custom JavaScript to Add a Dynamic Date

The Behaviors and Snippets panel don't always have just the right script for your needs. In this tutorial, you use custom JavaScript to add a dynamic date that displays the current date to the site visitor. Because this date is to be on most, if not all, of the site pages, you use an external page to store the script and simply link to the .JS page. When the browser encounters the `<script>` tag, it locates the .JS page to include its content in the current page. It's important to understand that when you use the linking method, both the page that uses the script and the actual .JS file need to be on the server and must maintain the exact path relationship as it exists when you link to the script. The alternative to linking is to embed the actual code in every page—and that's just not very efficient.

1. **In the Site panel, open the home page (**`index.cfm`**) from the stockimagenation folder.**

2. **Select the main large table and press the left-arrow key to get the cursor outside the table.**
   An easy way to select the outside table is to click in the margin and drag into the table.

3. **Use the Assets panel to insert a** `spacer.gif`**. Make the size 560x20.**
   This spacer is used to help position our date. The spacer is added to the top of the document.

4. **In the Assets panel. Click the Scripts icon.**
   The .JS file is an asset; therefore, Dreamweaver automatically categorizes it as such.

< T I P >

You are provided with a folder in your site files named scripts. The JavaScript for the date can be found here. You can write your own scripts or search the Internet for what you need. There are many free scripts available.

5. **Right-click (Ctrl-click)** `datescript.js` **and choose Edit.**
   This script creates arrays from variables and dynamically writes the concatenated expressions as "Today is Sunday, Jan. 5, 2003" (but uses the correct day and date, of course!).

6. **You don't need to edit anything, just take a look at the code so you can close the script.**

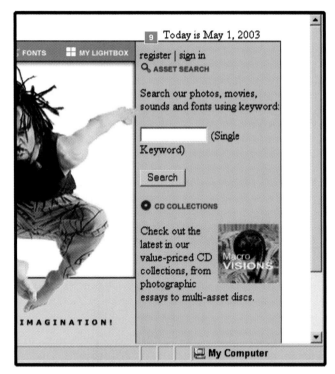

7. **Select the large spacer image you added at the top of the page.**
   Use your right-arrow key to move off the image.

8. **Right-click (Ctrl-click) the** datescript.js **filename in the Assets panel and choose Insert.**
   If you have your View Options→Visual Aids→Invisible Elements enabled, you can see the icon that represents the script that you inserted. You cannot see this script in action until you preview it in a browser.

9. **Save and preview the page in a browser.**
   Although the dynamic date appears kind of big and clunky now, you style its appearance in the next session when you learn to define and use Cascading Style Sheets. This script dynamically writes the tag that uses the style you define later.

Tutorial
» Installing Extensions

A lot of truly great functionality powered by JavaScript is yours for the taking in the form of extensions. Extensions are packaged scripts that add new tools to your Dreamweaver program, providing new behaviors, commands, or menu options. In this session you install some extension. In the next session, you make use of some killer extensions that are not only powerful, but are free! Yes, the folks at Project Seven give away these tools and you can quickly download and install them via your program's Extension Manager.

1. **In Dreamweaver, save and close any open documents.**

2. **Choose Commands→Manage Extensions.**
   This opens the Extension Manager. Many of the Macromedia applications are *extensible,* meaning you can extend the program by adding new features and functions through extensions.

<TIP>
If you ever have a problem with the Extension Manager (some people do), Windows users can open it from the Start menu.

3. **Open a browser and navigate to** www.projectseven.com.

<NOTE>
You can alternatively get extensions directly from the Extension Manager without leaving Dreamweaver by clicking the Macromedia (m's) icon. You are not going to Macromedia for this extension because those at Project Seven are updated faster.

4. **Click the Extensions button and scroll down the page when it opens.**

5. **Download the following extensions under the Free Extensions list by clicking the version link.**
   Save them in the Downloaded Extension folder inside the Dreamweaver MX application folder. However, you can save anywhere you like.
   > Animagic Layers
   > Auto Layers
   > ReDoIt
   > Scroller, Horizontal
   > Snap Layers

6. **Close the browser. Install the extensions directly from the Macromedia Extension Manager. Choose File→Install Extension or click the Install icon to open the dialog box.**

7. **Navigate to the folder where you saved the extensions (Dreamweaver MX) and select one. Agree to any disclaimers and such.**

8. **Repeat for all the extensions.**

   In later sessions, you use these extensions to build incredibly powerful and cool page elements without breaking a sweat!

<TIP>

There are lots of sites that offer both free and commercial extensions, but the most likely place to start is at the Macromedia Exchange (http://macromedia.com/exchange). You can review the available extensions without registering, but to download any extension, you must be a registered member. Registering is easy and free.

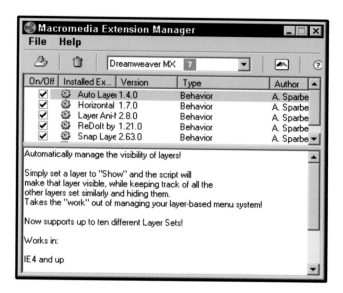

Extensions Management for All Platforms

Updating your Dreamweaver application or having to re-install it is not an uncommon task. When it's necessary, it's quite frustrating to have to re-install all those favorite extensions, especially if you have to go online and download them again. To guard against this, here's a tip. Keep your downloaded extensions in the Downloaded Extensions folder found in the Macromedia\Dreamweaver MX\ folder in your C:\ drive (for Macintosh users, this is the Macromedia\Dreamweaver MX folder wherever you installed your program). It's also wise to organize your extensions into folders according to their makers, as in PVII (project seven). This helps you later if you either need to re-install or update an extension. When you update or re-install Dreamweaver MX, an existing Downloaded Extensions folder remains as the application is updated or installed.

You might not want all your installed extensions active at all times. You can enable or disable extensions from the Extension Manager with ease. Just check or uncheck an installed extension. You can even delete an extension from the Manager by selecting it and clicking the Trash icon. This causes the extension to be

un-installed, which is different than disabled. Un-installing removes the reference to the extension from the list of extensions the next time you start the Manager but does not delete the downloaded extension package itself.

To see how an installed extension affects your Dreamweaver application interface, select the extension in the Manager. The area below the list of extensions should provide some details about where and how to use the selected extension. Additionally, most but not all extension dialog boxes contain a help button that provides more instruction about the extension.

Extensions for Macintosh Users

In some cases, File→Install Extension from the Extension Manager won't work to install extensions. Macintosh computers sometimes cannot "see" the extensions via the dialog box. Another method that seems to work well for Macintosh users is to simply double-click the downloaded extension's icon. Be sure to have Dreamweaver MX open at the time and the Extension Manager open, so you're ready to add the double-clicked extension to the correct program.

» Session Review

In this session, you learned to harness the power of JavaScript through the use of behaviors, snippets, and custom scripts. Although you didn't use the tools you installed with the extensions, you use them extensively in later sessions. The following questions test your knowledge from this session. The answers to the questions can be found in the tutorials noted in parentheses.

1. What is an event? ("Tutorial: Swapping Images for Rollover Buttons")

2. Where is a function typically written? (Session Introduction)

3. What does Macromedia (Dreamweaver) call an event combined with an action? (Session's introduction)

4. What are snippets and where are they stored? ("Tutorial: Building Snippets")

5. How do you edit a rollover button? ("Tutorial: Swapping Images for Rollover Buttons")

6. How do you install an extension? ("Tutorial: Installing Extensions")

7. Which behavior do you use to open a new browser window? ("Tutorial: Installing Extensions")

8. What is the JavaScript code used to close an open browser window? ("Tutorial: Installing Extensions")

9. How can you change which Events are offered for behaviors listed in the Behavior panel? ("Tutorial: Opening a Pop-Up Browser Window")

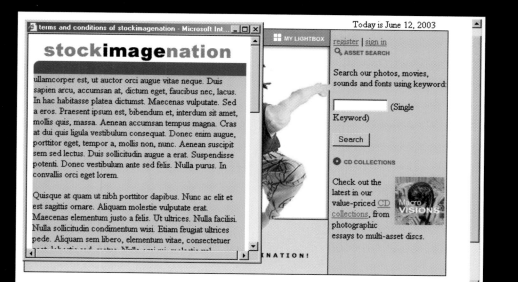

terms and conditions of stockimagenation - Microsoft Int...

stock**image**nation

ullamcorper est, ut auctor orci augue vitae neque. Duis
sapien arcu, accumsan at, dictum eget, faucibus nec, lacus.
In hac habitasse platea dictumst. Maecenas vulputate. Sed
a eros. Praesent ipsum est, bibendum et, interdum sit amet,
mollis quis, massa. Aenean accumsan tempus magna. Cras
at dui quis ligula vestibulum consequat. Donec enim augue,
porttitor eget, tempor a, mollis non, nunc. Aenean suscipit
sem sed lectus. Duis sollicitudin augue a erat. Suspendisse
potenti. Donec vestibulum ante sed felis. Nulla purus. In
convallis orci eget lorem.

Quisque at quam ut nibh porttitor dapibus. Nunc ac elit et
est sagittis ornare. Aliquam molestie vulputate erat.
Maecenas elementum justo a felis. Ut ultrices. Nulla facilisi.
Nulla sollicitudin condimentum wisi. Etiam feugiat ultrices
pede. Aliquam sem libero, elementum vitae, consectetuer

MY LIGHTBOX

register | sign in
ASSET SEARCH

Search our photos, movies,
sounds and fonts using keyword:

(Single
Keyword)

Search

CD COLLECTIONS

Check out the
latest in our
value-priced CD
collections, from
photographic
essays to multi-asset discs.

MacroVISIONS

INATION!

Using Cascading Style Sheets

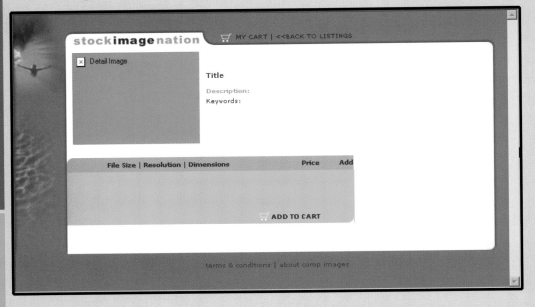

Cascading Style Sheets

The use of Cascading Style Sheets (CSS) is on the rise. Dreamweaver MX includes a lot of new and improved CSS features that are compatible with the World Wide Web Consortium (W3C) standards.

Cascading Style Sheets are probably one of the most important tools to learn in Web development. As a specification set forth by the W3C World Wide Web Consortium, CSS is a standard designed to separate the visual presentation of content from the actual structural markup—a language used to render structured documents like HTML and XML on-screen, on paper, and verbally, in speech.

What does this mean for you as a developer? It means that you no longer need to wrap a font tag around every block element to get the look you want. It means you can put the control of how your page appears into a single location.

One of the hottest new features in Macromedia Dreamweaver MX is the totally revamped CSS Styles panel and the vastly improved rendering of CSS within the Design view. Easier, more intuitive tools make learning and using CSS well worth your while. In fact, I guarantee that once you make the move to using CSS, you'll never go back!

TOOLS YOU'LL USE
Site window, Assets panel, CSS Styles panel, Snippets panel

MATERIALS NEEDED
Your stockimagenation root folder or the session11_starterfiles folder

TIME REQUIRED
90 minutes

Discussion

CSS Basics

A Cascading Style Sheet is a specification that uses its own syntax to write *rules* that control the appearance of content in a Web page. These rules are called *styles*, which together are collectively known as a *style sheet*. Style rules are governed by *the cascade*, which in turn, uses the principles of *inheritance*, *specificity*, and *importance* to determine which rule(s) apply where conflicting rules exist. A good bit of this discussion may go way over your head at first but read it anyway and try to grasp as much as possible. Everything here is done hands on throughout this session. Once you make your first style sheet it begins to sink in. After a few times you really begin to get the hang of it. It isn't nearly as intimidating as it may seem. You even get to look at the code later and it's amazing how straightforward and simple it is.

Cascading Style Sheets remove the extraneous markup that is added just to control how the content *appears*, leaving the HTML structural markup as it was originally intended. HTML is intended to tell a browser how to display your page. With CSS, the HTML can return to a purer form, uncluttered by markup. Cascading Style Sheets separate the appearance from the content. The content of a Web page includes the text, images, forms, and other coding that establishes what the page is about—what it is communicating. This is expressed through HTML codes and commands. How this content looks, its appearance, is handled by styles. Styles define the attributes of the content, such as the font, font size, paragraph alignment, and so on. What's great about style sheets is that you can style your text and positioning in a style sheet which all your pages can link to. When you need to make changes, all you need to change is one file!

< N O T E >
Although positioning with CSS is possible, it still isn't fully supported. Because you are testing for Netscape 4, you won't use that particular feature.

The Ever-Useful Cascade

Style rules can originate in an *external* page or *embedded* within the head of a specific page; style rules can even be defined at the block level or *inline*, although this practically defeats the advantages of using CSS. External style sheet(s) are linked or imported into a page. That page can also have both embedded and inline rules. It can even have more than one externally linked or imported sheet!

What happens when two different declarations are made for the same selector? The cascade also determines what happens when properties for a specific selector conflict; the general rule of thumb is that the "closest" rule's property value wins—although there can be exceptions to this. Given the same selector and property, an inline value overrides an embedded value, which in turn overrides an external value. If the declarations are in one or more linked or imported sheets, the style value in the last sheet read has precedence. This same principle means that the author's styles override default values provided by the browser (user-agent).

Inheritance

All HTML pages are governed by their structure—it's a key part of the basic markup. For example, you cannot put the body tag into the table tag; a paragraph may not contain a table, but table cells may contain paragraphs. These basic rules of structure create parent-child relationships between the elements in the page. Almost every element is either a parent or child, or both. This parent/child or ancestor/descendent relationship governs how CSS rules are applied to the page; it's not surprising that the major principle at play in these relationships is called inheritance. *Inheritance* is the mechanism for how style rules are applied, not only for the specific element, but for its descendents, too.

For example, if the body of a page is set to use a specific text color, all text in all elements should inherit that text color unless specifically set otherwise. This is the theory and should be the case, but of course, like all rules, there are exceptions—some due to special settings and some due to the vagaries of inconsistent browser support. As well, not all properties are inherited. Text color and size is inherited; border and box properties of margin and padding are not. Experience through practice and careful attention to reference resources helps you gain insight to this guiding principle of CSS.

Tutorial
» Creating a Practice Style

In this tutorial, you define your first style that is embedded in the HTML page. This page is to demonstrate a few principles only, you do not use it or save it.

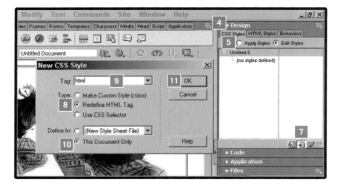

<NOTE>
An HTML tag is a selector, but the redefine HTML label tells you that you are going to change the default properties of the HTML tag you select.

<TIP>
Another good time to use embedded styles is when you need one separate style to make a site compatible with a certain browser. Another option is to link to two (or more) style sheets.

1. **Choose File→New, select a Basic page, HTML, and click the Create button.**

2. **In the Assets panel select the Image icon and select** leap_logo.gif **and insert it.**

3. **Preview in NN4, NN7, and IE6. You should see the margins all around the image.**
   Many designs require that your graphics have no margins in the browser. Because this is an appearance issue, you use a style to take care of the problem.

4. **Click the expander arrow of the Design panel group.**

5. **Click the CSS Styles panel tab to make it the active panel.**

6. **Click the Edit Styles button.**

7. **Click the Add (+) button.**
   The New CSS Style dialog box opens.

8. **Select the Redefine HTML Tag button.**

9. **Choose Html from the Tag drop-down menu.**
   Notice all the different HTML tags you can modify.

10. **Select the This Document Only button.**
    This embeds the style in the HTML page. Normally you don't want to do this, but for just one style it won't add too much to your page weight.

11. **Click OK.**
    The CSS Style Definition for HTML dialog box opens.

12. **Click the Box category.**

13. **In the Margin and Padding areas, leave Same for All checked.**

14. **Type 0 in the Top fields of both the Padding and Margin fields.**

15. **Click OK.**

You just made a style that changes the margin and padding of the HTML tag.

<NOTE>

Even though there is nothing in the Margin or Padding fields, browsers still add a few pixels by default. Unless you specifically set the margins to 0, you get the default.

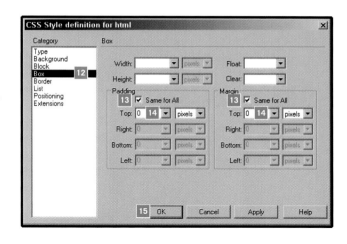

16. **Preview your work in all three browsers.**

Notice that in Netscape browsers you still see a margin. Netscape 4 isn't particularly good with CSS. You need to change the page properties in Dreamweaver.

17. **Choose Modify→Page Properties. In the margin fields (width, height, left, and right), type 0.**

You can change the text here as well, but don't do it! This would add code directly to the page for the color number and you do not want to do that. All the formatting code such as color are done using an external style sheet, thus removing the code from the page. You can add the page title here though.

<NOTE>

Margin width and height affect the margins in Netscape browsers. Left and Right margins affect Internet Explorer margins.

18. **Click OK.**

19. **Close the page without saving.**

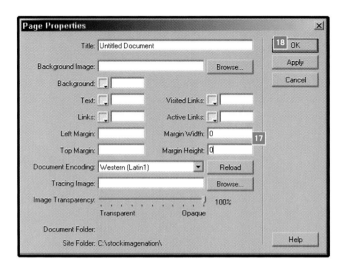

Tutorial
» Redefining HTML Tags

In this tutorial, you redefine a tag much like you did in the practice tutorial. This time, it's the `<body>` tag and you change more of its properties. You use a new style sheet for this site.

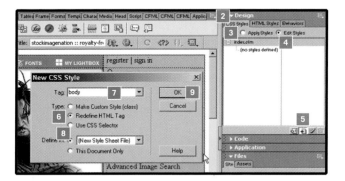

1. **Open the Site panel and double-click** `index.cfm` **(home page) to open it.**

2. **Click the expander arrow of the Design panel group.**

3. **Click the CSS Styles panel tab to make it the active panel.**

4. **Select the Edit Styles button.**

5. **Click the Add (+) button.**
   The New CSS Style dialog box opens.

6. **Select the Redefine HTML Tag button.**

7. **Choose body from the Tag drop-down menu.**

8. **Select (New Style Sheet File) in the Define In box.**

9. **Click OK.**
   The Save Style Sheet File As dialog box opens.

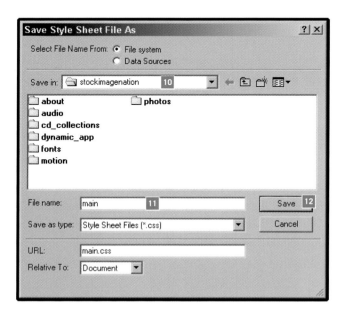

10. **Navigate to the html/stockimagenation folder.**

11. **Name the style sheet main.**

12. **Click Save.**
    The CSS Style Definition for Body in main.css dialog box opens.

13. **The Type category should be selected. From the Font menu, choose Verdana, Arial, Helvetica, sans-serif.**

14. **Choose a size of 10 and type** #333333 **for the color.**

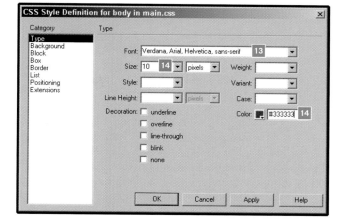

15. **Click the Background category.**

16. **Click the Background Color box and select white.**

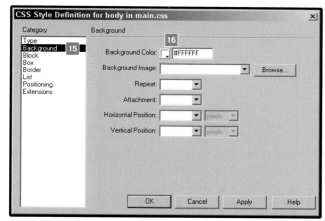

17. **Click the Box category.**

18. **Type** O **into both the Padding and Margin fields.**

19. **Click the Block category and set the Text Align to Center.**

20. **Click OK and preview your work in all three browsers**
    Notice that there is still a problem with the margins in Netscape.

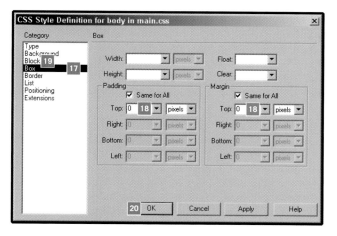

<NOTE>

Notice how all of the body text is now in Verdana but the font size isn't 10 px. Look at the bottom of the document; the text outside the table is Verdana and 10px. You only defined the body tag, not the p or td tags. You did not have to do anything to apply this style. It was applied automatically because of the selector you redefined, in this case, the body tag.

21. **Choose Modify→Page Properties and set all four margins to O. Click OK.**

CSS Rules

Each rule has two parts, a selector and the declaration. The selector is most often an HTML element such as H1, body, p, and so on. The declaration is a combination of properties and values. A declaration is always formatted as a property followed by a colon, and then a value, and ends with a semicolon. Each style sheet is made up of a series of rules. You don't need to know how to actually write the rules (although it's good to understand how they work) because Dreamweaver has a great interface that lets you choose the properties and values you want and then writes all the code for you. This illustration shows a bit of the main.css style sheet you are building.

```
body {
    font-family: Verdana, Arial, Helvetica, sans-serif;
    font-size: 10pt;
    color: 333333;
    background-color: #FFFFFF;
    margin: 0px;
    padding: 0px;
}
p {
    font-family: Verdana, Arial, Helvetica, sans-serif;
    font-size: 10px;
    color: 333333;
}
td {
    font-family: Verdana, Arial, Helvetica, sans-serif;
    font-size: 10px;
}
```

22. **In the CSS panel, click the New CSS Style icon.**
The New CSS Style dialog box opens.

23. **Select the Redefine HTML Tag button in the New CSS Style dialog box.**

24. **In the Tag, select p from the drop-down list.**

25. **Choose** main.css **from the Define In drop-down box.**
If you had more than one style sheet and the proper one wasn't listed by default, you select the one you want from the drop-down list.

26. **Click OK.**

27. **Set the following properties for the Type category:**
Font: Verdana, Arial, Helvetica, sans-serif
Size: 10px
Color: #333333
Leave the default settings for everything else.

28. **Click OK.**

29. **In the CSS panel, right-click (Control-click) the p style and select duplicate.**

30. **In the New CSS Style dialog box, change the tag name to td and click OK.**
You just changed the cell properties to be the same as the paragraph properties.

31. **Save your page and then view it in all three test browsers.**

32. **Select the Search button and notice its tag in the Tag Selector.**
The next thing you are going to do is set how the text on the button appears. This button uses an HTML tag of <input>.

33. **Add a new style.**

34. **Select Redefine HTML Tag. Select or type input for the Tag field and click OK.**

35. **In the Type category, enter** 11 **pixels for the type size.**

36. **In the Box category enter** 0 **into both the Padding and Margin fields and click OK.**
Notice how the button text changed.

37. **Save your page and preview it in all the browsers.**
Notice how the text renders differently in Netscape. It doesn't look bad, just different than Internet Explorer. Even the text field is longer in Netscape 7. It's difficult to control how forms look.

Tutorial

» Creating Custom Classes

In this tutorial, you replace the cell color of the column beneath the navigation area. Recall that it is a one-pixel cell containing a black background to produce the thin line. You make a CSS style that does the same thing. This separates the appearance of the document into the style sheet where it belongs.

1. **Click in the register I sign in cell and press the Tab key three times.**
   This gets your cursor into the 1x6 cell containing the orange line image.

2. **Click the `<td>` tag that appears before the `<img>` tag.**

3. **In the Property inspector, delete the background color.**

4. **In the CSS panel, add a new style.**
   The New CSS Style dialog box opens.

5. **Select the Make Custom Style (Class) button as the type.**

6. **In the Name field, type** .sbcol.
   Custom classes begin with a dot.

7. **Choose** `main.css` **from the Define In drop-down box.**

8. **Click OK to close the dialog box.**

9. **In the Definition dialog box, click the Background category and change the background color to #FF9900, which is orange.**

10. **Click OK.**
    You defined this specific `td` tag as a custom class because you don't want all the cells to be black. The class is defined; now you need to apply it to the cell.

Commenting Your CSS Code

Double click the `main.css` document in the Site panel to open it. This is the code for the styles you made so far. It's helpful to add comments to your code for co-workers as well as yourself. If you need to re-design the site, you might not remember what you did or why. Comments help solve that problem. Comments are added by starting with `/*` and ending with `*/`. Everything in between does not appear in a browser. You can comment your HTML code much the same way. The only difference is that HTML code starts with `<!-` and ends with `- >`.

In the `main.css` file, you can add a comment before the `<body>` tag that describes what the code is for. The comment would look like this:

/* SETS MARGINS FOR PAGE. TO SET NN4X, MARGINWIDTH, MARGINHEIGHT IS SET IN BODY TAG VIA HTML */

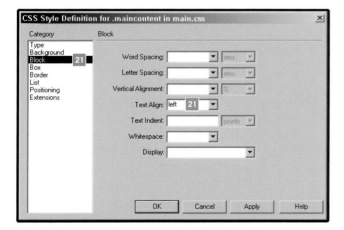

11. **In the Tag Selector, select the `<td>` for the sidebar column cell. Right-click (Control-click) and select Set Class→sbcol.**

12. **Test your work in all three browsers.**
    It looks great in all of the test browsers.

13. **Click an image in the nav bar and press the right-arrow key. Select the `<td>` tag in the Tag Selector.**

14. **In the Property inspector, remove the background color.**
    You may want to cut it instead of deleting it so you can paste it when you make the new style.

15. **In the CSS Panel, add a new style.**
    The New CSS Style dialog box opens.

16. **Select Custom Class, name it** .navbar **and click OK.**

17. **In the Background category, click the background color box and sample the blue from the buttons. Click OK.**
    You can also paste in the numbers you cut.

18. **With the `<td>` tag still selected, right-click (Control-click) and select Set Class→navbar.**

19. **Repeat steps 15 through 17 and name the new class** .sidebar. **Change the background to orange.**

20. **Select the `<td>` tag, delete background in Property inspector, and then set sidebar class to the following cells:**
    » Select the cell with register in it.
    » Tab four times to the thin orange line cell below the register cell. Right-click (Control-click) the `<td>` tag and select sidebar.
    » Click to place your cursor in the large sidebar area.
    » Select large men image; tab two times to be in the large sidebar column cell.

21. **Repeat steps 15 through 17 with these changes:**
    » Name the custom style .maincontent.
    » In the Background category set the color to white.
    » Select the Block category and select left for the Text alignment.

22. **Right-click (Control-click) the `<td>` tag before the `<img>` tag of the menu and set the class to maincontent.**

< N O T E >
The reason you set a class for this is that the content would inherit the center alignment of the `<div>` tag that surrounds this table. It doesn't affect the home page because there is no text content. Later, the images are removed and you use this structure as a template for other pages.

Tutorial
» Using Contextual Selectors

In this tutorial you make a style that controls only portions of the text. The class you made for the paragraph tag affects all paragraphs. Next you make a style that affects certain portions of text in the context of its use or location. You can apply separate classes to each paragraph if desired.

1. **In the CSS panel add a new style.**
   The New CSS Style dialog box opens.

2. **In the Type area, select Use CSS Selector button.**

3. **Name it** .sidebar p, **use the** main.css **style sheet, and then click OK.**
   This style affects the paragraph tag of anything using the sidebar class you defined previously. If you recall, you applied the .sidebar class to the <td> tag of the sidebar.

4. **In the Type category, enter** 150 **for the Line Height and select %** from the drop-down list.

5. **In the Block category, select Left for the Text Align option.**

6. **In the Margin column of the Box category, uncheck the Same for All option and enter these parameters (use pixels for all four measurements):**
   Top: 5
   Right: 5
   Bottom: 0
   Left: 5

7. **Click OK.**
   Notice that the text in the sidebar changed automatically. Because you altered an HTML tag, you didn't have to apply it.

8. **Preview in the browsers and save your work.**

9. **Add a new style.**

10. **Select Use CSS Selector and name it .maincontent p. Click OK.**

11. **Select the Block category and select Left for Text Align.**

12. **Select the Box category, uncheck the Same for All in Margin box, and enter the following:**
    Top: 5
    Right: 15
    Bottom: 0
    Left: 15

13. **Click OK.**
    This class controls the placement of text for the main content area when you don't have it filled with images.

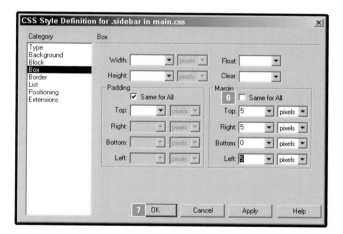

<NOTE>

A CSS Selector redefines or extends a class or HTML selector. You are still redefining HTML tags. The difference is that in Dreamweaver the CSS Selector option allows you to group tags and be more creative in the naming of the selector.

Tutorial
» Building Link Styles

In this tutorial, you create a style that affects the way the links look in each state using pseudo-class selectors. These selectors change the appearance of all hyperlinks using the <a> tag. Pseudo-class selectors are dynamic. They can be used to add rollover effects without images in browsers that support them. You see in this tutorial that it works in Internet Explorer 5.5 and Netscape 6.2. When defining more than one of the pseudo-class selectors, you need to do it in this order: a:link, a:visited, a:hover, and then a:active.

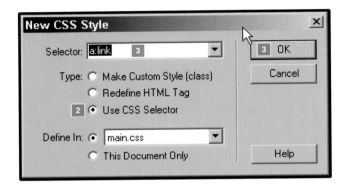

1. **Make a new style.**

2. **Select the Use CSS Selector button as the type.**

3. **Click the down arrow of the Selector field (for the name) and a:link and click OK.**

4. **In the Type category, type #003366 for the color and click OK.**

5. **Right-click (Control-click) the a:link style and select duplicate. Click the drop-down arrow and change the name to a: visited. Click OK.**

6. **Copy a:visited, and change its name to a:hover.**

7. **To edit the a:hover style, double-click its name in the CSS Styles panel.**

8. **In the Type category, change the font color to #993300.**

9. **Save and test your work in the browsers.**
   Pass your mouse over the links. You discover that the hover doesn't work in Netscape 4 but works fine in Netscape 7 and Internet Explorer.

Tutorial

» Building Contextual Link Styles

In this tutorial you create a class specifically for the links in the footer. This style affects the footer only—hence the name contextual link styles.

1. **Make a new style.**

2. **Select the Use CSS Selector type.**

3. **For the Name, type** .footer a:link **and click OK.**

4. **In the Type category, enter** 10px **for the font size, a color of** #666666, **and select None under Decoration.**

5. **Click OK.**

6. **Duplicate .footer a:link and rename it** .footer a:visited.

7. **Double-click .footer a:visited and change the color to #999999.**

8. **Duplicate .footer a:visited and name it** .footer a:hover.

9. **Double-click .footer a:hover and change the color to #FF6600. Select Underline in the Decoration area and then click OK.**

10. **Click inside the footer area.**

11. **Right-click (Control-click) the paragraph tag.**

12. **Select Set Class→footer.**
    Note that you didn't make a separate class named footer. You added it to the contextual links and it is automatically available as a class.

13. **Save and test in Internet Explorer and Netscape 7.**
    Notice that the CD Collections link in the sidebar is unchanged but the footer links have no underline and the hover can be seen.

14. **Test in Netscape 4.**
    It fairs relatively well. The underline is removed but there is no hover, which isn't a surprise because you saw in the previous tutorial that Netscape 4 doesn't support the hover feature.

15. **Save your file.**

Tutorial

» Inserting a Snippet and Testing the Page

In this tutorial, you insert the strict DOCTYPE snippets you made in Session 10, and then test the page to see the differences. You don't need to test the loose one because you are already testing with it. When there is no DOCTYPE present in your document (like this example), the loose DOCTYPE is automatically used. You see what problems arise when you use a strict DOC-TYPE. The following tutorial shows you how to fix them.

1. **Switch to code view and insert your cursor at the top of the page, in front of the** `<html>` **tag.**

2. **Press Enter (Return) to add a paragraph space. Press the keyboard up arrow to go back to the empty line.**

3. **Open the Snippets panel and open the CSS folder. Select the strict doctype and click the Insert button.**

<NOTE>
You must be in Code view to insert the snippet.

4. **Preview your work in each browser.**
   Notice that Internet Explorer looks fine and so does Netscape 4 because it simply doesn't understand the DOCTYPE and it is a quirks type browser. But what a mess in Netscape 7! What has happened is that the thin black line has expanded to make room for text with the image. In this case that happens to be a spacer image. Another problem is that between the men and the feet there is a `<br>` in the code so the extra space is generated.

<NOTE>
There are two modes that the browsers use to read and render your CSS: full standards mode and quirks mode. In quirks mode, layout emulates nonstandard markup that is required not to break existing content. In full standards mode, the behavior is described by the HTML and CSS specifications. The mode used is determined by the DOCTYPE in your page.

Tutorial
» Using a Block Display for Images

In this tutorial, you set the image tag to be a block element. The normal property for an image is inline and you can place text with it. Images display on the baseline like text. The default alignment for text is baseline, which keeps the descenders such as a g inside the table cell. But, as you saw in the preview with the strict DOCTYPE, the baseline for the image added space. If you make the cells containing the images block elements (block elements stack), the design meets the stricter DOCTYPE requirements.

1. **In the CSS panel, add a new style.**

2. **Select the Use CSS Selector type.**

3. **Name it** tr.decoration img **and click OK.**

4. **In the Block category, select Block from the Display drop-down menu and click OK.**

5. **Return to Design view and click to place your cursor in the orange register cell and tab once.**
   This puts you into the black line cell.

6. **Right-click (Control-click) the** <tr> **tag and set the Class to decoration.**

7. **Preview your work in Netscape 7.**
   Notice that there is still a space between the two images.

8. **Select the main image and then right-click (Control-click) the** <tr> **tag. Apply the decoration class.**

9. **Test and save the file.**

10. **Make a new style.**
    In the previous session you added some script which prints the date. This new style formats that text. You won't need to apply the style because the code in the script calls for the style to be added.

11. **Select Make Custom Style.**

12. **Name it** .date **and click OK.**

13. **In the Type category, enter** 10 pixels **for the size and a color of #666666.**

14. **Click OK.**

15. **Save and close the page.**

<NOTE>
If the images in Dreamweaver appear side by side, select the <td> tag and select No Wrapping in the Property inspector. This affects only how images appear in Dreamweaver.

<NOTE>
You can double-click the main.css file to see the code you added for the styles. In the Session 12 starter files, the main.css style sheet is commented for you. To use starter files, simply copy the html folder and paste it into your stockimagenation folder. Starter files are meant to be used at the beginning of any particular session you are having problems with. If you skipped sessions, you can pick up by using any starter file.

Tutorial

» Adding CSS to the Details Page

In this tutorial, you add the strict DOCTYPE to the page. You then get instructions for new types of styles that this page uses that vary from the home page. The styles that are the same as the home page are listed in Table 11.1 so you can use the previous instructions to add them if you like. All the styles are added in the details.cfm file in the session12_starterfiles folder if you decide not to add all the styles yourself. But the more you practice, the better you'll get.

1. **Double-click the** details.cfm **page to open it (in the dynamic_app folder).**

2. **Switch to code view and insert your cursor at the top of the page, in front of the** <html> **tag.**

3. **Press Enter (Return) to add a paragraph space. Press the keyboard up arrow to go back to the empty line.**

4. **Select the strict doctype in the Snippets panel and insert it.**

5. **Return to Design view. Redefine the HTML, body, paragraph, and cell tags and the link styles using the previous tutorials as a guide. In the New CSS Style dialog box, select This Document Only for every style you add for this page.**
   Table 11.1 lists the parameters to set for each style.

6. **Select the logo image and then the** <tr> **tag. Apply tr.decoration img.**

7. **Select each of the text links one at a time and add a null link in the Property inspector (**javascript:;**).**

Tutorial
» Creating Backgrounds Using CSS

In this tutorial, you add background color and background images using CSS. The cool thing about backgrounds and CSS is the fact that you can control how your images tile. You also see how to fix a problem Netscape 4 has with background images.

1. **In the CSS Styles panel add a new style.**
   The New CSS Style dialog box opens.

2. **Select Make Custom Style (Class) and name it .htile. Choose the This Document Only button and click OK.**
   This style is applied to the area behind the shopping cart. Notice how the black shadow isn't present along the bottom.

< N O T E >

Because you are embedding the style sheet, it also takes care of the Netscape issue of using a path relative to where the style is located.

3. **In the Background category, set the background color to #1C7BBD. For the background image, click the folder icon and browse to the images/details folder. Select** `details_htile.gif` **and open it.**
   The CSS Style definition for .htile dialog box opens.

4. **In the Repeat field, select repeat-x and click OK.**
   This tiles the image horizontally only.

5. **Select the logo image and tab over to the next table. Select the `<td>` tag before that table tag.**

6. **Delete the background color from the Property inspector.**

7. **Right-click (Control-click) the `<td>` tag and set the htile class.**

8. **Test your work in each browser.**
   Notice how the shadow is now there on the bottom of the cell in both Internet Explorer and Netscape. Don't worry about the other white areas you are seeing in Netscape; these are all background areas you add.

9. **Add a new style with these parameters:**
   Type: Custom Class
   Name: .vtile
   Background: color #1C7BBD, background image - detail_vtile, Repeat – repeat-y

10. **Click OK.**

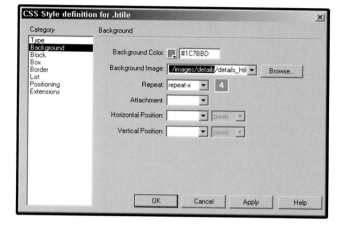

Background Images and Netscape 4

The CSS specification states that background image URL should be relative to where the style rule is defined. But Netscape 4X wants the URL relative to where the style is used. There are several ways to alleviate this problem.

» You can use an absolute URL if you know what it will be (`http://www. whatever.com/backgrounds/bk.gif`) but you can't view it on your local machine.

» You can save your style sheets in the same folder as the HTML page.

» You can add another declaration for body in the head of the document, which sets only the URL attribute. This is the simplest approach and is what you do here.

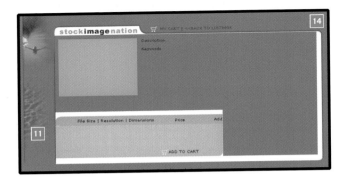

11. **Select the water image and press the right keyboard arrow key. Select the <td> tag and apply the vtile class. Repeat for the cell with the small image below the water image.**
    The background image has the shadow on the edges.

12. **Add a new style with the following parameters:**
    Type: Custom Class
    Name: .vtileright
    Background: color #1C7BBD, background image detail_vtileright, repeat-y

13. **Click OK.**

14. **Select the top-right corner image and then the right keyboard arrow key.**

15. **Select the <td> tag and delete the background image in the Property inspector.**

16. **Right-click (Control-click) and select Set Class→vtileright.**

17. **Select the bottom-right corner image and select its <td> tag. Apply the vtileright class to it.**

18. **Add a new style with the following parameters:**
    Type: Custom Class
    Name: .htilebtm
    Background: color #1C7BBD, background image detail_vtilebtm, repeat-repeat-x

19. **Click OK.**

20. **Click in the cell to the left of the bottom-right corner and delete the background image. Apply the vtilebtm class.**

21. **Add a new style with the following parameters:**
    Type: Custom Class
    Name: .ContentTable
    Background: color white

22. **Click OK.**

23. **Click to the right of the description area table to place your cursor outside the first table. Select the <td> tag.**

24. **Apply the ContentTable class.**
    This makes the table area white now.

25. **Preview your work in all three browsers.**
    The backgrounds have all been replaced using CSS styles.

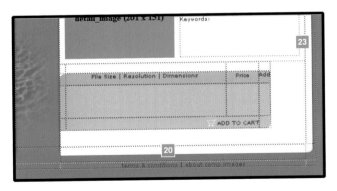

26. **Select the top left rounded corner image of the small orange table.**

27. **Select its <td> tag and set the Horz to Left and Vert to Top.**
    You may have noticed in Netscape that this image was aligned wrong.

28. **Add a new style with these parameters:**
    Type: Custom Class
    Name: tabletop
    Background: color dark orange (sample from top of orange table)

29. **Click OK.**

30. **Select the left corner image and then its** <td> **tag. If you have a background color added, delete it.**

31. **Click to place your cursor in each of the remaining cells of the top row and delete the background colors from each.**

32. **Click the** <tr> **tag.**
    The top row should be selected.

33. **Apply the tabletop class.**

34. **Add a new style with these parameters:**
    Type: Custom Class
    Name: orbody
    Background: color light orange

35. **Click OK.**

36. **Click in each of the cells for the next two rows and delete the background color in the Property inspector.**
    This is all of the lighter orange color. The only thing you see at this point is the dark orange top row, the right-bottom orange corner, and the shopping cart. Be sure that you select the corner image and then its <td> tag to remove the background color.

37. **Click in any cell of the second row (just below the dark orange) and select its** <tr> **tag. Set the class to orbody.**

38. **Repeat for the bottom row.**

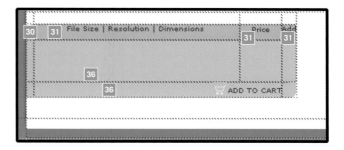

Troubleshooting Tips for Netscape

In Netscape, the table text can be misaligned for the bottom table. If it is, add a spacer.gif above the description text of *200X1* and one above *Add of 30X1*. There is already one for Price. To get the spacer on top, just place your cursor before the description text and press Shift-Enter. Then insert the spacer.gif image. For the ADD text, you don't need to add the break (Shift-Enter).

You might also see a short white line to the right of the terms and condition link area. To remove it, select the corner image, right-click (Control-click) on its <td> tag, and set the class to None.

I also discovered a couple of places that the background color wasn't removed from so you can check this as well. Place your cursor in the link cell (terms and conditions) and tab once to get into the next cell. In the Property inspector, if you see a background color, remove it. Also check the first column to the left of the link area (bottom-left cell) and if there is a background color, delete it.

If you see a small line under your right corner, select the image and change the Align in the Property inspector to Top. The cell should be set to Horz Right and Vert Top. The same cell settings are used in the shopping cart cell.

Tutorial
» Formatting the Text of the Details Page

In this tutorial, you add the rest of the styles to format the text in the description area and in the small orange table.

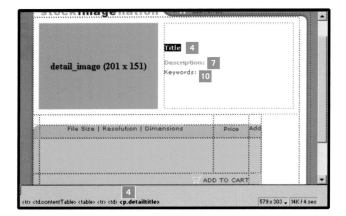

1. **Open the** details.cfm **page if you've closed it.**

2. **Add a new style with these parameters:**
   Type: Custom Class
   Name: .detailtitle
   Type: size 11 (type the number), Weight - bold
   Color: #003366
   Box: 0 Padding and Margin

3. **Click OK.**

4. **Click in the word Title and select its <p> tag. Apply the detailtitle class.**

5. **Add a new style with these parameters:**
   Type: Custom Class
   Name: .detailsubtitles
   Type: size 10, Weight - bold
   Color: #FF6600
   Box: Margin – uncheck Same for All and add all zeros except Bottom, which is 5

6. **Click OK.**

7. **Click the word Description, and then select its <p> tag. Apply the detailsubtitles class.**

8. **Add a new style with these parameters:**
   Type: Custom Class
   Name: .detailkeywords
   Box: Margin – uncheck Same for All and add all zeros except Bottom, which is 5
   Block: Align left

9. **Click OK.**

10. **Select the <p> tag for keywords and apply the detailkeyword class.**

11. **Add a new style with these parameters:**
    Type: Custom Class
    Name: .tablelabels
    Type: Weight - bold

12. **Click OK.**

13. **Select the <p> tag for the description area and the price and apply the tablelabels class.**

14. **Select the <td> tag for the Add cell and apply the tablelabels class. Repeat for the ADD TO CART cell.**

15. **Preview your file.**

16. **Save and close the file.**

Table 11.1: Parameters for Previously Discussed Styles

Name	Redefine HTML	CSS Selectors	Type	Background	Block	Box
html	X		Verdana..			Padding and Margin 0
body	X		Verdana..	Color #1C7BBD		Padding and Margin 0
p	X		size: 10 px, color: #333333			Padding and Margin 0
td	X		Verdana... size: 10 px, color: #333333			
tr.decoration img		X			Display: block	
a:link		X	color: #003366, decoration: none			
a:visited		X	color: #003366, decoration: none			
a:hover		X	color: #000000, decoration: none			

» Session Review

Now that you've learned how easy it is to control your text and images using CSS, let's see how much you've retained. The answers can be found in the tutorials listed in parentheses.

1. What is one of the purposes for using CSS? ("Discussion: CSS Basics")

2. Which panel set is the CSS Styles panel in? ("Tutorial: Creating a Practice Style")

3. When you defined the HTML tag and set the margins, why did it not work in Netscape? ("Tutorial: Redefining HTML Tags")

4. When creating a custom class, how is the name different? ("Tutorial: Creating Custom Classes")

5. How do you apply a class? ("Tutorial: Creating Custom Classes")

6. What is the order that you need to build link styles? ("Tutorial: Building Link Styles")

7. Is a link style a CSS Selector or a Custom Class? ("Tutorial: Building Link Styles")

8. Did you need to define a separate class of .footer to use it? ("Tutorial: Building Contextual Link Styles")

9. Which browser didn't support the hover technique? ("Tutorial: Building Contextual Link Styles")

10. What happened to the page when the strict DOCTYPE was applied? ("Tutorial: Inserting a Snippet and Testing the Page")

Session 12

Building the Site's Snap Menus

Today is June 19, 2003

HOME   PHOTOS   MOTION   AUDIO   FONTS   MY LIGHTBOX

register | sign in

Terms and Conditons
Link 1
Link 2
Link 3

ASSET SEARCH
Search our photos, movies,
sounds and fonts using keyword:

[   ] (Single Keyword)

Search

CD COLLECTIONS
Check out the
latest in our
value-priced CD
collections, from
photographic
essays to multi-
asset discs.

Macro
VISIONS

stockimagenation
GO AHEAD . SHAKE UP YOUR IMAGINATION!

Home | Photos | Motion | Audio | Fonts | My Lightbox

©copyright 2003 | all rights reserved
terms & conditions | about us

Discussion: **Understanding Layers**

Discussion: **Understanding How Snap Menus Work**

Tutorial: **Building the Menu Layers**

Tutorial: **Duplicating and Positioning the Menu Layers**

Tutorial: **Scripting Snap Menus with PVII Behaviors**

Tutorial: **Commenting Your DHTML Code**

Tutorial: **Scripting the onClick State of the Snap Menu's Buttons**

Session Introduction

In this session you build the Dynamic HTML (DHTML) menu system that is used throughout the stockimagenation site. Using extensions designed to add functionality to your Dreamweaver MX program, you combine Cascading Style Sheets (CSS) with JavaScript to display and interact with layers. You won't need to be a CSS or JavaScript wizard to do this because you take advantage of some pretty nifty Project Seven extensions (www.projectseven.com) that do a lot of the work for you. But while the grunt work is done for you, it's still important to understand how layers work and how the behaviors are used together to create the desired functionality—not only for the stockimagenation site, but for your own projects in the future.

In the process, you discover browser issues related to using layers and learn how to plan for and incorporate solutions to address these problems. To promote efficiency, you develop your elements in a way that makes updating them simple and site-wide.

» You learn to work with Dreamweaver's Layer panel, Draw Layer tool, and to use the Property inspector to name, position, and size layer <divs> for the menu system.

» You add HTML elements to your layers.

» You develop your elements in a way that promotes easy updates to the site and efficient re-use of existing structures.

» Using behaviors, you script the elements you built to appear and disappear in the desired location and on-demand.

» You organize your code and add comments to it that clearly explain each tag's purpose.

TOOLS YOU'LL USE
Layers panel, Property inspector, Code and Design views,
PVII Extensions (Snap Layers and Auto Layers extensions
from www.projectseven.com)

MATERIALS NEEDED
Your stockimagenation folder or the session12_starter files

TIME REQUIRED
90 minutes

Discussion

Understanding Layers

Before you begin to build the menu system, you should understand the nature of the tags and code you are using. In the sessions prior to this, you learned how to use HTML tags to lay out a page. In the process, you discovered how all elements naturally position themselves to the top and left of the page and only through HTML tags can you overcome this tendency. But you also encountered the limitations of HTML—no two elements can ever overlap. From the very beginning of the design, you used slicing, spacers, tables, and other tools to get exactly the right placement of page elements.

In this session, you learn how you can use a *layer* to create elements that *can* overlap other parts of the page. You used layers in Fireworks to position specific graphics above or below others; this is a similar concept, except that in an HTML page, a layer is created using CSS properties applied to the `<div>` tag—a very special selector that has no real properties of its own, except that it is a *block* element. Block elements are like paragraphs, tables, and lists, which display "stacked" as opposed to inline elements, which display side-by-side. When you apply CSS properties to the `<div>` tag, you can set values that affect the positioning of the `<div>` and any content within the tag.

< N O T E >

Although I use the term layer, the tag is `<div>`. In some incarnations of the Netscape browser, a proprietary `<layer>` tag was introduced by Netscape for the same use. However, even Netscape has deprecated that tag, which never worked in other major browsers.

How Layers Are Unique

Unlike normal HTML elements, layers *float* and can be positioned to nearly pixel-perfect locations or relative to another element or container. Layers make use of CSS positioning that removes them and their content from the regular flow of the HTML page, meaning they float.

Layers behave like documents when you add content to them. Remember how objects placed in the page always go to the top-left corner of the page unless you change the default behavior? A layer's content does the same thing. You can place almost any HTML tag or content in a layer, including text, images, tables, and lists. Any HTML element inserted into a layer in Design view has its code placed within the <div></div> tags for the layer in Code view. Layers also have a visibility property and can be visible or hidden; you can switch this on and off through the use of scripting. You work with other properties of layers as you build the site's menu system.

Layers Support in Browsers

You should keep in mind that CSS properties, and therefore layers, are supported only by version 4 and higher browsers. Although some earlier browsers did understand the <style> tag, most will ignore CSS positioning and simply display the <div> content inline. In addition, not all browsers implement CSS to the same specification, so rigorous testing is needed and cross-browser solutions are often required.

Discussion
Understanding How the Snap Menus Work

A Snap menu is just one of the many pop-up menu types in use in Web sites today. There are literally hundreds of pop-up menu methods, but few are as easy to design and build as those created in Dreamweaver MX with Project Seven's Snap Layers and AutoLayers extensions. Like most DHTML menu systems, Snap menus offer minimal clicking and maximum link choices in a very tidy space with an extremely small footprint. When activated, the menu appears, overlaying any content beneath it. Within the menu, you can display any number of text or image-based links and other content. When not in use, the menu disappears. When the page with the menus is loaded into the browser window, the menus are nowhere to be seen because their visibility is set to hidden. It's only when the user interacts with the navigation buttons that the menus are displayed.

Event-Based Scripting

Pop-up menus work by showing and hiding layers on-demand, triggering the show/hide with an *event*, which is typically a visitor's actions or the act of loading a page. The event used for the Snap menus you build in this session is the `onMouseOver` event. When the visitor moves the cursor over a main navigation button, the menu for that button appears and stays visible as the visitor enters the menu to click a link. If the visitor decides not to click a link or moves the cursor out of the menu, the menu disappears.

Two extensions supply the action that scripts how the menus appear and disappear and where the menus are positioned when events occur. The PVII AutoLayers and Snap Layers extensions add new behaviors into the Dreamweaver program that are accessed from the Behaviors panel. In the tutorials, you add behaviors to the buttons and other elements that control the menu pop-up and snap functions.

Events and actions (behaviors) attached to links in layers can be triggered only if the layer they are in is the *active* layer. Basically, that means it must be the first layer accessed beneath the visitor's cursor. For example, if two layers containing links are stacked one over the other, only the links in the top layer are clickable, even if you can see the other links in the bottom layer. The z-index property controls which layer is on top. It is possible to change the order of how layers are stacked or hide a layer to make one below it visible. In that case, the lower layer would become the active layer.

Absolute vs. Relative Positioning of Menus

Typically, a layer is absolutely positioned using Left and Top coordinates equivalent to positive values as measured from their container, most often the document itself. You can position layers with negative values, too. As measured from the document, this would be above and to the left of the top-left corner of the page. The buttons of the stockimagenation site are positioned relatively on the page.

The Snap menus you build are positioned at the start at 0,0, which translates to the top-left corner. However, you use the Snap Layers behavior to change each layer's position prior to displaying it, causing the menu to position itself relative to the button graphic it is associated with. What's cool about this? Well, as the page loads, the HTML layout is positioned as centered in the visitor's browser window. That's relative to the browser window's overall width, so the location of the button varies depending on each visitor's browser window width. The Snap Layer scripting changes the X,Y coordinates of a button's menu based on its location when the menu is called, which of course is after the page and button loads. That makes the position of the menu relative to the browser window too, if only indirectly.

The menu layer appears only after the visitor calls it (by moving the cursor over a button). The AutoLayers behavior is used to control visibility of menu layers, managing sets of layers to only display the ones needed at the time.

The Menucloser

A special invisible layer that contains a transparent image that is scripted also becomes visible when the menu for a button is revealed. This layer (menucloser) is invisible because a layer itself has no color by default. Layers are transparent unless given other properties or content to make the layer visible. The menucloser, which contains only a transparent GIF image, is beneath any active menu layer and is only encountered when the visitor leaves a menu layer because of the differences in size and positioning (X, Y, and Z) of the menucloser and any menu layer. As the visitor moves away from the menu and over the transparent gif of the menucloser layer, that image's behavior is triggered `onMouseOver`. The behavior (AutoLayers) hides all layers unless otherwise directed. There are design considerations when building a Snap menu, which is discussed in the appropriate tutorials.

Tutorial
» Building the Menu Layers

In this tutorial, you draw layers that are used for the menus in the stockimagenation site. To build each layer, you use the Draw Layer tool. You use the Layers panel and the Property inspector to name each layer and set its properties, from dimensions to coordinates to visibility. You learn how to work on hidden layers without resetting their visibility to visible so that you can add and manipulate layer content within.

Before you start this session, you might want to see the end result of the menus you build. It may help you understand what you are doing a bit better. The companion Web site for this book is at www.stockimagenation.com. Several of the links work. Whatever you build from using this book and/or the bonus sessions on the CD, works on the book's site.

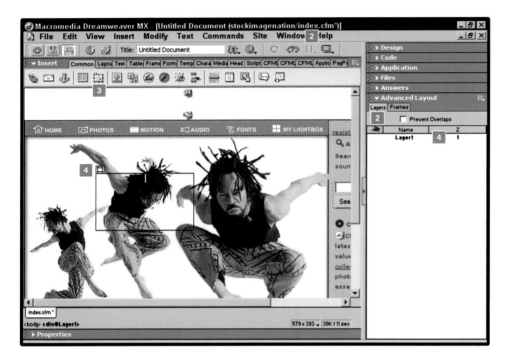

<NOTE>
The possible values for layer visibility are visible, hidden, and inherit. An open eye-icon means a layer is visible. A closed eye-icon means that the layer is hidden. No icon means that the layer inherits visibility from its parent container which, in this case, is the visible document.

1. **Open** index.cfm **from the html/stockimagenation directory.**

2. **Choose Window→Others→Layers or press F2 to open and activate the Layers panel.**

3. **Click the Draw Layer tool in the Insert bar to make it the active tool.**

4. **Anywhere in the page, click and drag downward and to the right—without releasing the mouse—to draw your first layer.**
   Don't worry about the size or location of the layer; you set these properties later. Take a look in the Layers panel. You should see Layer1 listed there. Notice that the z-index of this new layer is set at 1 and, under the eye-icon column (visibility), no value is shown.

5. **Click the Layer1 listing in the Layers panel.**
   This selects the layer. Notice that the Property inspector displays the various properties that are associated with layers, including the name of the layer.

6. **Double-click the Layer1 listing. Rename Layer1** menucloser **and then press Enter to set the name.**
   You could also use the Property inspector to rename the layer, changing Layer1 in the top-left corner of the inspector to **menucloser**. Again, you press Enter to change the name.

7. **Set the width (W) of the menucloser layer to 200px.**
   Each menu is 150px wide. Setting the menucloser layer to 200px enables you to position the menucloser so that part of it protrudes to the left and right of the menu that appears above it.

< N O T E >

Layer property values (lengths) can be fixed or relative but in either case, the px (pixels) or % (percentage) must appear directly after the unit amount (no spaces), as in 200px or 100%, not 200 px or 100%. Pixels (px) are the default and do not have to be included, although explicit code is clean code!

8. **Click inside the menucloser layer shape.**
   You see the cursor flash at the top-left of the layer. Any content you place in this layer gravitates to the top-left, too. If your cursor is not in the top-left then click on the left align option in the Property inspector (to the Right of the Italic icon).

9. **In the Assets panel, select** `spacer.gif` **and insert it.**

10. **While the image is still selected, use the Property inspector to set its width (W) and height (H) to** 200px.
   This might not expand your menucloser layer depending upon how big you made the layer in the first place. Just like any other container, content drives the true width and height of a containing tag. In this case, the image's width matches the layer's width. Notice that with the image selected, the Tag selector displays the `<img>` tag to the right of the `<div.#menucloser>` tag. You can use the Tag selector to select a layer, too.

11. **Click the** `<div.#menucloser>` **tag in the Tag selector. Remove the value in the height (H) field.**
   You want an empty field.

12. **From the Visibility (Vis) drop-down list, select hidden.**

<T I P>
When you click out of the layer and into the document, the layer's outline disappears now because the layer is hidden. To reselect the layer and to make it visible, click its name in the Layers panel. This makes the layer temporarily visible while you work on it. You don't need to reset the visibility to work in a layer.

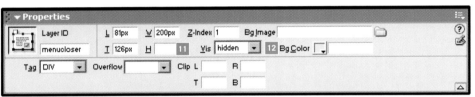

About Naming Layers

It's always wise to have naming conventions in place when developing a Web site, as has been discussed throughout this book. Layers are no exception to this rule. In fact, it is even more critical because layer names are IDs and must be unique. For this site (and as a personal preference) most layers are named using `LyrName`. `Lyr` is the start of each layer's name and another typically descriptive name is added, capping the first letter of that name. So, for example, the menu layer for the Photos button in the stockimagenation site is `LyrPhotos`. The only exception to this rule is the menucloser layer, for purposes that are explained later as you begin to apply the behaviors to script your menus.

13. **Use the Draw Layer tool to draw another layer anywhere in the page.**

14. **Name the new layer LyrHome and set its width (W) to 150px.**

15. **Click into your new layer. Add a table that is 150px wide, with 2 rows, 1 column and zero border, padding, and spacing.**

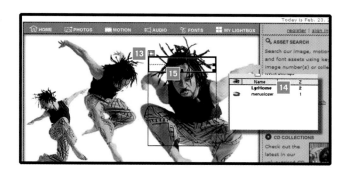

16. **Click to place your cursor into the first row of the table. From the Assest panel, insert** sm_arrow_home.gif. **Type** Arrow for Home menu **for the alternative text.**
    Most of the menus use the sm_arrow.gif graphic, but the first and last menus (Home and LightBox, which you make later) use their own arrow graphics for placement of the arrow relative to the icon of the button.

17. **Add a line break after the image.**
    The easiest way to do this when the <img> tag is still selected is to press the right arrow key and then press Shift-Enter (or Shift-Return) to add the <br> tag.

18. **Type** Links go here **and press Enter or Return to add a few paragraphs to the menu.**

19. **Tab to the next row of the table and insert the image** sm_btm.gif. **Type** Bottom menu **for the alternative text.**
    All menus use the same bottom image. In Session 11, you built your external and embedded styles for the stockimagenation site. The menus need a new style to supply lines along either side of the menu. A background image, set with CSS, is used to color in and create the lines, which matches up with the top and bottom images' lines.

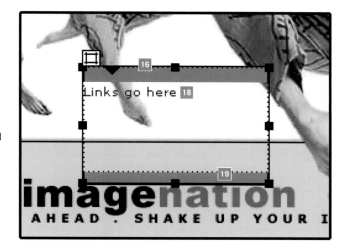

About the Layers Panel

Unless you have customized your panel groups, this may open the Advanced Design layer group with other panels included. The example images in this session show the Layers panel as part of the Design panel group. In fact, the Design group is customized to contain the CSS Styles, Behaviors, and Layers panels. See Session 8 for information about customizing your panels in Dreamweaver MX.

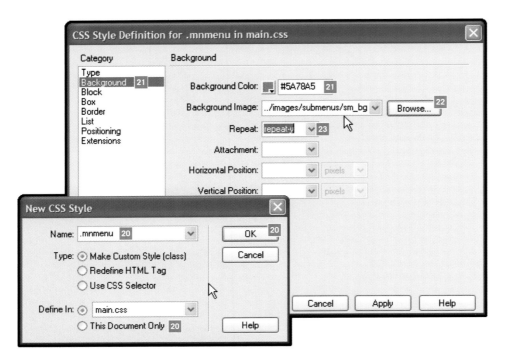

20. **Open the Styles panel and add a New Style. Select the Make Custom Style (class) button as the Type, and name it .mnmenu. Select This Document Only and click OK.**

21. **Select the Background category and change the background color to #5A78A5.**
    You can sample the button blue or simply type in the value.

22. **Click the Browse button and navigate to html/images/submenus/sm/sm_bg.gif and open it.**

Draw Layer vs. Insert Layer

There are several methods to adding a layer <div> to a page. When you use the Draw Layer tool to make a layer, the code for the layer is placed just below the opening <body> tag and above all other HTML structures. This is true no matter where you click when you drag and draw the layer. Another method of adding a layer div is accessed by choosing Insert→Layer. This, however, places the layer code within the current HTML structure — basically inserting it exactly where your cursor is inserted.

Because layer code should not be placed within elements like tables, you should always use the Draw Layer method unless you are inserting a layer within another layer or have a valid reason for using another method.

23. **Set Repeat to** repeat-y. **Close the CSS Definition dialog box and return to the layer.**

24. **Click inside the first row of the LyrHome table (it's okay to select the image). Use the Tag selector to select the <td> tag and set the class to mnmenu.**
    You should see the background image fill in the table cell.

25. **In the Layers panel, select LyrHome. In the Property inspector, remove its height (H) value. Set its visibility (Vis) to hidden.**
    The content in the layer keeps it open to the correct height.

<NOTE>
It's almost always best to remove the height for a layer because some browsers incorrectly render certain properties of a layer when the content exceeds the stated value. If no value is given, the content drives the height and "auto" is the value, which prevents any problems. Don't remove the height value for an empty label. Wait until you put content into it. Otherwise, the label collapses to zero height. If you should be unable to make a layer active (put your cursor in the label), click the layer name in the Layers panel and check the Property inspector to see the height and width values.

26. **Save your page and keep it open for the next tutorial.**
    You won't preview the page yet because your layers are not visible and there would be nothing new to see.

Tutorial
» Duplicating and Positioning the Menu Layers

To speed up the development process, you can copy and paste layer code and then modify the pasted layers, adjusting their position, content, and such. There are several methods to copying layers, but this one is pretty easy. In this tutorial, you copy LyrHome, pasting several copies of it that you modify and rename to make the additional menus. Keep your eyes open and pay attention to the Layers panel as you paste.

1. Select LyrHome **in the Layers panel. Once selected, click the layer's handle in the document.**

2. **Press Ctrl+C (⌘+C) to copy the layer.**

3. **Click off of the layer (**LyrHome**) into the document (try to avoid selecting any other page element) and press Ctrl+V (⌘+V) five times to paste five copies of the layer into the document.**
Before you do anything else, look at the Layers panel. You should see a total of six LyrHome layers listed even though you cannot "see" them in the document. Keep in mind that the pasted layers are positioned exactly where the original is, so you might not think you accomplished your task, but you have!

4. **Starting with the second** LyrHome **from the bottom, change the name of the layers (double-click each name and retype a new one) to match the following:** LyrBox, LyrFonts, LyrAudio, LyrMotion, LyrPhotos.

5. **Select** LyrPhotos. **In the document, double-click the arrow graphic and change its src to** sm_arrow.gif. **In the Property inspector change the Alt text to match the button.**

6. **Repeat step 5 for** LyrMotion, LyrAudio, **and** LyrFonts.

7. **Repeat step 5 for** LyrBox, **except you should select** sm_arrow_box.gif.

8. **In the Layers panel, Shift-click to select all of your menu layers and the menucloser layer.**

9. **In the Property inspector (be sure it is expanded to full view), set the left (L) and top (T) coordinates to 0. Press Enter to lock in the value and update the layer locations in the document.**

10. **Save your page and keep it open for the next tutorial.**
So far, you built the menu layers and styled the table that contains the menu options. A table is used to format the content of the menus and to facilitate adding the background tiling image to create the outline around the menu. The top graphic doesn't have an outline along the top, which creates the illusion that the outline below the buttons opens up to let the menu pop out. The arrow guides the visitor's eye down into the menu for that button. This is a classic use of composition as discussed in the early portions of this book.

Tutorial
» Scripting Snap Menus with PVII Behaviors

With the menu layers in place, you're ready to add behaviors to the navigation buttons (and other elements) that display and position each button's menu. You also script the action to hide the menus when they're not in use. The Snap Layers and AutoLayers extensions you downloaded and installed in Session 10 provide all the necessary code for your menus. It's so easy, you'll add Snap Menus to all your sites! The very first action sets up the menucloser so that it understands that any time a visitor's cursor moves over the image in the menucloser layer, the browser should hide all the layers associated with your menu system, including the menucloser layer. You should still be working in the `index.cfm` home page you modified during this session.

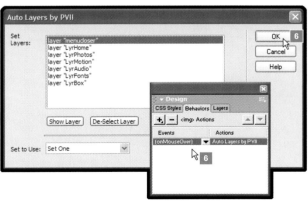

1. **Use the Layers panel to select the menucloser layer.**

2. **In the document, click to select the transparent GIF image in the menucloser layer.**
   A good way to determine whether the spacer image is selected is to look at the Property inspector. If you see the height and width of the image, it's selected.

3. **In the Design panel group, select the Behaviors tab to make it active.**
   If you don't see the Behaviors tab, choose Window→Behaviors.

4. **Click the Add (+) icon and set Show Event For to 3.0 and Later Browsers.**
   This doesn't affect the code you add to your page, except that it changes the default Event that is automatically selected for the Action.

   < T I P >
   If you leave Show Events For set to 4.0 and Later Browsers, the event selected won't be `onMouseOver`. The main reason that the event changes with 3.0 and later browsers is that earlier browsers just couldn't use any event other than `onMouseOver` — they did not understand other events associated with interacting with a link, be it text-based or image-based. This is a tiny but powerful trick to speed up the development process and should always be used when you know that all your behaviors need to be triggered by the `onMouseOver` event.

5. **Click the Add (+) icon again and select Studio VII→AutoLayers by PVII.**

6. **In the AutoLayers dialog box, click OK.**
   A layer may be selected but nothing is done to it. In this case, you want all layers associated with your menu to hide anytime the visitor mouses over the menucloser GIF, and any layer not set explicitly to *show* is *hidden*. When you OK the dialog box, check to see that the event is indeed (`onMouseOver`).

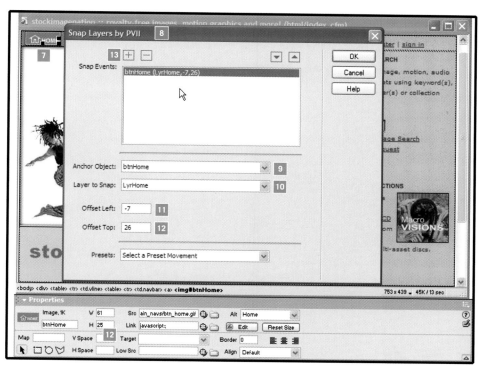

7. **Click anywhere in the document to deselect the menucloser. Then select the Home button.**

8. **Add (+) the behavior Studio VII→Snap Layers by PVII.**
   In the Snap Layers dialog box, you add two Snap Events. Notice that you can see the Swap Image behavior you added in Session 9.

9. **Choose btnHome from the Anchor Object drop-down menu.**
   The name of your buttons was added when you built the button rollovers in an earlier session.

10. **Choose LyrHome from the Layer to Snap drop-down menu.**
    Layer to Snap must always be a layer, which is obvious. The naming convention here makes it easier to be sure you are selecting a layer.

11. **Set the Offset Left value to** -7.
    This is -7px even though it isn't explicitly stated. The offset is relative to the anchor object (btnHome) and because it is negative, the left edge of the LyrHome is 6px to the left of the button's left edge. The Home button is actually 6px away from the left edge of the table border, but you have to add the 1px border. A spacer GIF (W=6px) sits to the left of the Home button. However, you want the menu to sit flush along the edge of the table, so -7px value moves the LyrHome menu over 7px to the left.

12. **Set the Offset Top value to** 26.
    Again, this is 26 pixels. The positive value places the layer (LyrHome) 26px below the button's (btnHome) top edge. A negative value would be above the top of the button. You always place the Layer to Snap in a way that it does not cover the button. Because the button is selected when you are working in the Snap Layers dialog box, it's easy to see the dimensions of the button. In this case, the buttons are 25px tall. Later, you see how the 1px difference between the layer placement and the button's bottom edge affects your design.

13. **Click the plus sign (+) in the top left to add a new Snap Event. In this case, the Anchor Object field remains** btnHome.

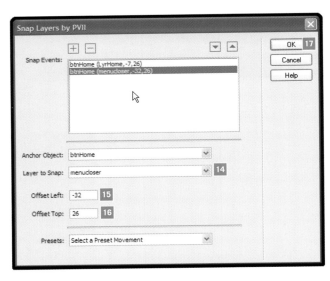

14. **Set Layer to Snap field to** menucloser.
    For every button, you always have a second Snap Event that affects the menucloser layer.

15. **Set Offset Left to** -32.
    The value of -32 represents the -7px plus the -25px discussed when setting the width of the menucloser layer (25px on both sides). Setting the left offset to -32 means that 25px of the menucloser layer is exposed on the right side of the LyrHome menu.

16. **Leave the Offset Top set to** 26.
    It's very cool that this friendly dialog box keeps the earlier values. It makes your job even easier!

17. **Click OK to close the dialog box. The Event should be** (onMouseOver) **by default.**

18. **With the Home button still selected, add (+) the behavior Studio VII→AutoLayers by PVII.**

19. **Select** menucloser **and click the Show Layer button. Click LyrHome and press the Show button again. OK the dialog box to close it.**
    Both behaviors should be set to (onMouseOver).

20. **Save your page and preview it in a browser. Test the menu button.**
    Your menus might not appear properly at this point. You may see a bit of the menu repeated to the right. You fix this shortly.

<NOTE>
Read the sidebar "Capturing the Cursor As It Exits" to understand why your menu sometimes doesn't hide as expected. In the following steps of this tutorial, you set up your other menu layers and fix the problem as described in the sidebar.

21. **Repeat steps 7 through 19 for each button, using the values supplied in Table 12.1.**
    Notice the Snap Layer Offsets for the LightBox button (btnMyBox) vary to place the menu more to the left of the button. This keeps the menu within the main content area and off the sidebar, as you see when you preview.

<NOTE>
It's much easier to repeat the button settings if you print the instructions and the table. In the session12 folder, you'll find a PDF file named buttonsettings.pdf.

Table 12.1: Snap Menu Settings

Button	Anchor Object I Layer to Snap	Offsets	AutoLayers to Show
btnHome	btnHome I LyrHome	L=-7, T=26	menucloser, LyrHome
+	btnHome I menucloser	L=-32, T=26	
btnPhoto	btnPhoto I LyrPhotos	L=0, T=26	menucloser, LyrPhotos
+	btnPhoto I menucloser	L=-25, T=26	
btnMotion	btnMotion I LyrMotion	L=0, T=26	menucloser, LyrMotion
+	btnMotion I menucloser	L=-25, T=26	
btnAudio	btnAudio I LyrAudio	L=0, T=26	menucloser, LyrAudio
+	btnAudio I menucloser	L=-25, T=26	
btnFonts	btnFonts I LyrFonts	L=0, T=26	menucloser, LyrFonts
+	btnFonts I menucloser	L=-25, T=26	
btnMyBox	btnMyBox I LyrBox	L=-50, T=26	menucloser, LyrBox
+	btnMyBox I menucloser	L=-75, T=26	

22. **Apply the AutoLayers behavior to the first spacer image before the Home button and the spacer image after the Lightbox button.**
Just click OK when the dialog box opens; you don't need to show anything.

23. **Save and test your page rigorously. Keep the page open for the next tutorial.**
If you have any problems, be sure to check the event for each action and check the Anchor Object and Layer to Snap for each button. Don't worry if you still see the repeated menu piece on the right side; it is taken care of in step 26 (if it's even a problem; it isn't always).

24. **In the CSS Styles panel, click the Add (+) button, select CSS Selector as the type, name the style** .mnmenu p, **select** main.css, **and click OK.**
This is to adjust the formatting of the content in each menu.

25. **Select the Box category, uncheck Same for All in the Margin area, and type T=3px I R=5px I B=0px I L=5px.**
You don't have to apply this style. Because paragraphs appear in each menu, the properties apply automatically. You do, however, have to tweak the paragraph code.

```
<tr>                                    26
    <td class="mnmenu"><p>
<img src="../images/submenus/sm_arrow_home.gif" alt="Arrow
for Home menu" width="150" height="13">
    26  <br>Links go here</p>
        <p> </p>
        <p> </p></td>
    </tr>
```

Finishing the Menus

To add the actual links to each menu, select the layer name and overwrite the text that says *Links go here*. Add the links by selecting the link name and use the point-to-file method from the Property inspector.

In Session 11, refer to the "Adding Contextual Link Styles" tutorial. You need to add three styles for the menu. For each style select CSS Selector and `main.css`. These are the style names and the changes in the Type category for each:

» .mnmenu a:link: Color #FFFFFF, Decoration none
» .mnmenu a:visited: Color #FFFFFF, Decoration none
» .mnmenu a:hover: Color #003366 and select underlined

26. **Select LyrHome in the Layers panel. Select the arrow graphic and then switch to the Split view (Show Code and Design view). Locate this code:**

```
<tr>
        <td class="mnmenu"><p>
<img src="../images/submenus/sm_arrow_home.gif
   " alt="Arrow for Home menu" width="150"
height="13">
            <br>Links go here</p>
            <p> </p>
            <p> </p></td>
        </tr>
```

Select the <p> tag in front of the <img src... tag and cut it (Ctrl+X / ⌘+X). Select the <br> tag in front of Links and paste (Ctrl+V / ⌘+V). The resulting code looks like:

```
<tr>
        <td class="mnmenu">
<img src="../images/submenus/sm_arrow_home.gif
   " alt="Arrow for Home menu" width="150"
height="13">
            <p>Links go here</p>
            <p> </p>
            <p> </p></td>
        </tr>
```

27. **Repeat step 26 for all menu layers except menucloser.**

Capturing the Cursor As It Exits

A major key to designing successful Snap menus is capturing the visitor's cursor as it escapes the menu. So far, when you move your cursor over the Home button, the menu displays. If you move to the left, right, or bottom of the menu as you exit, the menu hides. But when you move the cursor off the menu in an upwards direction, the menu remains visible. This is because nothing tells the browser to hide the menu. If the visitor's cursor "escapes" the menu and does not encounter the menucloser, the event to hide the menu is never called. Because of its dimensions, the menucloser is only accessible at the left, right, or bottom edges of the menu. When you design your menucloser, *always* make it wider and longer than the widest and tallest of your menus.

You cannot position the menucloser in such a way that it can capture all directions because the menucloser *cannot* be positioned over the button. When it's over the button, it's supposed to show the button's menu *and* the menucloser. As soon as it shows the menucloser, the cursor no longer is over the button, it's over the menucloser's transparent GIF, which is set to hide the layers (including menucloser). A dysfunctional flickering occurs as both behaviors

are fired one after the other. That's why you never position the menucloser over the button that calls it and why the menucloser cannot be responsible for hiding the menus in every instance. But the same scripting approach is used to capture the visitor's cursor when it leaves in any direction other than where the menucloser is positioned. In the case of the Home button, when the user moves up and right out of the menu or to the right directly from the Home button, the Photos button triggers a different menu to display while hiding any open menu. That is obvious as you script the next button.

The trick to successful Snap menus is to have some sort of image that *caps* your menu system in order to cover any backdoor exits from the menus and buttons. Your caps can be visible images or simply transparent GIFs (spacers) conveniently placed around the uncovered exits. In this design, there's a spacer to the left of the Home button (6x25), a spacer to the right of the LightBox button (7x25), and one that is placed above and outside of the table that contains the content (560x20). You simply apply the AutoLayers by PVII behavior to each of these transparent images just as you did before.

Tutorial
» Commenting Your DHTML Code

Keeping your code commented is always desirable when developing a Web site. A *comment* is descriptive text that you insert in the HTML code to explain the code or provide other information. The text of the comment appears only in Code view and does not display in the Web page in the browser. Special markup for HTML comments (<!— comment here —>) hide what is between the markup from the browser as it renders the page. HTML comments begin with <!— and end with - -〉.

Commenting code associated with DHTML elements is doubly important because the code is so complex and because the elements it creates are not part of the standard flow of the document. Although it isn't that hard for the average developer to read how paragraphs, tables, or lists appear in a page, a menu that changes position and sometimes isn't even visible might be confusing. Accidentally changing or deleting the menu's code can devastate your page.

In this tutorial, you add comments for each of the menu elements to make them more readily identifiable.

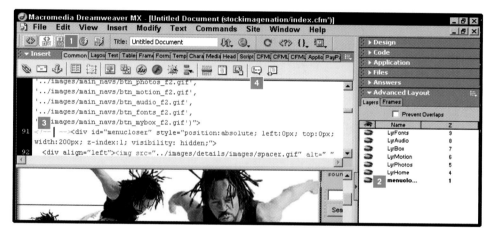

1. **Switch from Design view of the stockimagenation home page to Split view. Choose View→Visual Aids→Invisible Elements and select it if there is no check by Invisible Elements.**

<TIP>
You can control which view (Design or Code) is on top in Split view. To switch, select or unselect Design View on Top from the View menu. You can also adjust the room given to either view by dragging the border between the views. Wait until your cursor changes to drag.

2. **Click into the Design view portion. Use the Layers panel to select the menucloser layer or click the CSS icon that represents that <div> tag.**
You can select layers with the Layers panel only when Design is the active view. Clicking the layer or its icon should highlight the tag's code in Code view.

3. **In the Code portion, insert your cursor just to the left (the beginning) of the highlighted code.**
If you don't place your cursor before the code, the comment is added to the end of the code, which you don't want.

4. **Click the Comment icon in the Common panel of the Insert bar to add a comment.**

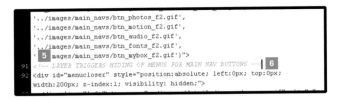

```
'../images/main_navs/btn_photos_f2.gif',
'../images/main_navs/btn_motion_f2.gif',
'../images/main_navs/btn_audio_f2.gif',
'../images/main_navs/btn_fonts_f2.gif',
' 5 mages/main_navs/btn_mybox_f2.gif')">
91  <!-- LAYER TRIGGERS HIDING OF MENUS FOR MAIN NAV BUTTONS -- 6
92  <div id="menucloser" style="position:absolute; left:0px; top:0px;
    width:200px; z-index:1; visibility: hidden;">
```

Table 12.2: Menu Code Comments

Layer	Comment
menucloser	LAYER TRIGGERS HIDING OF MENUS FOR MAIN NAV BUTTONS
LyrHome	LAYER CONTAINS MENU ITEMS FOR HOME BUTTON
LyrPhotos	LAYER CONTAINS MENU ITEMS FOR PHOTOS BUTTON
LyrMotion	LAYER CONTAINS MENU ITEMS FOR MOTION BUTTON
LyrAudio	LAYER CONTAINS MENU ITEMS FOR AUDIO BUTTON
LyrFonts	LAYER CONTAINS MENU ITEMS FOR FONTS BUTTON
LyrBox	LAYER CONTAINS MENU ITEMS FOR LIGHTBOX BUTTON

5. Type the following statement (between the inserted comment tags): LAYER TRIGGERS HIDING OF MENUS FOR MAIN NAV BUTTONS.

6. Insert your cursor just after the closing comment markup and press Enter or Return to move the menucloser code to the next line.
   You now have a Comment icon in front of the CSS icon for the menucloser layer. This makes for more readable code.

< T I P >
The example shown uses all uppercase text so that it stands out from the generally lowercase code markup. If you use uppercase code, try using all lowercase comments.

7. Click back into Design and select LyrHome in the Layers panel.

8. Insert your cursor just before the highlighted code in the Code portion of the view.

9. Insert a set of comment tags and add LAYER CONTAINS MENU ITEMS FOR HOME BUTTON.
   Add a return after the comment, just as you did with the previous comment, to place the LyrHome code on the next line.

10. Repeat the commenting process for each of the menu layers, using the comments provided in Table 12.2. Save the page and keep it open for the next tutorial.

11. To edit your comments, select a Comment icon and change the comment text in the Property inspector.

Tutorial

» Scripting the onClick State of the Snap Menu's Buttons

As a final touch, many developers like to have their rollover buttons stay clicked while the site visitors move their cursor to the Snap menu. Currently, this doesn't happen because when you move off the button to the menu, the (onMouseOut) event for the rollover button is set to restore the previous button state. In fact, the key to stopping this behavior is to remove that action from each of the buttons. Of course, you have to set up some remote rollover effects on all the buttons, the menucloser, and the "cap" images that are set to hide the menus as well.

1. **Select the Home button.**

2. **Select its Swap Image Restore Action in the Behaviors panel and delete it by pressing the minus (-) button. Repeat this step for all the buttons.**

3. **Preview the page.**

   The problem here is that the button states don't restore, but you want each button's normal or up state to restore when the visitor leaves that button's menu, goes to another button, or leaves any button without going to a menu.

4. **Select the Home button and double-click its Swap Image action in the Behaviors panel.**

   In the Images list of the Swap Image dialog box, btnHome is already selected and a small asterisk appears just after it. You change the rollover state of all the buttons except the Home button.

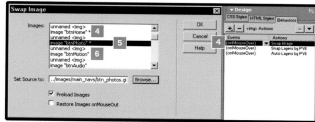

5. **In the Images list, select btnPhoto and press the Browse button. Navigate (if necessary) to the main_navs folder and select btn_photos.gif, which is the up or normal state of the Photos button.**

   You are changing the states of the buttons other than the Home button so that only the Home button is black (rollover color) when you are on that page.

< N O T E >

You are scripting a remote rollover.

6. **While you are in the Swap Image dialog box, repeat step 5 for every button (except Home), selecting its name from the list and browsing to locate and select its up state (not the _f2 state). Scroll to find all the button images. When *all* the remote rollover states for the buttons have been set, click OK to close the dialog box.**

7. **Repeat steps 4 through 6, selecting the Photos button.**

    In this case, you set the remote rollovers for all buttons except the Photos button.

8. **Repeat steps 4 through 6 for the remaining buttons, each time scripting the remote rollover steps for all buttons except the one that you selected to double-click its Swap Image action.**

    You also need to set each button to swap to its up state if the visitor moves over the menucloser's GIF or any of the "cap" GIFs, which you do next.

9. **In the Layers panel, select menucloser. Select the GIF in the menucloser layer by clicking inside it.**

10. **In the Behaviors panel, click the plus sign and add a Swap Image behavior to it.**

    In this case, you set the remote rollover states for each of the main navigation buttons, selecting each button's name and browsing to locate its up state (not the _f2 state). Be sure to do all the buttons while this dialog box is open.

11. **Before you click OK to close the dialog box, uncheck the Preload and Restore functions!**

    If you miss one, you can always double-click the action to add the missed button.

12. **Repeat steps 9 through 11 for the two end cap spacers, setting the remote rollover (f2 image) for all the buttons for each spacer.**

13. **Save and test your page.**

    Now the active button should remain in its over state until users leave the menu, encounter the menucloser, move over another button, or encounter any of the capture spacers.

» Session Review

In this session, you added more functionality to your Dreamweaver MX program through the addition of more behaviors. The new features came from the PVII behaviors you downloaded and installed in your program. You built the Snap menus used by the stockimagenation site, adding layers and scripting them to display on-demand. You also set up the behavior that controls the positioning of the menus relative to their respective buttons. Test what you have learned by answering the following questions. Answers can be found in the tutorials noted in parentheses.

1. Which tag is typically used for layers? ("Tutorial: Building the Menu Layers")

2. Which behaviors are used to script Snap menus? ("Tutorial: Building the Menu Layers")

3. How do you access the layers you've added to a page? ("Tutorial: Building the Menu Layers")

4. How do you set the absolute position of a layer? ("Tutorial: Duplicating and Positioning the Menu Layers")

5. How do you write an HTML comment? ("Tutorial: Commenting Your DHTML Code")

6. Which action causes the state of the navigation button to return to its up or normal state? ("Tutorial: Scripting the onClick State of the Snap Menu's Buttons")

7. When you set an image state for any graphic other than the one that is currently selected, which type of rollover is this called? ("Tutorial: Scripting the onClick State of the Snap Menu's Buttons")

8. How do you edit an existing Swap Image action? ("Tutorial: Scripting the onClick State of the Snap Menu's Buttons")

Session 13

Automating with Library Items and Templates

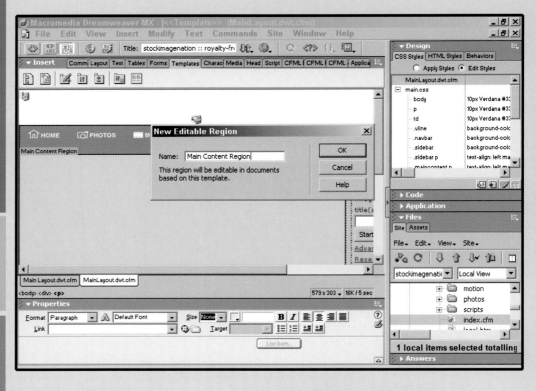

Tutorial: **Building a Library Item**

Tutorial: **Saving the Design as a Template**

Tutorial: **Adding a Table**

Tutorial: **Building Pages from Your Template**

Tutorial: **Adding an Optional Editable Region**

Automating in Dreamweaver

Locating, opening, and editing every page when changes are required to one specific element can be a time-consuming task. Fortunately, you can use Library items to build page elements that are easily updated. Making a Library item allows you to open a single, original source, make your edits, and then save and update every occurrence of the item in all site pages! Macromedia Dreamweaver MX then does all the grunt work of updating and maintaining accurate paths to images and files.

A Library item is stored code. You build a Library item by selecting page elements and clicking New Library Item. The code is copied to a new text file. You drag Library items from the Assets panel to your pages. To edit a Library item, you simply double-click it in the document or in the Assets panel, make changes, and save. Dreamweaver gives you the option of updating any instances of the item. If you choose to update, Dreamweaver looks through every page in the site, substitutes the new code in the original file, and again adjusts and maintains the proper paths. Any updated page that is not open is automatically saved. Open documents are modified but not saved; if you close an updated page, you are asked to save it.

In this chapter, you learn how to use Library items to build page elements that are easily updated. You also learn how to work with Dreamweaver templates to add more pages to a site while maintaining a consistent, editable layout. Templates act like Library items *at the page level*. You can use them to lock down or modify multiple elements.

TOOLS YOU'LL USE
Site window, Template panel

MATERIALS NEEDED
Your stockimagenation root folder or the starter file in the session13 folder

TIME REQUIRED
60 minutes

Tutorial
» Building a Library Item

In this tutorial, you make a Library item out of the footer area of the home page. Library items are very powerful and save you a ton of time when you need to update the links of the footer area. As a site grows, the links inevitably change.

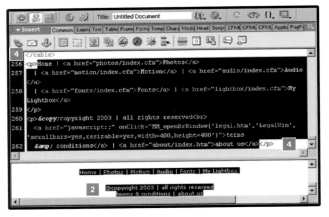

1. **Open the** stockimagenation index.cfm **page.**

2. **Highlight the entire footer area.**

3. **Switch to Code and Design view.**
   You need to check the code to be sure that any alignment tags get selected. Here, the paragraph tags surround the selection that needs to be included.

4. **Click to place your cursor in front of the** <p >Home **tag. Press the Shift key and click after the** </p> **(closing tag) to select the entire footer area.**

5. **Open the Assets panel and click the Library icon.**

6. **From the Library Options pop-up menu, select New Library Item.**

7. **Click OK for the warning that styles aren't saved with the item.**

<NOTE>
When saving a Library item that uses a class style, Macromedia Dreamweaver MX alerts you that the Item might not appear as designed when used. This is true if the destination page doesn't have the class defined as a style rule; in the example used in this session, the destination pages are linked to the style sheet.

8. **Type** footer **for the name.**
   When the name area in the Assets panel is highlighted, just type the new name. Notice the Library item in your page; it is highlighted in yellow to denote that it's a Library item.

<NOTE>
If you want to add Library items to pages, you simply insert them from the Assets panel. To edit a Library item, double-click it and footer.lbi opens.

9. **Save the page.**

Tutorial
» Saving the Design as a Template

In this tutorial you make a template out of the home page. The actual home page won't become a template because there is only one page exactly like it. But the basic page design becomes a template for the interior pages.

1. **With the** `index.cfm` **page open, choose File→Save As Template.**

2. **Name it** MainLayout **and click Save.**

3. **Change back to Design view. In the Insert panel, click the Templates tab.**

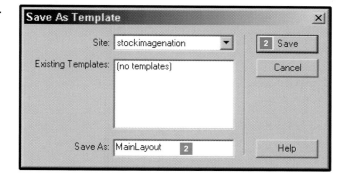

4. **Select and delete the large image and the feet. The background will be black. To change this, make a new style with these parameters: Custom Class, name it .background, background category make the color #CCCCCC (a light) gray, and OK. Right-click the** `<td>` **tag and set the class to background.**

5. **Select the** `<td>` **tag for the images cell.**

6. **In the Template panel, click the Editable Region icon.**
   An *editable region* is an unlocked area in the template and pages based on a template. All templates should contain at least one editable region to be useful.

7. **Name it Main Content Region and click OK.**
   Don't worry if one of the menu layers shows up when you select the `<td>` tag.

8. **Press Tab once. In the Assets panel, insert line1.gif.**
   This replaces the black thin line with a bit of the finger color in it.

9. **Press Tab once more and delete the image.**
   This deletes the fingertips. You have already applied the orange background so now it's just orange.

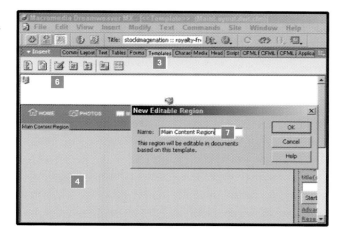

< N O T E >

Changes made to the editable region in the template do not result in updates to these regions in pages based on the template. Changes do, however, affect any subsequent pages created from the template.

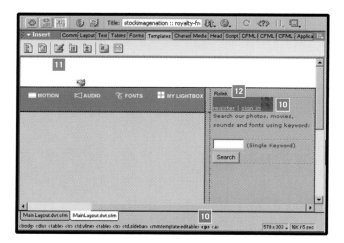

10. **Select the register I sign in text and then its** <td> **tag.**

11. **Click the Editable Region icon.**

12. **Name it Rslink and click OK.**
    Notice the blue tab added to the template with the name. This does not show in a browser.

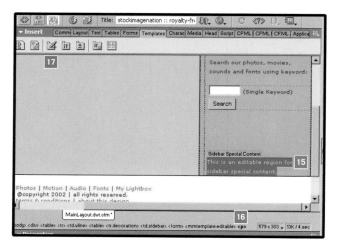

13. **Delete the CD Collections icon.**

14. **Delete the CD image.**

15. **Highlight the text and type** This is an editable region for sidebar special content.

16. **Click in the new text and select its** <p> **tag.**

17. **Click the Editable Region icon and name it Sidebar Special Content. Click OK.**

18. **Select the footer and click the Editable Region icon.**

19. **Name it footer and click OK.**

Tutorial

» Adding a Table

In this tutorial, you add another table and a couple of styles. This table can be used for banners or special content.

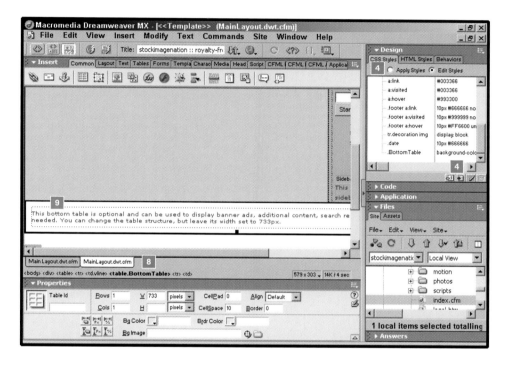

1. **Click in the orange sidebar area and then select the `<table>` tag that precedes it.**

2. **Press the keyboard right-arrow key.**

3. **Choose Insert→Insert Table and use 1 row, 1 column, 733 pixels, and all zeros. Click OK.**
   The table stacks below the main content area and above the footer area.

4. **Open the CSS Styles panel and add a new style.**

5. **Select Make Custom Style and name it .BottomTable in** `main.css`. **Click OK.**

6. **Use the following parameters:**
   Background: Cor #FFFFFF
   Box: 0 for padding and margin
   Border: Style – Solid, Width 1 pixel, Color #000000

7. **Click OK.**

8. **Right-click (Control-click) the table tag and apply the BottomTable class.**

9. **Click inside the table and type** This bottom table is optional and can be used to display banner ads, additional content, search results, and so on: whatever is needed. You can change the table structure, but leave its width set to 733px.

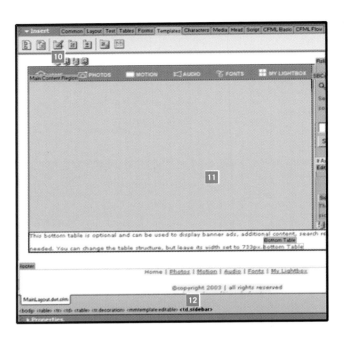

10. **Select the table and click the Editable Region icon. Name it Bottom Table Content and click OK.**
    See the illustration; it shows all the editable regions defined so far.

11. **Back in Design view, click in the content area (where the men used to be) and press Tab two times.**
    This positions your cursor in the large thin sidebar column.

12. **Click the `<td sidebar>` tag in the Tag Selector.**

13. **Click the Template tab of the Insert bar.**

14. **Click the Editable Region icon.**

15. **Name it SBCol Image.**

16. **Save your file.**

How Templates Work

When two or more pages in a site use a common layout, it makes sense to create a master document—or template—that contains the shared elements to use as the basis of pages you build for a site. Macromedia Dreamweaver templates take this concept much further with features to manage path structures and update pages, *plus* a whole range of options for designating both locked and editable elements in pages based on the template.

As it does with Library Items, Dreamweaver builds a special folder to hold Template Assets. Templates are saved as .DWT files into a *Templates* folder that the program adds at the root level of the site. Special markup in HTML pages based on a Dreamweaver template allows the program to locate and update parts of pages when modifications are made in the template file.

Dreamweaver templates are like Library items on a *page* level. But, where a Library item is completely locked down, a template contains both locked and editable regions. Locked template

regions cannot be edited in pages based on the template; only specially designated editable regions can be individualized on a page-by-page basis. You can also specify optional and repeating areas, if needed, to accommodate data-driven, dynamic pages based on your template.

Locked and editable regions only affect the pages that are based on the template; everything in a template file is editable. However, only changes made in locked regions of the template are updated in the related pages. This makes perfect sense when you think about it—editable regions are not updated by the template because each page's editable regions probably contain page-specific content! Like Library items, the code for pages based on a template is solely contained in the HTML page; the original template and Templates folder are not required on the Web server. When you update pages based on a template, you must save and upload all modified pages to the Web server.

Tutorial
» Building Pages from Your Template

In this tutorial, you learn how to open a new page using an existing template. You also learn how to apply a template to the placeholder pages you made previously.

1. **Choose File→New.**

2. **Click the Templates tab in the New Document dialog box.**

3. **In the Templates For area, select your defined site.**

4. **In the Site area, select the template name (mainlayout).**

5. **Click the Create button.**
   Notice that you now have a copy of the template page.

6. **Choose File→Save As and navigate to the html/stockimagena-tion/photos folder. Save it as** index.cfm.

7. **Click OK to overwrite the placeholder file.**

8. **In the Site panel (window), open the audio file and double-click the** index.cfm **to open it.**

9. **Type** Content goes here.
   This page is just a placeholder page with no content yet.

10. **Choose Modify→Templates→Apply Template to Page.**

11. **Be sure Update Page when Template Changes option is checked. Click Select.**
    Because the page now has content in it, the Inconsistent Region Names dialog box opens so you can tell it where to put the current content.

12. **Select the Document Body region text.**

13. **In the Move Content to New Region drop-down list, select Nowhere.**
    When you see this dialog box after applying a template, you most frequently want to choose the Nowhere option.

14. **Click OK.**
    Notice that the page now looks exactly like the template.

15. **Open each of the index pages in the following folders and choose Modify→Templates→Apply Template to Page: About, Audio, CD collection, Fonts, Motion, Lightbox.**

16. **Close and save each** index.cfm **page.**

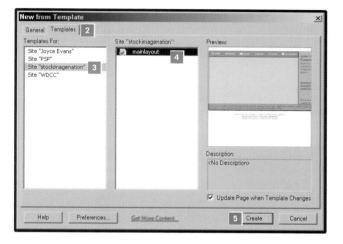

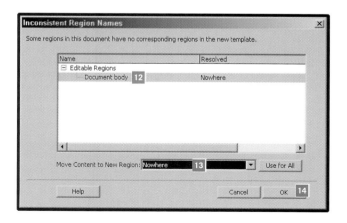

Tutorial

» Adding an Optional Editable Region

In this tutorial, you add an optional editable region. An optional region is just that—optional. This is a portion of the page, such as a sidebar area, an image, or even a navigational element that is used on some pages, but not others. Optional regions are controlled by conditional statements and can be set so that the region is editable or not.

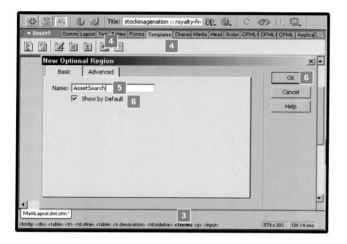

1. **Open the** `MainLayout.dwt` **template page again (it's in the Template folder).**

2. **Select the form Search button.**

3. **In the Tag Selector, click the** `<form>` **tag (**`form#SearchForm`**).** This will select the entire form. You are going to make the form editable (optionally).

4. **Click the Templates tab and select the Editable Optional Region icon. Be sure you click the icon that says Editable not just Optional.**

5. **Name it AssetSearch.**

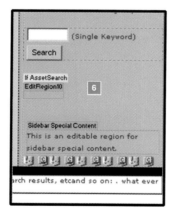

6. **Leave Show by Default selected and click OK.**
   Notice at the bottom of the column that there is now a label for If AssetSearch and Editable Region 10.

<NOTE>

To update the template, choose File➜Save and click Yes in the dialog box that appears. Click Close in the Update Pages dialog box. Open any of the `index.cfm` pages and note that Region 10 is now visible.

» Session Review

Now that you understand a bit about how templates work and how powerful they are for site consistency, it's time to test your retention. The answers can be found in the tutorials listed in parentheses.

1. Do you make entire pages into Library items? ("Tutorial: Building a Library Item")

2. What is the best use of a Library item? ("Tutorial: Building a Library Item")

3. Where are Library items saved? ("Tutorial: Building a Library Item")

4. Where do you find the Template panel? ("Tutorial: Saving the Design as a Template")

5. What do you do if you want a region to be editable? ("Tutorial: Saving the Design as a Template")

6. How do you make a new page from a template? ("Tutorial: Building Pages from Your Template")

7. Is an optional editable region visible on the other pages using the template? ("Tutorial: Adding an Optional Editable Region")

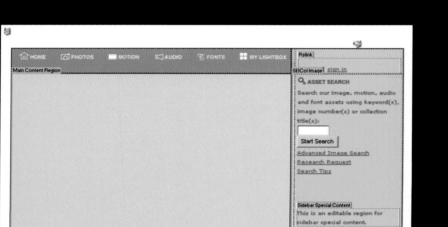

HOME | PHOTOS | MOTION | AUDIO | FONTS | MY LIGHTBOX

Rslink

Main Content Region

SBCol Image | sign in

ASSET SEARCH

Search our image, motion, audio and font assets using keyword(s), image number(s) or collection title(s):

Start Search

Advanced Image Search
Research Request
Search Tips

Sidebar Special Content

This is an editable region for sidebar special content.

If AssetSearch
EditRegion10

Bottom Table Content

This bottom table is optional and can be used to display banner ads, additional content, search results, etc. what ever is needed. You can change the table structure, but leave its width set to 733px.

ooter

Home | Photos | Motion | Audio | Fonts | My Lightbox
©copyright 2002 | all rights reserved.
terms & conditions | about this design

Scroller Region

Part V

Building a Web Application in Dreamweaver

Building Dynamic Web Pages

Building a Web Application in Dreamweaver MX

The hottest topic in Web design today is dynamic site content. At this point, you have been building *static* pages. You used some *client-side* scripting to produce dynamic, interactive elements, but the content has been statically defined in the Web page. References to images, movies, or any other content, including text copy in the page, is "hard-coded" using HTML tags. The content is the same for every visitor until you (the developer) change the code and replace the page on the Web server.

By contrast, the content of a dynamic, or *data-driven*, Web page is all or partially undefined until the visitor requests the page. Page content is pulled from a data source, typically a database, at the time of the visit, so it's possible to have more, less, or even *different* content based upon how the database records have changed. Application logic uses server-side scripting to collect, store, and display content based on input from the site visitor. Dynamic content is always up-to-date and relative.

TOOLS YOU'LL USE
Applications panel group, Site Definition panel (window), a Web browser, ColdFusion MX Server

MATERIALS NEEDED
From the accompanying CD-ROM, you need the session14 directory and files

TIME REQUIRED
30 minutes

Discussion

How Data-Driven Pages Work

The pages you built in the previous sessions have all been static. You added images and text, built links, and even used *client-side scripting* through Dreamweaver JavaScript behaviors to build some pretty amazing page elements, including dynamic HTML menus. Now you use *server-side scripting*, which is application logic that runs on the server before a page is returned to the user's Web browser, to build pages with dynamic or data-driven content. To understand the difference, first look at how a Web server is used to serve a static page.

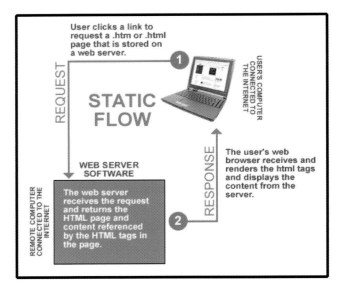

The static page contains hard-coded content. When an image is required, the <img> tag includes information about where to find the image <img src="path to image on web server">. If the page needs to display 10 images, 10 tags are required.

By contrast, an image in a data-driven page might use application logic to set the image src (source). In this sense, the content is partially undefined until the moment the page is requested. Special tags are used to tell the server where to find the database, what type of database it is, and which table of the database to use to get the information about the image. The Web server uses special application server software that understands the type of logic used and that can communicate through a database driver with the database.

A data-driven page typically uses a different page extension to trigger the Web server to scan the page for possible processing. The extension determines which server-based support method is used to decode the page. Dreamweaver MX supports Active Server Pages and ASP.NET (.ASP, .ASPX), ColdFusion Markup Language (.CFM or .CFML), JavaServer Pages (.JSP), and Hypertext PreProcessor Pages (.PHP) scripting environments. The Web server sends the page to the application server, which uses information included in the page's logic to request data from a database table. The scripting commands are stripped from the page and replaced with whatever HTML tags are necessary to display the content. Then the page is sent to the Web server. The Web server, in turn, delivers the page and content to the user's browser.

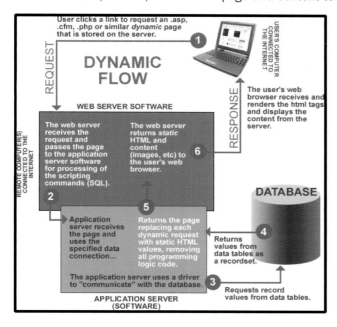

The data-driven page, for example, can be set up using the `<img src="">` tag, too, but instead of inserting the path to the image, all or part of the path is defined as a record in a database. It might look something like `<cfoutput query="rsShowCDs"><img src="images/cd_collection/ #rsShowCDS. CDThumbs#" width="85" height="85" hspace="5" vspace="5" border="1"></cfoutput>`. Additional commands might surround the image tag to tell it to repeat for all the related records contained in the database. One image, 10 images, or 10,000 images—it wouldn't matter because the application server would add enough HTML to display as many images as referenced by the database records. The example given uses ColdFusion markup, and although other scripting languages would look a little bit different, the concept is the same. Most languages use *SQL* (Structured Query Language) to build a *recordset*, which is a subset of data, by querying the database for data that matches a specific set of parameters.

Using a Database

A *database* is a collection of data records. Data is typically stored as a record in a table with *columns,* sometimes called *fields*, for each data type. A perfect example of a database is your e-mail program's address book. Each person or company listed is a record. Its data fields (columns) might be name, address, city, state, e-mail address, and so on. Simple, huh? Imagine the address book as a table with rows and columns and you get the concept of what a database table looks like. But there's more depth to it; a database can contain more than one table.

You don't need to build a database to build a site in this book because I've supplied you with one. For your own site, you need to either alter the one given you or build your own. If you are unfamiliar with databases, a good place to start is *Database Design for Mere Mortals* by Michael J. Hernandez.

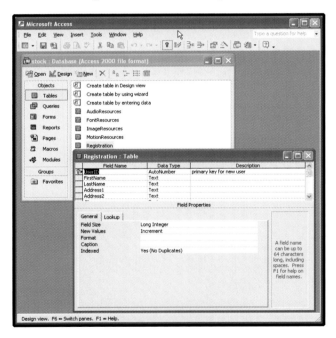

The project database is an Access 2002 database and contains many tables, including the Registration table seen in the figure. Access is a Windows-only program and is typically purchased as part of the Microsoft Professional Office Suite. However, you don't need Access to use the database when building the project site in Dreamweaver MX because you are supplied one in your original site starter files.

What You Need to Build Data-Driven (Dynamic) Pages

To build data-driven pages in Dreamweaver MX, you need a Web server, an application server, and a database. You've got the database. The Web and application servers required depend upon the scripting environment you use for development and whether you develop locally or remotely. In this case, you use ColdFusion, a fairly simple to learn, tag-based scripting language by Macromedia. ColdFusion MX Server is required to process the ColdFusion Markup tags. ColdFusion MX Server (Developer Edition) is free to download at Macromedia and ships with both the Studio MX and Dreamweaver MX programs. However, it is only available for Windows. There is a complex solution for MacOSX using CFMX for J2EE, but it is quite involved and way beyond the scope of this book. J2EE is a Java Server.

Development Solutions

You have two basic choices for developing the data-driven pages in this book: You can develop locally (Windows-only) and deploy later to an online Web server with CFMX support or you can develop using a remotely-hosted ColdFusion MX server. Macintosh users must take the former route and Windows users, eventually, also need to publish to the same setup. One of the most difficult issues that beginners deal with when starting to build data-driven pages is going from local development to remote publishing. You won't be able to see your dynamic text or images until they are tested at the server level. The local development solution requires a Windows computer with either IIS (Internet Information Services) or PWS (Personal Web Server). If you aren't sure whether your computer has IIS or PWS, follow the directions given in Appendix C. If you have a Windows ME or Windows XP Home Edition operating system, your computer doesn't support IIS or PWS. You need an upgraded system or you can use a remote development solution. If you determine you have IIS or PWS up and running on your Windows computer, you need to install ColdFusion MX Server (Developer Edition) as a stand-alone Web server. Again, follow the directions given in Appendix C.

Develop Locally, Deploy Remotely

When you opt to develop dynamic pages locally, you must add information about what server model you use, where the testing server (application server software) is located, where your pages are stored on the Web server, and the access method for moving pages back and forth from the local root folder to the remote root folder. So far you've defined your *local root folder* and begun to build your pages. You selected ColdFusion as a server model, effectively choosing the application logic and page extension (.CFM) you planned to use for the site. But because you were not yet adding ColdFusion tags and did not need application server software to process your pages, you did not have to move your pages to a Web server, and did not have to add any information about Web servers, application servers, or databases. Now you do.

You edit your site definition to create and choose a *remote root folder* in the CFusionmx\wwwroot directory of your ColdFusion MX server (which serves as both Web and application server). You select Local/Network as your *access method* for moving pages back and forth between local and remote roots because both folders may be on the same computer or network. You define a data source (DSN) using ColdFusion Administrator to select the database stored in the CFusionMX\wwwroot\stockimagenation\database directory. Dreamweaver MX uses this information to allow you to connect to your database and preview your pages locally.

Develop and Deploy Remotely

Eventually, all developers must define a remote Web and application server to publish their pages. In fact, the most common question new developers have is how they should "transfer" their sites so that they work when uploaded to the hosted Web server. It isn't really that much different from local development, but it does require that you be connected to the Internet to transfer and preview your pages. You use FTP (File Transfer Protocol) to move files from your *local root* to the *remote root* folder on the remotely-hosted Web server. You provide information about the hosted Web server directory account and specify the folder where your pages are stored (just as you would in local development) in the site definition dialog box in Dreamweaver MX.

< N O T E >
You can get by with ColdFusion 5 for this book's project. You won't use any ColdFusionMX-only features.

Local and Remote Site Structure

Although it may seem like the local root folder comes first and then the remote root folder is built, the truth is that you need to know the structure of the remote root before you begin to build your site because you want the local and remote roots to use the same directory structure. Dreamweaver MX helps you maintain this "mirrored" site structure as you upload and download files and folders between the two root folders. This is especially critical when working with a database because you don't typically want your database to be accessible to the general public—you don't want them to be able to download it. You do want them to be able to view pages that access the database and that is done through a database connection. The connection defines the type and location of the database, so it's easy to see why the structure locally needs to be the same as remotely, whether you use the local Web server (localhost) of IIS, PWS or ColdFusion, or a remotely hosted Web server. The path needs to be the same. Fortunately, when using Dreamweaver MX, this information is contained in a special file that is included into each dynamic page prior to processing. When you change where the database is located, you only need to change the path used by the connection.

ColdFusion Hosting

A remote development solution for developing ColdFusion pages requires a hosting company that supports ColdFusion MX and, in this case, Access database. One really great company is CrystalTech (www.crystaltech.com), the company that hosts the book's project site (www.stockimagenation.com). They charge reasonable prices and don't require a contract. Best of all, they have great support and provide excellent features in the form of a Control Center where you can manage your account.

Examples using CrystalTech's easy-to-use control panels and site structure are used in the tutorials for this session along with the local development steps and examples. Typically, ColdFusion support costs a little bit more than ASP and other options, but CrystalTech is fairly reasonable for the developers who really want to improve their skills with ColdFusion.

Unfortunately, free ColdFusion hosting is scarce because the popularity of the program has increased. You can see a list of hosting companies with their support for various technologies in this Macromedia Tech Note; http://www.macromedia.com/support/dreamweaver/ts/documents/web_hosts_mx.htm.

When searching for a ColdFusion hosting company, there are certain features that are ideal:

>> ColdFusion MX support

>> Database connections — an unlimited number of ODBC connections is ideal

>> The capability to create your own DSNs

>> At least 100MB of disk space and a very high transfer rate (GBs are not unusual)

>> 24x7 technical support by e-mail *and* by phone

Tutorial
» Defining a Local Web and Testing Server

If you use a Windows computer with IIS or PWS and ColdFusion MX Server installed and want to develop locally, follow the steps in this tutorial to edit your site definition to include the required information about your local server setup.

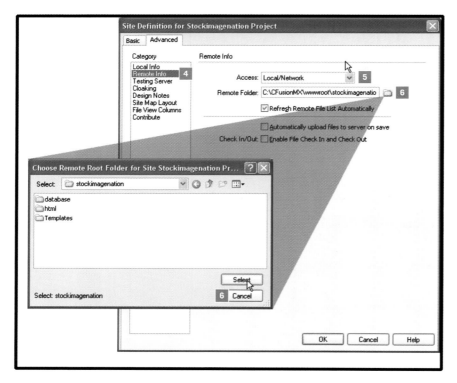

1. **Be sure that you have IIS or PWS installed and running and that you install ColdFusion MX Server.**
   Read the instructions in Appendix C.

   < N O T E >
   Windows ME and XP Home Edition do not support IIS or PWS. You need to upgrade to work with a database locally. You can, however, use a remote solution as described earlier. Skip this tutorial and use the next one to set up your remote solution.

2. **In Dreamweaver MX, press F8 to open the Site panel (window).**

3. **Choose Site→Edit Sites. Click the Edit button in the Edit Sites dialog box.**

4. **Select the Advance Site Setup tab; then select the Remote Info category.**

5. **Click the menu arrow for the Access field and select Local/Network.**
   Because both the server and your local root are on the same computer, you can simply transfer files from one directory to the other. If the computer serving as the Web server were a part of a local network, you'd also use this method of access.

6. **Click the folder icon by the Remote Folder field and navigate to C:\CFusionMX\wwwroot\. Add a new folder named stockimagenation in the wwwroot directory. Open the new folder and select it for the remote site root.**
   You transfer files to this folder in a later tutorial.

7. **Switch to the Testing Server category.**

   You already selected the ColdFusion server model in an earlier session.

8. **Select Local/Network from the Access menu.**

   Dreamweaver should automatically point the testing server folder to the same folder as the remote root. The URL prefix tells Dreamweaver what to append in front of the page address when you preview in your browser. Remember, if you are working locally, dynamic pages must go through Dreamweaver to your local server for processing of the application logic. The URL Prefix uses http://localhost:8500/stockimagenation/. 8500 refers to the port that ColdFusion MX Server uses to serve the pages. All Web servers require a port. You see the same thing in the address line of the browser when you preview your pages.

9. **Click OK to close the Site Definition dialog box. Click the Done button in the Edit Sites dialog box to save the changes and return to the Site panel.**

10. **Keep the site open.**

    Windows users who are developing with this method should read, but not complete, the next tutorial. Macintosh users and Windows users who want to develop using a remote Web server need to use the next tutorial.

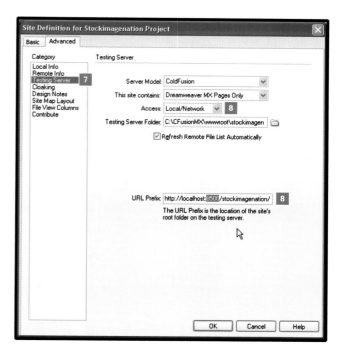

Tutorial
» Defining a Remote Web and Testing Server

This tutorial takes you through the steps of defining a remote Web and testing server. Macintosh users and Windows users who want to set up a remote solution should work through this tutorial. If you are developing locally, do not complete this tutorial. It's still a good idea to read it for future knowledge.

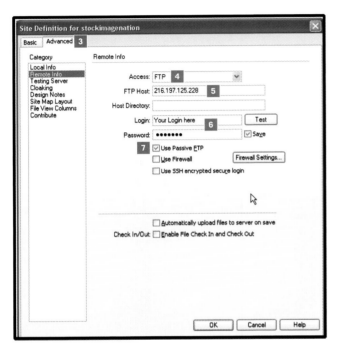

1. **In Dreamweaver, press F8 to open the Site panel (window) and make sure your stockimagenation site is active.**

2. **Choose Site→Edit Sites. When the Edit Sites dialog box opens, click the Edit button.**

3. **Click the Advanced tab to use categories. Select the Remote Info category.**

4. **Choose FTP from the Access menu.**

5. **Type in the name of your domain, its IP address, or whatever your hosting company says is required for the host server.**

<NOTE>
For CrystalTech, this is entered as *yourdomain.com* or *.net* or *.org*, where"*yourdomain.com*" is, of course, your domain's name and type. If you just signed up for an account at CrystalTech, they send you an IP address that you can use until your domain name is transferred or propagated over the Internet. CrystalTech assigns an IP address to each "virtual" server (domain account) using shared hosting and sends you the information for FTP right after you sign up.

6. **Add your FTP login ID (username) and password.**
   If you enter your password here, it is saved in the Dreamweaver program. If you prefer not to save it or run the risk of someone else using it from this computer, you are prompted for it each time you connect to the remote Web server.

7. **Select the Use Passive FTP check box.**
   This allows your service provider's FTP server to set the data port for file transfers when Dreamweaver attempts to connect to your site. Many providers set their servers up this way for better security control.

8. **Switch to the Testing Server category.**
   You already selected the ColdFusion server model.

9. **Choose FTP from the Access menu.**

10. **Press Test if you are online and want to test the connection.**

11. **Click OK to close the Site Definition panel (window) and keep Dreamweaver MX open for the next tutorial.**

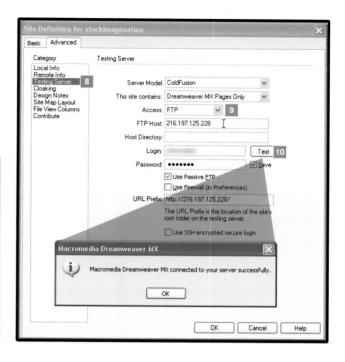

URL Prefix

Dreamweaver MX correctly adds the information you supplied in the Remote Info category to the fields for the testing server. Most of the time (99%) this is the correct information. Some servers actually have a wwwroot folder that must be set as the host directory in both the Remote and Testing category dialog boxes. If this happens to be the case for your hosting company, you might find that Dreamweaver MX adds the extra directory to the URL prefix, resulting in an incorrect URL. To fix it, simply remove the /wwwroot addition from the URL prefix and then test to see that the testing server connection still works (by pressing the Test button).

Tutorial
» Transferring Files to the Web Server

Whether you develop locally or remotely, your files (including the database) need to be stored on the Web server. In both cases, you use Dreamweaver MX's Site panel (window) to move the files. For the remote setup, you must be online and able to connect to the remote Web server.

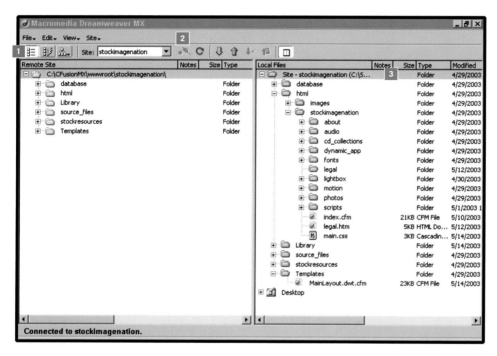

1. **Press F8 to bring up the Site panel (window) and expand it to view both the local and remote root folders.**

   For Windows, click the Expand/Collapse icon that looks like the Site panel when expanded. For Macintosh, use the small white arrow found at the bottom-left edge of the Site window.

2. **Connect to the Web server.**

3. **Select the root folder in the local files and click the Put icon (the blue Up arrow) to place all your files onto the remote Web server.**

   You get a message asking if you are sure you want to put the entire site. Click OK. Once the files are transferred you can delete the source_files folder and the stockresources folder from the remote location if you are short on hard drive space.

4. **Click the Expand/Collapse button to return the Site panel (window) to its collapsed state.**

   You moved the database to the remote Web server.

<TIP>

If you work locally (using Local/Network), Dreamweaver MX includes text that says you should press the *Refresh* icon to view your remote root folder. If you work remotely (FTP), Dreamweaver gives you a message to press the *Connect* icon to connect to the hosted Web server.

<NOTE>

Whenever you add new files or folders to your site, you should move them to the Web server, especially if they are required by the dynamic page you are working with. When you preview, Dreamweaver doesn't automatically upload all the necessary dependent files to the server so that they are available. It is better to be proactive with this than to rely on any program to do this for you anyway!

Put and Get

The process of moving your files is the same whether you are using a Local/Network or FTP connection, except that you must be connected to the Internet when using FTP. Put moves selected files or folders from the local root folder to the remote root folder. The other arrow is Get, which moves selected files or folders from the remote root folder to the local root folder. If you select a file buried within several directories, Dreamweaver MX adds the required directories to maintain the same structure as the originating root folder. This is Dreamweaver MX at its best and one of the main reasons you define a site. Dreamweaver doesn't require "mirrored" file structures; you can easily drag and drop files from one root to another using any folder you like, but mirrored structures make sense to maintain paths to images and pages and for that reason. Dreamweaver does, when using Put and Get, build whatever folders are needed to maintain the structure.

The Database Folder and NTFS File Permissions

When using server-side scripting to add, modify, or delete records in a database, the proper permissions must be set on the database folder to allow your pages to interact with the database. When working remotely, most Web hosting companies provide a specific database folder with the proper permissions applied. You simply upload your database to that folder and everything works well. If you delete this folder or plan to use a different folder, you might need to request that the administrator set permissions on the new folder. CrystalTech provides its clients with panels to view and set permissions on folders in their accounts.

If you are developing locally on a Windows XP, 2000, or NT computer, you want the folder permissions for "everyone" accessing the database folder to be set to read and execute. Because you're the owner of the computer, you have full control over this folder. Consult your IIS or PWS Help files for more information about how permissions affect reading, writing, and executing scripts.

Tutorial

» Specifying the RDS Login for ColdFusion Server (Windows Only)

RDS stands for Remote Development Services and you must configure this in the integrated development environment (IDE) of Dreamweaver MX prior to setting up a DSN (Datasource Name) for working with your database. The RDS login is enabled in ColdFusion MX Server by default and you had to enter a login password when you installed it. Now you simply log in from Dreamweaver.

1. **Use the Site panel to open the home page (**index.cfm**) in the html/stockimagenation folder.**

2. **Press Ctrl+Shift+F10 to bring up the Databases panel in the Application panel group.**
   If you don't have a page open when this panel opens, the links inside are grayed out.

3. **Click the RDS login link (number 4).**

4. **Type your RDS login and press the OK button.**
   The information in the Databases panel changes after you login to reveal some pre-defined Data Sources.

Tutorial
» Adding a ColdFusion Datasource (Locally-Windows Only)

In this tutorial, you create a DSN (Datasource Name) to add a data source to your Dreamweaver environment. If you develop locally (Windows XP Pro, NT, or 2000) and install ColdFusion MX Server (per the instructions in Appendix C), you use ColdFusion MX Administrator to add a data source. Developers using a remotely hosted Web server should skip this tutorial and complete the next one instead.

1. **In Dreamweaver, press Ctrl+F10 to bring up the Bindings panel in the Application panel group.**

2. **Open** `index.cfm` **(the home page).**

3. **Click the data source link (number 5 on the list).**
   This opens the ColdFusionMX Administrator, which was installed when you installed ColdFusion MX Server (Developer Edition) using the instructions provided in Appendix C.

4. **Enter the Login password you set up when you installed ColdFusion MX Server and Login.**

5. **In the Data Sources screen, type** stock **into the Data Source Name field and choose Microsoft Access as the Driver type.**

6. **Click the Add button on the Microsoft Access screen.**

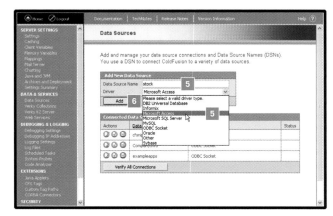

7. **Click the Browse Server button for the database file and navigate to your C:\CFusionMX\wwwroot\stockimagenation\database folder and select the** `stock.mdb` **database file.**

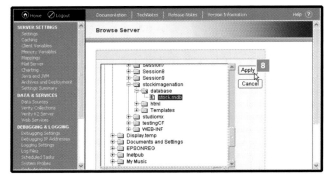

8. **Click the Apply button, which returns you to the previous screen with the path set in the Database File field.**
   The path to the database is included in the DSN you are creating. The path is C:\CFusionMX\wwwroot\stockimagenation\database\stock.mdb.

9. **Click the Submit button to build your new DSN.**
   The new data source is available in your Data Sources table. The small icons to the left of each data source allow you to edit, verify, and delete the data source.

10. **Log out and close the CFMX Administrator. Return to Dreamweaver MX.**
   You can close the home page in Dreamweaver. Because you have your DSN set up locally, you won't need to complete the next tutorial, but keep in mind that it contains the steps you follow when you are ready to move your site to a remote Web server for publishing.

Tutorial
» Adding a DSN on the Remote Web Server

Unfortunately, most hosting companies don't allow customers to add their own DSNs and require you to e-mail or contact their support staff to have the DSN created for you. CrystalTech does allow you to create your own DSNs, which is why I think that they are an outstanding CFMX hosting company. If you purchased an account there, this tutorial walks you through the steps of creating the DSN online. If your hosting company does allow you to create DSNs but the company is not CrystalTech, much of what is shown may vary, but the concepts are the same. And, if you're required to ask for the DSN to be created, the concepts also apply, including where you locate the database and how it is named.

It's important that you use the suggested name because all references to DSNs or connections in the following sessions indicate using this DSN.

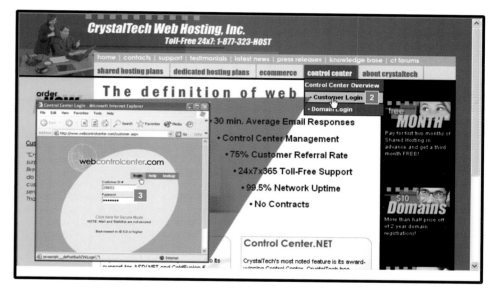

1. **Open a Web browser (the examples use Internet Explorer 6) and go to** `www.crystaltech.com`.

2. **From the Control Center button menu, choose Customer Login.**
   This pops open a new window with the customer login form.

3. **Enter your customer ID and login information as given in the e-mail that CrystalTech sends when your site has been set up. The customer ID is a number. Log in.**

4. **In your Control Center, choose Site Admin→DSN Admin.**

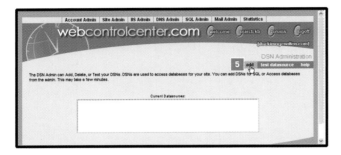

5. **In the DSN Admin page, click the Add button.**

6. **When the page refreshes, choose Access from the Database Type menu.**
   This refreshes the page again to add new fields to the form.

7. **Scroll down to the File Path field and select the database folder, and then click the Select button just below the field.**
   When the page refreshes, you see the stock.mdb database file you uploaded earlier.

8. **Click once on the stock.mdb file in the File Path field.**

9. **Set the DSN Name to stock and add your Username and Password (twice, to verify).**
   The Username is not your customer ID. It is the FTP login name that CrystalTech sent you via e-mail. For security purposes, the username is deliberately wrong in the example shown.

10. **Press the Save button to the upper right of the form.**
    When the page refreshes (it may take a minute), you are returned to the DSN Admin page where your current datasources field displays your new DSN.

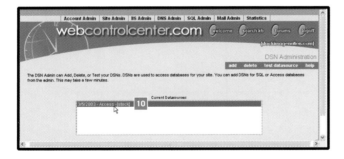

» Session Review

In this session, you added information about the remote Web server and selected a server access method. You added the same information in the Testing Server category of the site definition to create a URL prefix for your site. Finally, you set up a DSN either locally using ColdFusion MX Administrator or remotely through a hosting company such as CrystalTech. Test what you have learned with these questions. Answers can be found in the tutorials noted in parentheses.

1. What is a remote root folder? ("Tutorial: Defining a Local Web and Testing Server")

2. Why must you place your pages on a Web server? ("Tutorial: Defining a Local Web and Testing Server")

3. If you decide to develop remotely, which access method do you choose? ("Tutorial: Defining a Remote Web and Testing Server")

4. What is a DSN? ("Tutorial: Specifying the RDS Login Information for ColdFusion Server").

5. Which language is used to communicate with a database? ("Tutorial: Specifying the RDS Login Information for ColdFusion Server")

6. What does the Put command do? ("Tutorial: Transferring Files to the Web Server")

7. Is the DSN name on your hosting server a unique name different than your local server? ("Tutorial: Adding a ColdFusion Datasource")

CrystalTech Web Hosting, Inc.
Toll-Free 24x7: 1-877-323-HOST

home | contacts | support | testimonials | latest news | press releases | knowledge base | ct forums

shared hosting plans   dedicated hosting plans   ecommerce   control center   about crystaltech

Control Center Overview
- Customer Login
- Domain Login

The definition of web

- 30 min. Average Email Responses
- Control Center Management
- 75% Customer Referral Rate
- 24x7x365 Toll-Free Support
- 99.5% Network Uptime
- No Contracts

free **MONTH**
Pay for first two months of Shared Hosting in advance and get a third month FREE!

$10 **Domains**
More than half price off of 2 year domain registrations!

Control Center Login — Microsoft Internet Explorer

File   Edit   View   Favorites   Tools   Help

Address http://www.webcontrolcenter.com/customer.aspx

webcontrolcenter.com

login   help   lookup

Customer ID #
29653
Password
••••••••

Click here for Secure Mode
NOTE: Mail and Statistics are not secured

Best viewed in IE 6.0 or higher

Control Center.NET

CrystalTech's most noted feature is its award-

Displaying Dynamic Data

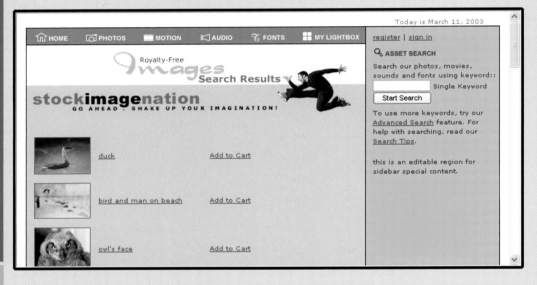

Recordsets and Dynamic Content with ColdFusion MX

In this session, you learn how to build a *recordset*—a subset of information pulled from a database—and use it to dynamically display content in your page. *Recordsets* are created through *Structured Language Queries* (SQL) that ask for specific data from the tables of a database. Tables may contain a lot more information than you need for any one page.

Queries can be used to compare and return data records against specific criteria. The database contains columns for AssetID, AssetFileName, AssetDesc, and Keywords. For example, you can build a query to request the ID, filename, and description of all assets that have a keyword of flower. The recordset returned by the query contains *only* this information about assets records that match the criteria. The table also contains pricing and other details about assets, but that information is not included in the recordset. Using a recordset means that less contact with the database (and therefore the Web and application server) is required; the recordset is placed into temporary memory for quick recall. When the data is no longer needed, the recordset is destroyed and the memory released.

Dreamweaver MX contains an easy-to-use recordset builder that offers a simple or advanced interface for defining queries. As you work through the tutorials, you see just how easy it is to build SQL statements to display records returned by a search page; to display dynamic images, text and links; and to request the server build enough HTML structures to display the returned data.

TOOLS YOU'LL USE
The Databases panel, Bindings panel, Server Behaviors panel,
Insert→Application Objects menu choices, the Recordset Builder

MATERIALS NEEDED
Your stockimagenation root folder or the session15_starterfiles folder

TIME REQUIRED
90 minutes

Discussion

ColdFusion Markup and SQL Basics

ColdFusion Markup Language is a tag-based language like HTML, making it simple to write and understand. When you build a ColdFusion page, you are building a *ColdFusion Template*. This kind of template isn't like a Dreamweaver MX Template; it doesn't contain the same kind of markup used in Dreamweaver to update pages. Instead, it's an HTML page that contains *CFML* markup. A .CFM page opens and closes with the same tags as any .HTM page:

```
<html>
  <head>
  <title></title>
  </head>
  <body>
    <cfoutput> Today is #DateFormat(Now(),
        'mm/dd/yyyy')# </cfoutput>
  </body>
</html>
```

CF tags are embedded into the HTML of the page by Dreamweaver MX as you build queries with the Simple and Advanced Recordset Builder dialog boxes.

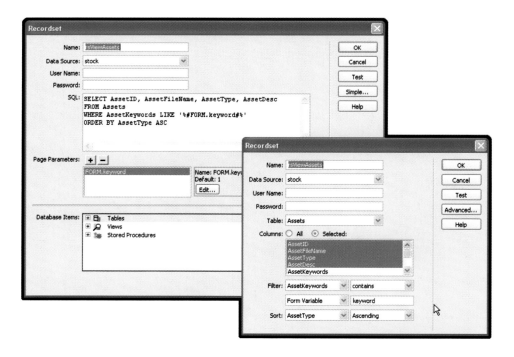

To better understand what the builder is doing, it helps to have at least a rudimentary knowledge of basic SQL elements. If you don't completely understand everything listed, don't worry—the idea is just to introduce you to the vocabulary and concepts of SQL and basic CFML.

The Building Blocks of SQL

Commands are the verbs of the Structured Query Language (SQL) and are task-oriented. Commands determine the type of operation you perform. The four basic commands you use in Dreamweaver MX are SELECT, UPDATE, INSERT, and DELETE. Commands are used to build queries. A *clause* refines an SQL query. Common clauses include FROM, INTO, WHERE, ORDER BY, GROUP BY, JOIN, and SET. *Operators* are used to construct compound conditional and comparison expressions. They perform calculations and make comparisons between expressions.

Table 15.1: Operators

Operator	Description
=	Equal to
<>	Not equal to
<	Less than
>	Greater than
<=	Less than or equal to
>=	Greater than or equal to
+	Plus (as in addition)
-	Minus (as in subtraction)
/	Divided by (division)
*	Multiply by (multiplication)
AND	Conditional-both must evaluate to true
OR	Conditional-one or both must evaluate to true
IN	Value is in a list
LIKE	Used in wildcard comparisons, contained in
EXISTS	Tests for a nonempty recordset
NOT	Ignores a condition

Why is it important to build a vocabulary of SQL terms? Imagine reading the stock market pages in a newspaper; if you didn't understand a little bit about the symbols and jargon used, you couldn't make heads or tails of the information and certainly couldn't use the information to purchase stocks! The same can be said about SQL and ColdFusion Markup. Understanding even a little bit of what each element represents allows you to "read" the code Dreamweaver inserts into your pages as you build queries.

Take a look at this query:

```
SELECT LastName, FirstName
FROM Registration
WHERE LastName = Jones
```

You can read that, can't you? And you understand exactly what is being done because you understand the basic command (SELECT), clause (FROM), and operator (=). The rest of the code references specific parts of a database: a table and data columns. Additional concepts to understand are *literal, expression, parameter,* and *variable.* Don't panic! This is stuff you actually already know, even if you think you don't.

A *literal* is a symbol or letter that stands for itself, as opposed to representing something else. For example, in some programming languages, $ indicates the end of a line of code, but as a literal, $ means dollars. Literals, in CFML, are generally surrounded by double quotes, which mean that what is contained within is to be used *as is,* without evaluation (literally).

In its most basic form, an *expression* is a single element, like 5, John, cat, or WhichAsset. When combined with operators, (compound) expressions evaluate data. For example, 1 + 1 = 2 is a mathematical compound expression; John is 6'4" and Bob is 5' 9". 6'4" is greater than 5'9". All of these are expressions. Expressions are the building blocks of CFML.

A *variable* is a name associated with data. It stores or contains a value. The values can change over time (it can vary—get it? variables). There are many kinds of variables, from local (which apply to the current page) to session (which apply to the visit). Variables in ColdFusion are used to "hold" information like a cup holds water or tea or coffee. The cup's purpose is the same, even if the contents change. In this session, you use form and URL variables to pass information from page to page.

Finally, a *parameter* is a measurable factor that is used to include or exclude data in a recordset. For example, you can use the parameter Form.LastName, which holds the variable value entered by the site visitor into the form field LastName, to include or exclude matching data in a query, basically saying something like "give me all the data for a record where the record's LastName column matches Form.LastName.value." The value is measurable.

ColdFusion Markup

In practice, you probably won't be writing CFML tags by hand—not yet anyway. But there are some tags and basic syntax that it helps to understand. Most (but not all) CFML tags are pairs; they have an opening and closing tag. `<cfoutput></cfoutput>` is the one you see most often. This pair tells the ColdFusion engine to write what is between the tags. You use this tag when you want an expression evaluated and written, as in

```
<cfoutput> Today is #DateFormat(Now(), 'mm/dd/yyyy')#
</cfoutput>
```

You might notice the pound signs surrounding the expression. Pound signs are used to separate expressions from literals. "`Today is`" is a literal that is simply written without evaluation, whereas #DateFormat(Now(), 'mm/dd/yyyy')# is an expression requiring evaluation. Pound signs occur around variable names because they require evaluation, too.

Luckily for you, you don't have to know this stuff to build ColdFusion pages. (I knew you'd like that!) In most cases, Dreamweaver MX adds the necessary tags and places pound signs around your expressions where needed. If you want to see the resulting CFML added to your page by Dreamweaver after you insert or bind data to a page or add a server behavior, you can select the text, image, or other object that uses the CFML and use Dreamweaver's Quick Tag Editor to see the code.

But just as you should seek to familiarize yourself with HTML tags to better understand what you are building, so should you buddy up with CF tags. You hand-write them before you know it!

Tutorial
» Building a Recordset

To obtain the data that is dynamically displayed in your ColdFusion template (page), you must query the database. In Session 14, you set up the DSN to the stock.mdb database. In this tutorial you develop a search results page to display the data returned from a search query. To start this tutorial, you use your Dreamweaver template to build a new page in the dynamic_app folder.

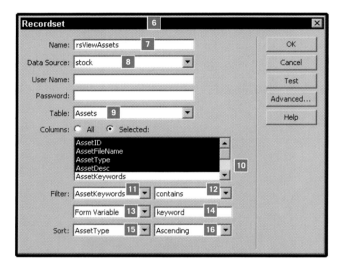

1. **Press F11 to bring up the Assets panel and click the Template Assets icon.**

2. **Right-click (Ctrl-click) the MainLayout template and choose New From Template.**

3. **When the new document opens, choose File→Save As. Navigate to the html/stockimagenation/dynamic_apps folder and save the page as** search_results.cfm.

4. **Change the page title to** stockimagenation :: search results.

5. **If the Bindings panel isn't open, press Ctrl+F10 (⌘+F10) to open it.**

6. **Press the Add (+) button and choose Recordset (Query).**
   This opens Dreamweaver's Recordset Builder, typically in its Simple mode. If yours is in the Advanced mode, click the Simple button found on the right side of the dialog box.

7. **Name your new recordset** rsViewAssets.
   It's common to use rs (for recordset) to start the names of recordsets. This makes it easy to identify your recordsets.

8. **From the Data Source menu, choose stock.**
   The Data Source menu contains all data sources defined in ColdFusion Administrator.

9. **Choose Assets from the Table menu.**
   Other tables in the database are listed here, too, but Assets is already selected because it is first in the database.

10. **In the Columns area, select Columns. Shift-select the first four columns, including AssetID, AssetFileName, AssetType, and AssetDesc.**
    Whether you choose All or Selected, you are invoking the SQL command SELECT. So far, you've completed the basics of building a simple recordset to SELECT all the data from the four columns chosen from the Assets table. But you won't be displaying all the data—remember, this page is going to return results from a search.

11. **From the first Filter menu, select AssetKeywords.**
    Filtering includes or excludes data based on some criteria.

12. Use the second Filter menu to select contains.

This is a menu of *operators* and *clauses* used in SQL. Contains is selected because the AssetKeywords column contains one *or more* keywords but the keyword form field contains only one keyword. Because the words will not be an exact match, the operator cannot be EQUALS (= or EQ).

13. In the third Filter menu, choose Form Variable.

This menu offers options for selecting all kinds of data sources, from form variables to URL parameters to cookies or even entered values.

14. In the final Filter field, type keyword.

The search form (in the sidebar of almost all the site pages) contains a field named keyword. When the form is submitted using the POST method, the value of the keyword field is posted as `Form.keyword.value`.

15. In the first Sort menu, select the AssetType column.

Sorting allows you to modify how the results or data set is returned to the page. Sorting writes a *clause* using ORDER BY.

16. In the second Sort menu, choose Ascending.

If the data is numerical, ascending starts with the lowest value, as in 1, 2, 3. Because the AssetType column contains words, ascending writes them as audio, font, image, and movie—the four types of assets provided by stockimagenation. But the advantage of sorting allows assets to be grouped by their AssetType.

17. Click the Advanced button on the right side of the Recordset Builder dialog box to see what your SQL looks like in a more revealing interface.

The Advanced mode displays the actual commands, operators, and clauses you've written by making choices in the Simple mode's menus.

18. Press the Edit button in the Page Parameters fields. Type the value purple and click OK to close the dialog box.

Because this SQL statement requires a parameter, you add a default value for testing purposes.

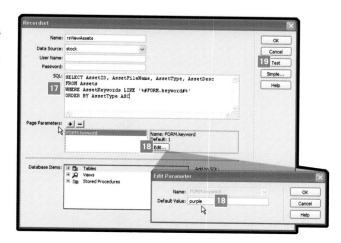

<NOTE>

A form variable is obtained when a form is posted to the page called by the action attribute.

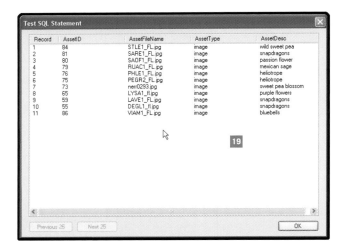

19. **Press the Test button.**
    Using your default parameter, a set of data is returned in the Test SQL Statement window. Click OK to close this test window.

20. **Click OK to close the Recordset Builder window without going back to the Simple mode.**
    Switching back to Simple mode can reset the page parameter value to 1.

21. **Select the** search_results.cfm **page from the dynamic_app folder and press the Put button at the top of the Site panel. Click Yes to save the page. When asked if you want to include independent files, click No.**
    Remember, the saved page must reside on the server to test it, whether using a local or remote server. In this case, there's nothing to see, so you won't test your page just yet.

22. **Keep this page open for the following tutorials.**

Tutorial

» Displaying Dynamic Text

In this tutorial, you insert a data column in your page to display recordset data as dynamic text. Because the query may return one or more records, you build a new structure to hold the data so that it can be repeated as often as needed to display all results. You modify the existing `search_results.cfm` page a bit and insert a table with rows that later repeat as needed.

1. **Click to place your cursor in the main content region.**

2. **Open the Assets panel.**

3. **Insert the image** `img_searchresults.gif`. **Type** Image for Search Results and Stockimagenation logo **for the alternative text and click OK.**

4. **Press your right Arrow key to move past the image and insert a new table with one row, three columns, zero padding and border, 10px of spacing, and a width of 300px.**
   The width is incidental and you ultimately remove that value to create a table whose width is set by the data it contains.

5. **Insert your cursor into the second cell of the table.**

6. **In the Bindings panel, expand the Recordset to expose all the data columns available.**

7. **Select AssetDesc and press the Insert button at the bottom of the panel.**

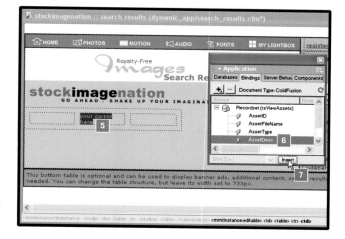

8. **Insert your cursor into the third table cell and type** Add to Cart; **then select it and give it a null link (type** javascript:; **into the Link field or select it from the Link History).**

9. **Select the** `<table>` **tag using the Tag selector and remove the Width value in the Property inspector.**

10. **Save your page and use the Put button to move it to the Web server. Keep the page open for the next tutorial.**

Tutorial

» Inserting a Dynamic Image

Each asset contains an image thumbnail, whether it is an actual photo or movie animation (for photographic and motion assets) or an icon (for audio or font assets). In this tutorial, you use the AssetFileName data column to display the actual thumbnail for the asset. The most common mistake beginners make, whether they are using ColdFusion, ASP, or any other server model, is that they try to display the image by inserting the data column, just as you did with the dynamic text. But if you think about this method, you can figure out why it won't work. Using that method, the expression is evaluated and the actual text of the value is inserted, which is not exactly what you wanted. For example, if the AssetFileName evaluates as `mydog.jpg`, that is what you would see (literally)—not the image whose *source* is `mydog.gif`.

When you set up a database table to use image assets, you aren't actually storing the image. You could do just that but not all databases allow it and it also requires a ton more space, making your database very large indeed. Instead, you make decisions about how to *reference* the image. Many new developers try to store the entire path to the image. Does this make sense? It doesn't, really, because you first have to know the exact site structure prior to entering the data into the database and secondly, if you decide to change the structure of the site or the location of the image or the location of the page referencing the image, you're forced to change all the values in your database. Yikes! Instead, you simply reference the filename of the image and build a relative path structure in Dreamweaver. This way your path structure is relative to the page *wherever it is*, is updateable by Dreamweaver's outstanding site management tools and doesn't affect the database values whatsoever!

1. **Insert your cursor into the first cell of the table you built in the previous tutorial.**
   If your cursor is in a different cell or it's hard to click into the collapsed cell, simply Tab (forward) or Shift+Tab (backwards) from other cells until you are back in the first cell.

2. **Press the Insert Image object button in the Common tools of the Insert bar.**

3. **Navigate upwards out of the html directory to the AssetResources folder and into the thumbs directory.**
   At this point, you should see ../../../AssetResources/thumbs/ in the URL field of the dialog box.

4. **Copy the URL path.**

5. **Select Data Sources at the top of the dialog box.**
   Instead of folders, you are offered the recordset you built with your SQL.

6. **Expand the recordset listing and select AssetFileName.**
   Now the URL path reads
   `<cfoutput>#rsViewAssets.AssetFileName#</cfoutput>`, which tells the ColdFusion engine to evaluate the expression to determine the image source file.

7. **Insert your cursor before the expression (in front of <cfoutput>) and paste the URL path you copied in step 4, and then OK the new URL. Click OK.**
   You just created a relative dynamic path, and Dreamweaver can manage the path structure if you should decide to reorganize the pages in the site.

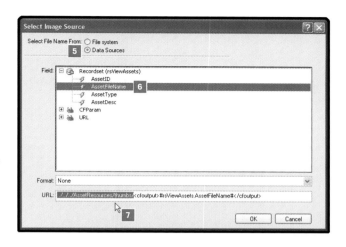

8. **Click Cancel when the Alternative text dialog box opens. For this image you add the alt text in the Property inspector. Type** stockimagenation **in the Alt field.**
   If you enter the alt text in the accessibility dialog box, the code is placed inside the `<cdoutput>` tags, but when you enter it in the Property inspector, it's placed outside the ColdFusion tags, which in this case make a difference.

`<NOTE>`
Did you notice that this image doesn't have a width or height? Because you cannot know the required width or height, you don't enter a value at all. This allows the image to be whatever width and height it is. If a value were entered and was not the actual width and height of whatever record is displayed, the image would be distorted to fit the entered values.

9. **To dynamically add the asset type to the Alt Text description, keep the dynamic image selected and click to Code view.**

10. **Insert your cursor just after stockimagenation (and before the quote mark) in the Alt Text string and add a space, followed by two colons (::) and another space.**

11. **Open the Bindings panel and select the AssetDesc data column. Click and drag it to the code view and drop it just after the space you added in the Alt text string.**

12. **Press the Enter (Return) key to add a space and then select AssetType in the Bindings panel and drag it to Code view.**
    The figure shows what the code looks like when you are done.

13. **Switch to Design view and save the page. Put the** `search_results.cfm` **page to the Web server.**

14. **Preview it in a browser. Click OK to update the file on the testing server.**
    You should see one image and if you hover over it, you should see the Alt text. Notice that the Alt text attached to the image in the database displays automatically behind the text you added.

15. **Select the image, in the Property inspector type** 1 **for the Border, and enter** 2 **for both vspace and hspace.**
    Normally, you do this sort of thing with CSS, but Netscape 4x hates the Border property and seldom does the right thing when it is applied via CSS.

    < N O T E >
    Box and Border are not well-supported in Netscape 4x. The combination causes this browser to treat the border and box as a separate element from the image, displaying the box and border below the image.

16. **Open the CSS Styles panel and add a new style. Select Make Custom Class, name it .dynamicdisplay in the** `main.css` **style sheet, and click OK. Select the Block category and select Text Align - Left and OK the dialog box.**

17. **Click on the search results page title image; then select the** `<td>` **to the left of the** `<img>` **tag in the Tag selector. Apply the class dynamicdisplay.**
    This forces the data table to align left. It was aligning center because the tables are inheriting the align=center from the `<div>` tags that encompass the entire layout.

18. **Save and preview the page. Keep the page open for the next tutorial.**

Tutorial

» Adding a Dynamic Link to Open a Details Page

In the search results page, different assets are returned based on a keyword search. Chances are that the site visitor will want to examine one or more of the returned assets in detail. To show asset details, you'll build a link to pop open a new browser window to display the details.cfm page you built in Session 9. That page will be used to display additional data for whichever asset that the visitor selects. The *detail* page knows which asset to display because you'll pass the AssetID value as a URL parameter. A URL parameter is information passed via a URL link in the *master* page.

Dreamweaver MX contains a built-in Application Object that builds a similar set of pages that are called Master-Detail page sets. The problem with using the Application Object is that code is inserted into the page in a rather uncontrolled manner. If you're using a pre-existing page, the code is inserted at the bottom of your existing HTML — probably not what you want. You've already built the master page — all that remains is to pass a parameter that contains a unique key for the asset to the details page. A unique key in an Access database is a primary key. When you build a database, you should always incorporate a primary key to clearly identify a record. In this case, the AssetID data column has been included in the rsViewAssets recordset. You'll start by building a null link and using Dreamweaver's built-in Open Browser Window behavior to pop open the new browser window, then go on to make the page that loads dynamically selected by passing the variable WhichAsset. The detail page's recordset will read the current value for WhichAsset and filter its data results by the AssetID passed.

1. **Select the dynamic text reference in the second table cell ({rsViewAssets.AssetDesc}) and use the Property inspector to create a null link. Type** javascript:; **into the link field or choose it from your Link History.**

2. **If the Behaviors panel isn't open, press Shift+F3 to open. Click Add (+) and select the behavior Open Browser Window.**

3. **In the Open Browser Window dialog box, click the Browse button and select** details.cfm **from the dynamic_app folder.**

4. **Click the Parameters button to the right of the URL field.**

5. **Insert your cursor just below the Name heading and type** WhichAsset.

6. **Tab to move your cursor below the Value heading and click the Dynamic Data icon (yellow lighting bolt) next to that field.**

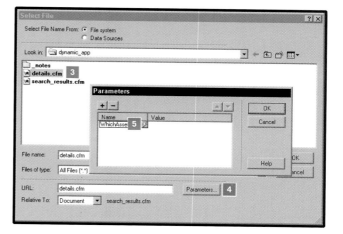

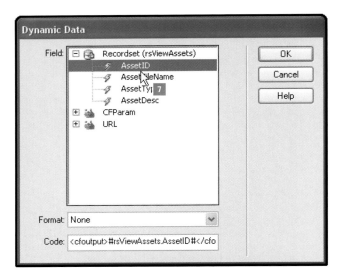

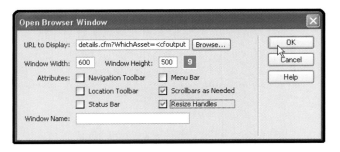

7. **In the Dynamic Data dialog box, expand the recordset (rsViewAssets) and select AssetID.**

8. **OK all the dialog boxes and return to the Open Browser Window behavior window.**
   The URL in the URL to Display field is dynamic; it should now read details.cfm?WhichAsset=#rsViewAssets. AssetID#, which passes the WhichAsset parameter for the specific asset whose link was clicked.

9. **Set the Window Width to** 500 **and Height to** 500. **Give the visitor a scroll bar and a resize option and close the Open Browser Window dialog box.**

10. **If you don't see** onClick **in the Behaviors panel, click the arrow in the center of the behavior and select** onClick. **If you don't see this option, select Show Events for and select 4.0 and later Browsers. Now select** onClick.

11. **Save your page, put it to the Web server, and preview it in a browser. Try clicking the link.**

    Although the details page doesn't yet display the dynamic content, the link is working. Now you want the image to be clickable, too.

12. **Click into the text link in the search page and select the <a> tag from the Tag selector.**

13. **Press Ctrl+T (Cmd+T) to call the Quick Tag Editor, which should open to the Edit Tag function.**

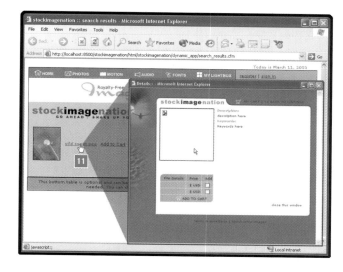

14. **Select and copy all the code within the tag except for the angle brackets, and then click back into the document.**

    The Editor closes.

15. **Select the dynamic image and type** `javascript:;` **into its link field.**

16. **Select the <a> tag for the image and press Ctrl+T to open the Quick Tag Editor.**

17. **Replace <a> href="`javascript:;`"> with the copied code.**

    ```
    <a href="javascript:;"
    onClick="MM_openBrWindow('details.cfm?WhichAsset=<cf
    output>#rsViewAssets.AssetID#</cfoutput>',
    '','scrollbars=yes,resizable=yes,width=600,height=50
    0')">
    ```

18. **Save and put the page to the Web server. Preview it to test the image link.**

    Next you replace the static references of the details page with dynamic ones.

19. **Close your** `search_results.cfm` **page.**

Tutorial
» Using URL Parameters to Pass AssetID to the Details Page

Now you're ready to use the data passed in the URL parameters of the links in the search_results page. You can use the AssetID to build the recordset to pull all the data for the asset and then use the information to create a dynamic page title, display a dynamic image, and so forth.

1. **Open** details.cfm **from the dynamic_app folder.**

2. **In the Bindings panel, add a recordset. Click the Simple button if it's present; if not, you are already there. Use the following settings; then close the recordset dialog box:**
   > Name: rsViewAssets
   > Data Source: stock
   > Table: Assets
   > Columns: All
   > Filter: AssetID = URL Parameter AssetID (fields 1-4)
   > Sort: None

   After you close the Recordset dialog box, a new data source is added to the Databases folder. Setting AssetID equal to a URL parameter causes Dreamweaver to add the CFML code for <CFParam>, a method it uses to store the variable.

3. **Double-click the image placeholder, be sure File system is selected, and then navigate to the AssetResources/medium folder.**

4. **Copy the URL path.**

5. **Select Data Sources and expand the recordset to choose AssetFileName.**
   Sound familiar? This is just what you did in the search page.

6. **Paste the copied folder path in front of the dynamic code in the URL field and close the dialog box. Remove the width and height for the placeholder image.**

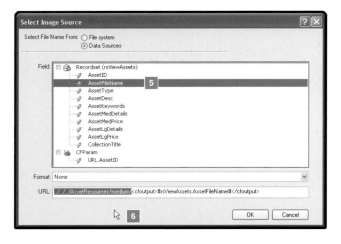

7. **Select Title paragraph in the document.**

8. **In the Bindings panel, select AssetFileName and click the Insert button.**
   The dynamic reference replaces the static text.

9. **In the document place your cursor at the end of the Description label and press Enter (Return). Select AssetDesc in the Bindings panel and click the Insert button.**
   If the new dynamic text is red, set the class to None using the Tag Selector.

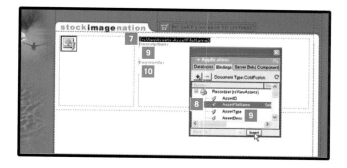

10. **In the document, place your cursor at the end of the Keywords label and press Enter (Return). Select AssetKeywords in the Binding panel and click the Insert button.**

11. **In the orange detail table, highlight File Size | Resolution | Dimensions and type File Details.**
    The title was changed after the page was initially developed, which happens in real life.

12. **In the orange detail table, insert your cursor in the cell below the table header (File Details). In the Binding panel select AssetMedDetails and insert it.**

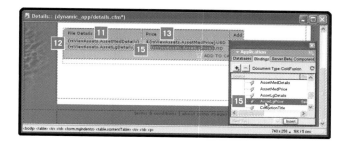

13. **Tab over to the next cell and type $USD. Insert your cursor between the dollar sign and USD and insert AssetMedPrice.**

14. **Right-click (Control-click) and select Table→Insert Rows or Columns. Select Row, 1 and Below the Selection and click OK.**

15. **Repeat steps 11 and 12 in the next row, using AssetLgDetails and AssetLgPrice.**
    See how easy this is?

16. **Choose View→Head Content.**

17. **Select the Page Title icon and switch to Code and Design view.**

18. **Insert your cursor just after the static title text (detail ::).**

19. **In the Bindings panel, select AssetFileName and click the Insert button.**

20. **Save your page and upload (Put) it on the Web server and close it.**

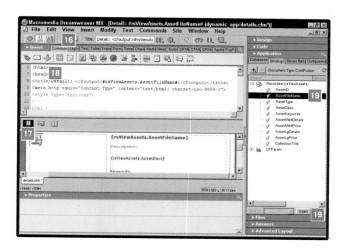

Tutorial
» Using the Repeat Region Server Behavior

Now you use a Server Behavior to show more than one record in your `search_results.cfm` page. A Server Behavior is application logic that is pre-defined in Dreamweaver MX. You can access Server Behaviors from the Server Behavior panel.

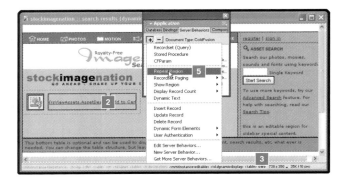

1. **Open** `search_results.cfm` **from the dynamic_app folder and switch back to Design view.**

2. **Insert your cursor into the table with the dynamic image.**

3. **Use the Tag selector to select the** `<tr>`.

4. **Press Ctrl+F9 (⌘+F9) to open the Server Behaviors panel.**
   You should see all the server-side scripting (behaviors) you already added to this page in the Server Behaviors panel. Now you add another behavior to repeat the table row for all records.

5. **Click Add (+) and select Repeat Region.**

6. **In the Repeat Regions dialog box, select Show to All Records and click OK.**
   Paging, which is what you would have to do if you show sets of results, involves more complex structures that require passing variables from page to page. You get an opportunity to do this later.

7. **Save the page and move it to the Web server.**

8. **Preview the page in a Web browser. Close the page.**
   Now the page displays lots of assets (images) that match the default purple search value. Now it's time to set up the search form to populate the parameter with a real keyword.

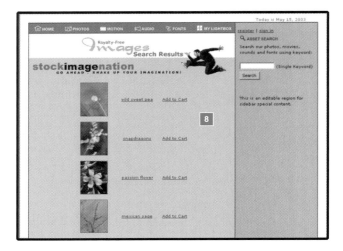

Tutorial
» Passing the Keyword via a Form Post

Every main page in the site has a simple search form in the sidebar, including the search_results page. In this brief tutorial, you empower the search form in the home page (stockimagenation/index.cfm) to call the search_results.cfm page. You repeat the process in the Main Layout template so that all future pages have the search form set up.

1. Open index.cfm from the stockimagenation folder.

2. Select the Single Keyword text in the sidebar.

3. Select the <form#search> tag using the Tag selector.

4. Press the Browse folder icon next to the Action field in the Property inspector and navigate to the dynamic_app folder.

5. Select search_results.cfm and OK the dialog box to close it.

6. In the Property inspector make sure that the method is POST. Post passes the form values via form variables.

7. Save your page and upload it to the Web server.

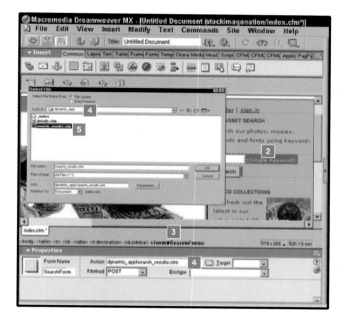

8. Preview the home page and enter the word turtle into the keyword form field and press the Search button.
   You should have at least three results for turtle.

9. Close the page.

10. Press F11 to open the Assets panel and click to the Template Assets.

11. Double-click MainLayout.dwt to open it. Repeat steps 2 through 8.

12. Save your template and update when asked. Close the update dialog box.

13. Open search_results.cfm and double-click the recordset in the Bindings panel.

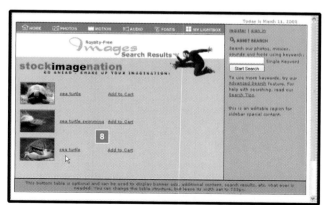

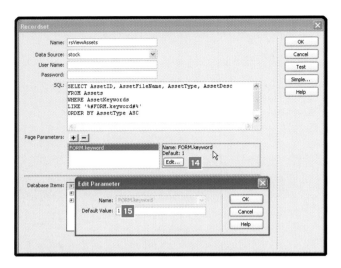

14. **Switch to Advanced mode and click the Edit button for the Page Parameters.**

15. **Replace purple with the number** 1.

16. **Close the recordset builder and save the page.**

17. **Put the** search_results.cfm **page to the server.**

18. **Preview the home page and type** frog **into the search field. Press the search button.**

    When the keyword search doesn't return results, the visitor gets an empty page. While it isn't a problem, it also isn't very user-friendly. In the next tutorial, you add some text to be displayed when the results produce nothing.

Tutorial

» Using the Show Region Server Behavior

To provide a more user-friendly experience, you add some text to the `search_results.cfm` page that only displays when no results are returned. One way to think about no results is to remember that the results, if there are any, are contained in a recordset. If there are no results, the recordset is empty. Dreamweaver MX includes a server behavior that shows or hides a region, such as a paragraph of text, based on whether the recordset is empty or not.

1. **Open `search_results.cfm` if it isn't already open.**

2. **Select the image in the main content area.**

3. **Press your right Arrow key to move to the right of the image and add a new table using these values:**
   Rows: 1
   Columns: 1
   Width: 300px
   Padding: 0
   Spacing: 10px
   Border: 0

4. **Type the following into the single-celled table:** Sorry, your keyword did not produce results. Try a new keyword in the search field in the orange sidebar.

5. **Select the new `<table>` tag in the Tag selector.**

6. **From the Server Behaviors panel, click (+) select Show Region→If the Recordset is Empty. OK the dialog box to select rsViewAssets.**
   Now if the recordset returns no results, the new message displays. If there are results, the region does not display.

7. **Delete the *Add to cart* text from the table with the image placeholder.**
   This page contains thumbnails only and won't be used to make the actual purchase.

8. **Save the page and upload (Put) it on the Web server.**

9. **Use the Site panel to select the home page. Press F12 to preview it.**

10. **Enter frog as the keyword and press the search button.**
    Just as before, no assets match the keyword frog, so your new message is displayed.

11. **Use the sidebar search form to enter the keyword bird and submit the search again.**
    This time, the recordset is not empty, so the message isn't shown. Instead, your search_results includes many assets.

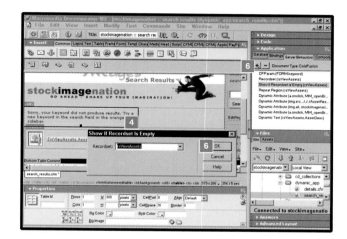

» Session Review

In this session, you really learned a lot. You learned how to gain access to your database information and how to display it as text, images and links. You learned how to use data columns in lots of places, including the title tag and alt text. Using server behaviors, you learned how to get the application server to add HTML to display all records in a database and to show a region based on the state of a recordset. You increased your vocabulary of terms, adding terms like expression, literal, operator and clause. You also learned how to pass parameters and how to build path structures that are both relative and dynamic. Wow. Congratulations! Now test your knowledge. The answers can be found in the sections noted in parentheses.

1. What is a recordset? (Session Introduction)

2. What is a common prefix for a recordset name? ("Tutorial: Building a Recordset")

3. When you pass information from a form with the POST method, what are you passing? ("Tutorial: Passing the Keyword via the Form Post")

4. What is an expression? ("Discussion: ColdFusion Markup and SQL Basics")

5. What is the CF tag that tells the ColdFusion engine to write what is between the tags? ("Tutorial: Inserting a Dynamic Image")

6. How do you preview your dynamic page in the Dreamweaver MX workspace? ("Tutorial: Inserting a Dynamic Image")

7. Where do you access the Repeat Region and Show Region functions? ("Tutorial: Using the Repeat Region Server Behavior")

Adding a Shopping Cart

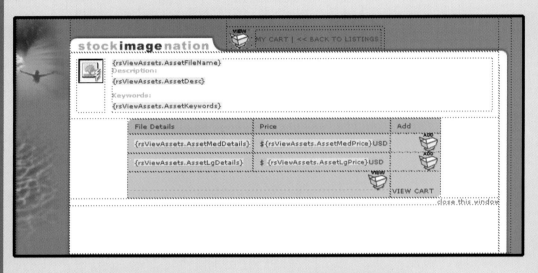

Tutorial: **Getting a PayPal Account**

Tutorial: **Installing the WebAssist Extension**

Tutorial: **Preparing the Orange Table for the Cart Buttons**

Tutorial: **Adding the Cart Buttons**

Tutorial: **Passing Dynamic Data to the Cart**

Selling on the Internet

Selling something via your Web site can be extremely easy as you see in this session. You learn how to accept payments using PayPal. PayPal is a Web-based service that allows individuals and small companies to act as if they had merchant accounts; that is, to accept credit cards and online checks in payment for products and services. I've used PayPal for years and have been very happy with them. You don't need a merchant account for credit cards nor a secure certificate. A company named WebAssist has made an extension to Dreamweaver that provides linkage to the PayPal service. The extension is provided for you on this book's CD-ROM. Using the extension you discover how very easy it is to accept payments online. You even see how you can customize the PayPal shopping cart a bit. By using PayPal your buyer adds purchases to the shopping cart on your site. At checkout, they are brought to PayPal's secure server. From there the buyer checks out. Once checkout is finished the buyer automatically returns to your site to a page that you specify.

TOOLS YOU'LL USE
WA PayPal shopping cart extension, Code view

MATERIALS NEEDED
Your root folder or the session16_starter files (`PayPal303.mxp`
in the session16/Extension folder. `checkoutsuccess.cfm`,
`checkoutsorry.cfm`, `checkout_logo.gif`,
`detail_cart.gif`, and `detail_cart_lt0.gif`)

TIME REQUIRED
60 minutes

Tutorial
» Getting a PayPal Account

You need to sign up to get a *free* PayPal account. A free personal account is available, but if you want to receive payments from your Web site, you have to upgrade to the Premier or business account. The only fee is a per-transaction fee. At the time of this writing, it was 2.9 percent and 30 cents per transaction fee.

1. **Go to www.paypal.com.**

2. **Click the Signup for your Free PayPal Account link.**

3. **Click the Business link.**

4. **Fill in the appropriate information for your business and click Continue.**

5. **You are presented with more forms to fill out. Fill them out and be sure to read the User Agreement and Privacy Policy. Check the boxes to state you've read them; then click Sign Up.**

6. **You are sent to a page that tells you an e-mail will arrive and what you need to do.**

<N O T E>

Of course, for people to buy your product or service, it has to be available for viewing on the Web. This means that your site has to reside on a host that, in this example, provides support for a ColdFusion scripting engine. You used Crystaltech in Session 14 as an example. When you are finished building your shopping cart application, you need to transfer your files to the server.

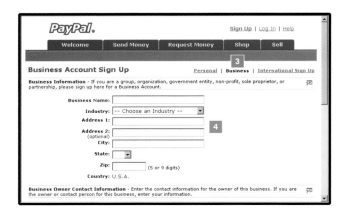

Tutorial
» Installing the WebAssist Extension

WebAssist (www.webassist.com) has allowed its PayPal extension to be placed on the CD-ROM for you. But you still want to go to the Web site to check out their great tutorials and other products. You use the free PayPal version of the shopping cart. When you are ready for a more complex shopping cart or require more functionality, check out the WA e-cart solution from WebAssist.

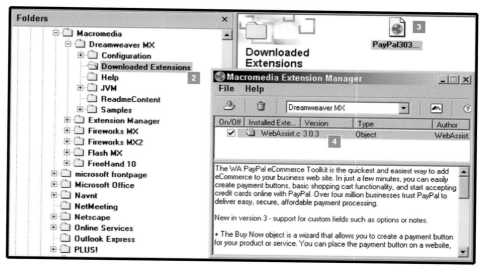

1. **Navigate to the session16/Extension folder and copy the** PayPal303.mxp **file.**

2. **Open your Dreamweaver/Dreamweaver MX/Downloaded Extensions folder and paste into it.**

3. **Double-click the** PayPal303.mxp **filename and it automatically opens the Extension Manager and installs the extension for you.**

4. **Click the Accept button and your extension is installed and shows up in the Extension Manager.**

<NOTE>
You don't have to put your downloaded extensions in the Dreamweaver folder to work; you can store them anywhere. This is just a good folder to use to help organize your extensions. Once you install the extension, Dreamweaver puts it in the Dreamweaver Downloaded Extensions folder.

Tutorial

» Preparing the Orange Table for the Cart Buttons

In this tutorial you add the Add and View Cart buttons to the `details.cfm` page to make it interact with PayPal, thereby allowing users to add items to their cart and to check out.

1. **Open the html/stockimagenation/dynamic_app folder.**
   Skip step 2 if you are using the session16_starter files.

2. **In the Site panel, scroll to the bottom and you see a folder for your desktop or your computer. Open this and navigate to your CD drive or anywhere you may have saved this book's CD files. In the session16 folder you see** `checkout_logo.gif`. **Select it and drag it to your stockimagenation/dynamic_app folder.**

   < N O T E >

   When you navigate to the CD from the Site panel, notice that there is a lock by the image name on a PC. Even if you copied the files from the CD to your PC, the files would still be locked. By dragging the file from the CD within Dreamweaver and dropping it in the appropriate folder, you avoid this issue.

3. **In the dynamic_app folder, double-click** `details.cfm` **to open it.**

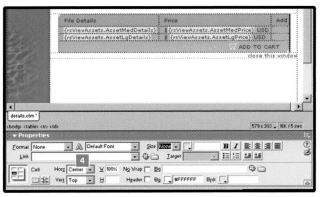

4. **Click in the bottom orange table and select the** `<td>` **tag to the left of the** `<table.ContentTable>` **tag. In the Property inspector, change the Horz field to Center.**
   The table is now centered in the space available.

Tutorial
» Adding the Cart Buttons

In this tutorial, you add the buttons that enable users to view and add items to the cart. If you are using the session16_starter files, you can skip step 1.

1. **In the Site panel, go to the desktop and navigate to the CD-ROM. Locate the session16 folder. Select the following files and then drag them to the html/stockimagenation/dynamic_app folder of your root:**

       checkoutsuccess.cfm
       checkoutsorry.cfm
       detail_cart.gif
       detail_cart_lt0

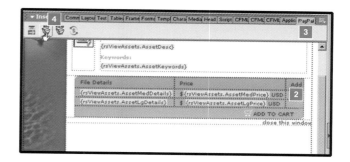

2. **Click in the first light orange cell below the ADD label to place your cursor.**

3. **From the Insert panel, click the PayPal tab that was added when you installed the extension.**

4. **Click the Add button.**

5. **Fill in your PayPal e-mail name if you have it set up already.**

6. **Click the PayPal link at the bottom to register if you haven't done so yet.**

<NOTE>
You can click the Help button at any time for more instructions.

7. **Click the Next button.**

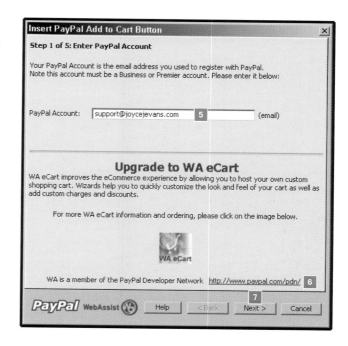

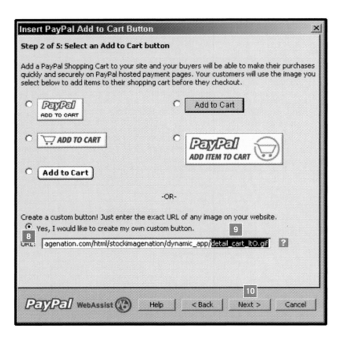

8. Click the "Yes, I would like to create my own custom button" option.

9. In the URL field type www.stockimagenation.com/html/stockimagenation/dynamic_app/detail_cart_ltO.gif.
   That is a capital O not a zero at the end of the name. This links to the image in the dynamic_app folder.

10. **Click Next.**

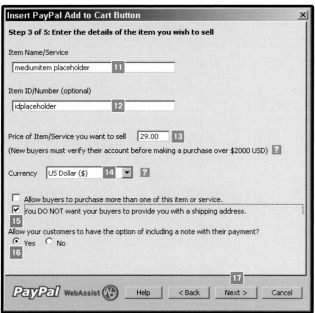

11. **In the Item Name/Service field, type** mediumitem placeholder. You change this later in the code to connect it to your database so that the item name is filled in dynamically. Don't worry; it's easier than it sounds.

12. **In the Item ID field, type** idplaceholder.

13. **Type** 29.00 **for the price.**

14. **Select the currency option that you want.**

15. **You can select one of the options that follow if you want.**
    In the example, 'You DO NOT want your buyers to provide you with a shipping address' is selected because there is nothing to ship.

16. **Select Yes if you want the customer to be able to leave additional instructions or a note.**

17. **Click Next.**

18. **Enter the path of your logo image. After the https://, enter the secure part of the path (get from your hosting server) and then the file path to the image, which is:** `stockimagenation/ dynamic_app/checkout_logo.gif`.
    For PayPal, the image must be 150x50. This is one of the images you transferred to the dynamic_app folder.

If you don't have a secure server setup for your site, you see a warning when you enter PayPal. It in no way makes the site unsecure, but it could scare your buyer away. Do not use a logo unless you can put it on a secure server somewhere.

19. **Click Next.**

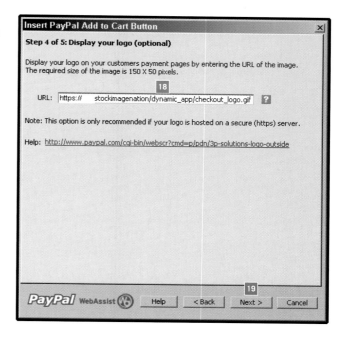

20. **In the first URL field type the path to the page that the buyer sees after they complete their purchase. The path is** `www.stockimagenation.com/html/ stockimagenation/dynamic_app/ checkoutsuccess.cfm`.

21. **In the second URL field type the path of the canceled or unsuccessful purchase. It's the same as step 20 except change the filename to** `checkoutsorry.cfm`.

22. **Click Next.**

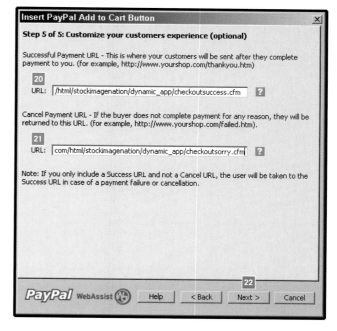

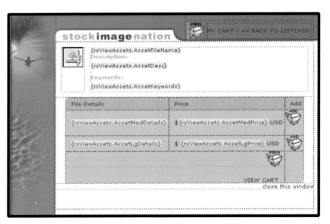

23. Click the Finish button after you review the list of items you added.

There is now a shopping cart icon in your Dreamweaver page. It is replaced with the cart image once your site is uploaded.

24. Repeat steps 3 through 23 for the next Add button with these changes:

Step 11: change the name to
largeitemplaceholder

Step 13: price of 39.00

25. In the bottom row of the orange table you can go ahead and delete the cart and text.

26. Select and delete the cart at the top of the page in the blue area.

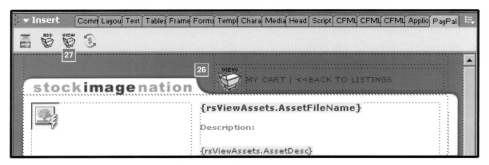

27. In the Insert panel (PayPal tab), click the View icon.

28. Click Next.

This screen is filled out from the last time you used it.

29. In the next screen select that you want to use a custom button and enter the URL of the same cart image (www. stockimagenation.com/html/stockimagenation/ dynamic_app/detail_cart.gif). Click Next.

You want the blue background instead of the orange.

30. Click Finish.

31. In the CSS Styles panel, click the Add a New Style button.

32. Select Redefine HTML tag. Type or select form in the Tag field, and then select This Document Only. Click OK.

This takes the extra padding out from around the last form you added (and any other form on this page).

33. Select the Box category and type O for both the Padding and the Margins. Click OK.

34. Save and test in all browsers.

Tutorial
» Passing Dynamic Data to the Cart

In this tutorial, you edit the code to make it so the shopping cart buttons know which item to add.

1. **If you closed the details page, double-click** details.cfm **to open it.**

   You are going to be working just a bit with the code, but it's really easy.

2. **To help you locate the proper code, select the first Add button in Design view.**

3. **Click the Code View icon.**

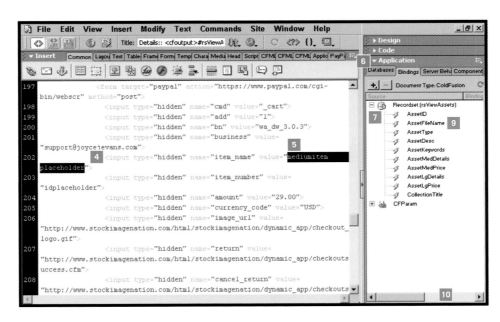

4. **Scroll up and find this code:**

```
<input type="hidden" name="business" value=
"support@joycejevans.com">
              <input type="hidden"
name="item_name" value="mediumitem placeholder">
```

5. **Select the words *mediumitem placeholder* and delete them.**

6. **Expand the Application panel group.**

7. **Click the Bindings tab and click the plus sign next to Recordset.**

8. **Make sure your cursor is between the quotes ("") where you deleted the placeholder text.**

9. **Select AssetFileName.**

10. **Click Bind.**

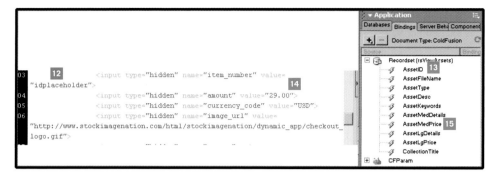

11. **Look at the new code; it now shows**

    ```
    <input type="hidden" name="item_name"
    value="<cfoutput>#rsViewAssets.AssetFileName#</cfout
    put>">
    ```

    The placeholder text has been replaced with the code that binds the button to your database.

12. **Locate and delete idplaceholder.**

13. **In the Bindings panel, select AssetID and then click the Bind button. The code now appear as:**

    ```
    <input type="hidden" name="item_number"
    value="<cfoutput>#rsViewAssets.AssetID#</cfoutput>">
    ```

14. **Highlight the price of 29.00 and delete it.**

15. **Select AssetMedPrice and bind it.**

16. **In the code for the price, place your cursor before** <cfoutput... **and type** Medium. **Add a space and type the Pipe symbol (I) and another space. The code looks like:**

    ```
    <input type="hidden" name="amount" value="Medium |
    <cfoutput>#rsViewAssets.AssetMedPrice#</cfoutput>">
    ```

    You added the word Medium so you can identify it in the shopping cart.

17. **Repeat for the second Add button except change the price to 39.00 and add the word Large.**

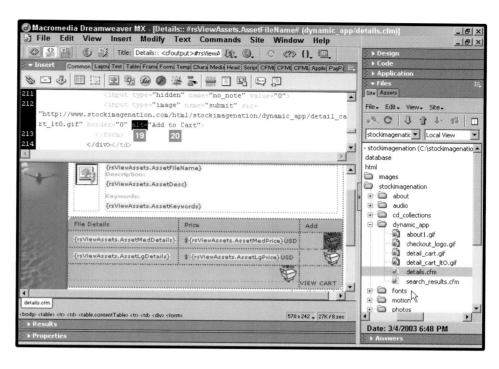

18. **Select the first Add button again in Design view.**

19. **Switch back to Code view and locate**

    ```
    alt="Make payments with PayPal - it's fast, free and
    secure!">
    ```

    This is PayPal's `alt` tag and is far too long. You can edit it.

20. **Delete the text between the quotes and type** Add to Cart.

21. **Replace the Alt text for each button including the View cart buttons.**

22. **Save your page. Upload it to your server and test it. To test:**

    » Go to the home page on your server (or use www.stockimagenation.com).

    » Type one of these words into the search field: **flower, bird, shell, turtle, duck, mountain.**

    » Select one of the images.

    » On the details page, click one of the Add buttons.

    PayPal automatically opens a new window. You can continue to browse the site and add to the cart. The PayPal window stays open. But if the user closed it, clicking the View button or Add button again opens it.

23. **After testing you may notice that the Add text and the carts don't look very good. Click behind Add and type** to Cart.

24. **Switch to Code view and locate the** `spacer.gif` **you see just before the Add to Cart text. Change it from 30 to 100.**
    I had you do it in Code view because it's very difficult to select in Design view.

25. **Click inside the cell with each cart and change the Horz to Center.**

26. **Now you can select the spacer above the Add to Cart text, press the right-arrow key, and press Shift-Enter (Return).**

27. **Select the spacer by the Price text; press Shift+Enter.**
    Do this only if your Price label isn't centered properly. Mine wasn't. Also note the spacer size and be sure the height is still 1. For some reason after being selected, my spacers would change to 8.

28. **Save and upload the file again and test it.**

» Session Review

Now that you saw first hand how easy it is to add a shopping cart to use with PayPal, it's time to test your retention. The answers can be found in the tutorials noted in parentheses.

1. Do you need a merchant account to get a PayPal account? ("Tutorial: Getting a PayPal Account")

2. Does it cost you anything to sign up for a PayPal account? ("Tutorial: Getting a PayPal Account")

3. What does the WebAssist cart extension cost? ("Tutorial: Installing the WebAssist Extension")

4. Where is a good place to save the extension? ("Tutorial: Installing the WebAssist Extension")

5. Why did you delete the form from the details page? ("Tutorial: Preparing the Orange Table for the Cart Buttons")

6. What is the advantage (particularly for Windows users) of transferring files from the CD to your hard drive using the Site panel? ("Tutorial: Preparing the Orange Table for the Cart Buttons")

7. Can you use your own buttons for the PayPal shopping cart? ("Discussion: Adding the Cart Buttons")

8. Can you use currency other than USA? ("Tutorial: Adding the Cart Buttons")

9. What do you need to consider if you are using a Logo on the PayPal page? ("Tutorial: Adding the Cart Buttons")

10. Why did you add the word Medium to the price tag? ("Tutorial: Passing Dynamic Data to the Cart")

Before You Publish

Get Ready for the World

Now that your site is complete you want to do a few things to be sure that it is working properly. The first thing you should do is add meta tags into the <HEAD> section to provide a description and keywords about your site. Search engines use this information to categorize your site. Then, you use Dreamweaver utilities to spell check and link check the pages in your site. After you are sure that your site is free of errors, you upload and synchronize your local and remote sites. You learn how Dreamweaver makes it easy to handle changes to individual pages or to the site structure itself. You learn how to repair broken links. Finally, you see how to save time by uploading only the changed pages to your remote site.

TOOLS YOU'LL USE
Site panel, Head category of the Insert bar

MATERIALS NEEDED
Your root folder or the session17_starterfiles folder

TIME REQUIRED
45 minutes

Tutorial
» Adding Meta Information

If you want users to find your Web site, you must list the site with the various engines and insert keywords and descriptions into your Web page. These keywords and descriptions help the search engine categorize your Web site.

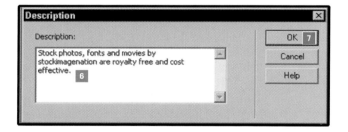

1. **Open the** `MainLayout.dwt` **template page and click the Head tab in the Insert menu. Click anywhere in your document.**
   The head content is invisible to users; they can't see what you enter, but what you enter can determine how a search engine categorizes and places your site.

2. **Click the Keywords icon.**

3. **Type these keywords into the keyword dialog box:** stock photos, royalty free, stock movies, fonts, Flash movies.
   You can add more than this. The key is to add the main words you think a user might type into a search engine when trying to find your type of site. Start with the most important words. Separate each keyword by a comma.

4. **Click OK.**

5. **Click the Description icon.**
   The Description dialog box opens.

6. **Type this description:** Stock photos, fonts and movies by stockimagenation are royalty free and cost effective.
   Use as many keywords as possible. This is the description that appears in many search engine listings.

7. **Click OK.**

<NOTE>
In step 1, you click into the document prior to adding the keywords because we discovered that the code is added above the DOCTYPE declaration instead of in between the head tags where they belong if the cursor isn't in the document.

<NOTE>
In step 6, do not click the keyword or description icons again to modify keywords or descriptions. This only adds another set of keywords and descriptions to the <head> of the document.

Do not use a certain word multiple times; this is considered spamming the search engine. Many search engines do not index your site if you do this.

8. **Click File→Save (or Save As) to save your work. When the dialog box opens asking you to update all the pages using this template, choose to do so.**
   This puts the meta tag information into every document. It's a good idea to edit the individual meta tags and place more specific keywords for specific pages.

Tutorial
» Testing Your Site Locally

Now that you feel you are done with your site, it's time to test it out prior to uploading it to a hosting server.

1. **Open the** `MainLayout.dwt` **document.**

2. **Select Commands→Cleanup HTML.**

3. **Select the various options available to cleanup.**
   For this page, I accepted the defaults, leaving Non-Dreamweaver comments and Remove Dreamweaver Special Markup and Special Tags unchecked. If your page really takes too long to load, you may want to remove the Dreamweaver special markup. But if you do so, the templates and Library items won't update. What you can do alternatively is make a duplicate of the root folder, one that's kept intact with Dreamweaver special markup and one with it removed. You can then upload the version with the removed markup and use the copy for future editing.

4. **Click OK. Save the template and update all the pages using it.**
   The Cleanup summary dialog box opens telling you what was removed (one nested tag and nine comments were removed). Because you designed this site in Dreamweaver using proper techniques, you won't get much of anything removed. But if you are working with someone else's page or one from other applications, you may be removing a lot of items.

   `<NOTE>`
   If you find you are working with a Word HTML file, be sure to run the Commands→Cleanup Word HTML filter. You'll be amazed at how much garbage can be removed safely.

5. **Repeat for all pages that you feel need cleaning up.**
   I ran it on the pages not using the template, `details.cfm`. Nothing was cleaned up; `search_results.cfm` had one tag and `index.htm` had nothing.

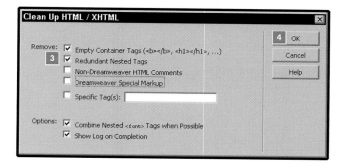

Keyword Usage

About 90% of Web hits are generated from a major search site. Knowing this, it is very important to choose your keywords wisely. The frequency of the keywords in a particular document can also influence your search rankings. Try to use some of your important keywords in the title of your page as well as in the document itself. Some engines even check the `<alt>` tag text so use it wisely as well. For more information on coding your meta tag information, visit these sites:

Search Engine Watch: www.searchenginewatch.com

Web Developer:
www.webdeveloper.com/html/html_metatag_res.html

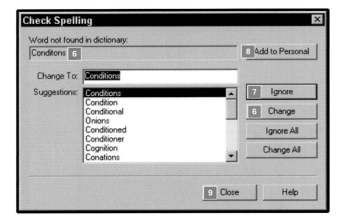

6. **On every page check your spelling by choosing Text→Check Spelling. Run it on the template. If you used the starter files, you'll find *Conditions* spelled wrong in one of the links.**
   Any misspelled words appear in the Check Spelling dialog box. You can use the suggested spelling, select one from the suggested list, or type your own change in and click the Change button.

7. **You can also click the Ignore button if it's something you don't want to change.**

8. **If it's something that occurs often, you should click the Add to Personal button to add the word to the dictionary. This way it won't keep coming up as misspelled.**

9. **When the spell checking is done, click the Close button to close the dialog box.**

10. **Do a spell check on every page and try to look out for misused words. These won't be found by a spell checker.**

11. **Check the download speeds of your pages by looking at the right side of the Status bar.**
    You can change the connection speed to test.

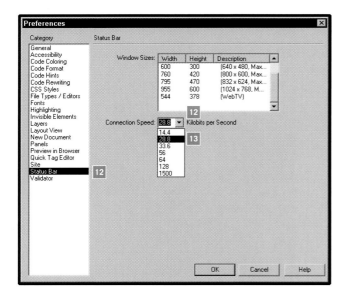

12. **Choose Edit→Preferences and select the Status Bar category. Click the drop-down menu for Connection Speed.**
    You should check your pages for download speed for the connection speeds you think your users are using.

13. **Select the desired speed and then click OK.**

< N O T E >

When you check the status bar and it shows a long download time, you need to optimize your images further or even perhaps make them smaller, use less of them, or whatever it takes to get the load time acceptable. Remember that users are very impatient. But also be aware that on some sites the load time is longer, but it is expected. For example, a site such as stockimagenation deals with displaying images. A user is aware of this and expects the extra time to load pages full of images. But you can do things to help out such as putting fewer images on a page and breaking the content into logical chunks instead of trying to put too much on one page.

Tutorial
» Running a Site Report for Links

In this tutorial, you run a site report for checking broken links in the MainLayout template as well as for checking the external links site wide.

1. **If you closed the template page, open it.**
    You run several reports on this page.

2. **Click Window→Results→Link Checker.**
    Notice that below the Property inspector a new panel group docks itself. This is the Results panel group with seven categories. Be sure that the Link Checker tab is selected.

3. **Look in the white field for the report results.**
    The area is blank because none of the links are broken on this particular page. Now you can check the entire site.

4. **Click the arrow next to the Show field to access the options for the Show drop-down list.**

5. **Click Broken Links.**

6. **Click the arrow near the green arrow icon.**

7. **Click Check links for entire site.**
    If you are using the session17_starterfiles, you see a few image links for the `legal.htm` page and one for the `search_results.cfm` page.

8. **Click inside the text of the first link. A yellow folder appears. Click it and browse to the html/images folder; select the correct image.**

9. **Repeat for each broken link, navigating to the folder that contains the correct image.**

10. **Look along the bottom of the Results panel group.**
    Notice there are 248 orphaned links. This means that these items are not linked to anything.

11. **Click the arrow for the Show field and click Orphaned Files.**
    For the most part, the orphaned links are images that are added dynamically to the page.

12. **Save any files you have open or haven't saved.**

13. **Back up your root folder. Now is a good time burn your site to a CD or other backup media.**

14. **Select the Templates folder in the Site panel and choose Site→Cloaking→Cloak.**

15. **Upload your site to a hosting server.**

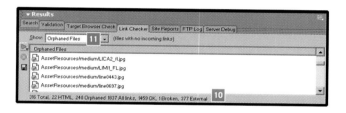

< N O T E >

In step 9, I have a file for the `search_results.cfm` page claiming a broken link. It's for the thumbnail images. Because this page has been uploaded to the server and tested, I'm going to assume it is a good link and coming up because of the server code added.

< N O T E >

In step 9, if you have other broken links that you happened to miss, click the yellow folder and locate the correct image or document and select it. When it is fixed it disappears from the list.

< N O T E >

In step 14, a message box opens telling you that cloaking (or hiding) this item does not affect how you use the template in your local site. It simply hides the folder from being uploaded to your server. You can do this to any folder such as source files. You don't need your large PNG files uploaded to the server.

Tutorial
» Synchronizing the Local and Root Folders

In this tutorial, you see how you can make changes to your local site and then automatically make the same changes to the remote server. This tutorial assumes you have uploaded your site to a hosting server.

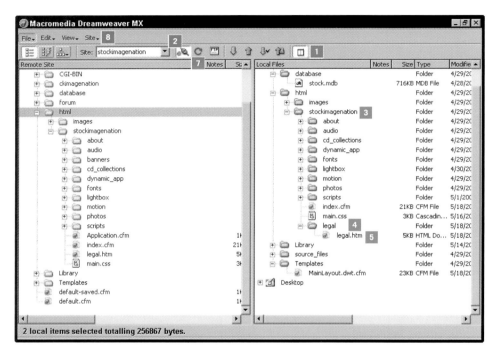

1. **Click the Expand/Collapse icon if the Site panel isn't open to view the Remote and Local views.**

2. **Click the Connect button to connect to the remote server.**

3. **Right-click the** stockimagenation **folder and click New Folder (Local View).**

4. **Name the new folder legal.**

5. **Click and drag the legal.htm page into the new legal folder.**

6. **Click Update to update all the files and their links.**
   Do not do this from any other location such as Windows Explorer. It only works if you do the moving from within the Site panel.

7. **Click the Reconnect button if you lost your connection.**

8. **Click Site→Synchronize and click the entire site.**

9. **Click the Delete remote files not on local drive option to select it.**
   This deletes the legal.htm files after they are placed in the legal folder.

10. **Check the report that opens. Leave everything checked.**

11. **When it's done synchronizing, you can choose to save a log and/or click Close when you are done.**
    Notice that the Remote site folder now looks just like the Local view folder with the legal folder and the legal.htm page in it and not in the stockimagenation folder where it was.

12. **Click the Disconnects from Remote Host icon.**

13. **Click the Expand/Collapse icon to return to the workspace.**

14. **Double-click** legal.htm **to open it.**
    Notice that all the images are still intact, even though the file moved. That's because Dreamweaver updated all the links to images when you moved them. If you did this outside of your root folder, all the image links would be broken.

15. **Test every page and look for any messed up tables, graphics, misused words, page titles, and so on.**

» Session Review

Now that you've checked your links and cleaned up the code a bit, it's time to see how much you remember. Answers can be found in the tutorials noted in parentheses.

1. Where are keywords and descriptions placed in the document? ("Tutorial: Adding Meta Information")

2. What are descriptions used for? ("Tutorial: Adding Meta Information")

3. What happens if you remove Dreamweaver Special Markup from your site? ("Tutorial: Testing Your Site Locally")

4. How can you get a frequently used word not to come up in the spell checker? ("Tutorial: Testing Your Site Locally")

5. How can you tell how long it will take for a page to load in a user's browser? ("Tutorial: Testing Your Site Locally")

6. What does cloaking do? ("Tutorial: Testing Your Site Locally")

7. What happens when you use the Site panel to move a file (page) to a different folder? What happens if you use Explorer? ("Tutorial: Synchronizing the Local and Root Folders")

8. How can you upload just the changed files in a site? ("Tutorial: Synchronizing the Local and Root Folders")

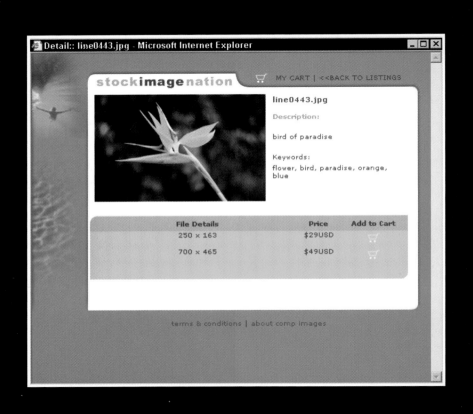

Appendix A

What's on the CD-ROM

This appendix describes the contents of the CD-ROM that accompanies this book. For the latest and greatest information, please refer to the ReadMe file located on the root of the CD-ROM. Here is what you will find:

- » System Requirements
- » Using the CD-ROM with Windows and Macintosh
- » What's on the CD-ROM
- » Troubleshooting

System Requirements

Make sure that your computer meets the minimum system requirements listed in this section. If your computer doesn't match up to most of these requirements, you might have a problem using the contents of the CD-ROM.

For Windows 98, Windows 2000, Windows NT, Windows Me, or Windows XP

- » PC with a Pentium III class III or 4 or better processor
- » At least 64MB of total RAM installed on your computer, 128MB recommended
- » At least 280MB of free hard drive space

» A color monitor with at least 800 x 600 resolution and a 16-bit video card

» A CD-ROM drive

For Macintosh

» Macintosh OS computer with a G3 or G4 PowerPC processor running OS 9.1, OS 9.2, or OS X

» At least 64MB of total RAM installed on your computer, 128MB recommended

» At least 320MB of free hard drive space

» A color monitor with at least 800 x 600 resolution and a 16-bit video card

» A CD-ROM drive

Using the CD-ROM with Windows

To install the items from the CD-ROM to your hard drive, follow these steps:

1. Insert the CD-ROM into your computer's CD-ROM drive.

2. The interface launches. If you have autorun disabled, click Start→Run. In the dialog box that appears, type **D:\start.exe**. Replace **D** with the proper letter if your CD-ROM drive uses a different letter. (If you don't know the letter, see how your CD-ROM drive is listed under My Computer.) Click OK.

3. A license agreement appears. Read through the license agreement, and then click the Accept button if you want to use the CD—after you click Accept, the License Agreement window won't bother you again.

4. The CD interface appears. The interface coordinates installing the programs and running the demos. The interface basically enables you to click a button or two to make things happen.

Using the CD-ROM with the Macintosh OS

To install the items from the CD-ROM to your hard drive, follow these steps:

1. Insert the CD-ROM into your CD-ROM drive.

2. Double-click the icon for the CD-ROM after it appears on the desktop.

3. Double-click the License Agreement icon. This is the license that you are agreeing to by using the CD. You can close this window once you've looked over the agreement.

4. Most programs come with installers; for those, simply open the program's folder on the CD-ROM and double-click the Install or Installer icon. *Note:* To install some programs, just drag the program's folder from the CD-ROM window and drop it on your hard drive icon.

What's on the CD-ROM

The following sections provide a summary of the software and other materials that you will find on the CD-ROM.

Tutorial Files

All the tutorial files that you use when working through the tutorials in this book are on the CD-ROM in the folder named "Tutorial Files." Within the Tutorial Files folder are subfolders containing the tutorial files for each session. In each session subfolder are all the files referenced in that session, including a starter file to use with that session if you need it.

Copy the files from your CD to your hard drive. The main file you need to copy right away is the stockimagenation_site_start folder. Once you copy it to your hard drive, rename it stockimagenation. Windows users have to right-click the folder and select Properties. Uncheck the Read-Only option and close. The book refers throughout to the site on your hard drive. If you make a mistake and need to back up, you can always start with the various session starter files. Just open the appropriate folder, copy its contents, and paste into your stockimagenation root folder on your hard drive. Or you can define a new site and point to a copy of the session starter file you want to use so you don't rewrite your working root folder.

Movies

Some concepts are difficult to show in a book, especially for beginners. In the areas that I think may be particularly difficult, I've included movie tutorials in the movies folder. To use them, you need a media player that plays MOV files. Windows and Macintosh machines both should be able to read these files. Double-click on the filename, and the appropriate player (if present) opens.

Software

The following applications are on the CD-ROM:

» **Mystical lighting, demo version.** A plug-in with great lighting effects.

» **DreamSuite, demo version**. A plug-in suite or stand-alone application.

» **Color Schemer, trial version for the PC.** Helps you develop color schemes.

» **ColorWrite, freeware software for multiple platforms.** Helps you come up with color schemes.

» **SmartDraw, trial version.** Flowcharting software.

» **WA PayPal eCommerce Toolkit, trial version.** A shopping cart extension.

>> **Linx Flash Editor, demo version.** Helps you easily edit Flash movies.

>> **SWfX, demo version.** Helps you easily create Flash text movies.

>> **ColdFusion MX Server, Developer Edition.** Helps you serve dynamic data to the users.

>> **Dreamweaver MX.** Premiere Web page authoring tool.

>> **Fireworks MX.** Image editing software for creation and optimization of images destined for the Web.

>> **Xenofex.** Demo version of Alien Skins plug-in; features many special effects.

Trial, demo, or evaluation versions are usually limited either by time or functionality, such as being unable to save projects. Some trial versions are very sensitive to system date changes. If you alter your computer's date, the programs will "time out" and be no longer functional.

Troubleshooting the CD

If you have difficulty installing or using any of the materials on the companion CD-ROM, try the following solutions:

>> Turn off any antivirus software that you may have running. Installers sometimes mimic virus activity and can make your computer incorrectly believe that a virus is infecting it. Be sure to turn the antivirus software back on later.

>> Close all running programs. The more programs you are running, the less memory is available to other programs. Installers also typically update files and programs; if you keep other programs running, the installation might not work properly.

>> Reference the ReadMe file. Please refer to the ReadMe file located on the root of the CD-ROM for the latest product information at the time of publication.

If you still have trouble with the CD-ROM, please call the Wiley Product Technical Support phone number: (800) 762-2974. Outside the United States, call 1(317) 572-3994. You can also contact Wiley Product Technical Support at www.wiley.com/techsupport. Wiley Publishing will provide technical support only for installation and other general quality control items; for technical support on the applications themselves, consult the program's vendor or author.

To place additional orders or to request information about other Wiley products, please call (800) 225-5945.

Appendix B

Web Design
Do's and Don'ts

The following list is meant to be a quick check-list to use when you are designing a site. Refer to this list now and then as you begin to learn Web design. The items featured on the list are some of the more common features that most professional Web designers agree upon.

» **Use ALT tags**—Always include alternative text for images. This allows screen readers to read a description of the image and makes your site more accessible. The alternative text can also be viewed in most browsers before the image loads.

» **Reduce file sizes**—Optimize your images by reducing color and size to the smallest file possible. If it's a photograph, consider cropping it to the most vital part to help add interest and reduce the size of the image. Use Fireworks (or an image editor) preview feature to see the results of your optimization. Get the file as small as possible.

» **Design above the fold**—Above the fold is the part that users see without scrolling (This term comes from newspapers; the front page above the fold is the part that is seen first, and the most important part in catching the reader's attention.) Be sure to have all links and vital information in the first screen. You can have more that is below the fold but be sure that all content is important and pertinent.

» **Provide good navigation**— User interfaces have been a topic of study and controversy since the world began, or at least since computers had monitors. Set up your navigation scheme in a manner that makes sense to your users. Study sites that you find easy to navigate, and figure out why the navigation scheme appeals to you. Then use your insight on your site.

» **Choose your content wisely**—Include only pertinent content. Break up large pieces of text into smaller readable chunks. Be sure that you include large articles on pages that are printable.

» **Make it easy to find home**—Include a way home from every page.

» **Include page titles**—Be sure to give every page a title name. An untitled document isn't very professional and doesn't help your search engine ratings. Many search engines use words in your title to index your site. Be sure you use a few of your top keywords in the title. Include a title in the content of the page so the readers know where they are.

» **Use Cascading Style Sheets**—Use CSS style sheets to format your text. It makes your site more accessable and is easier to edit when needed.

» **Test in all applicable browsers**—Always test your site in all the browsers your audience will be using before making the site live. You can install multiple versions of Netscape but only one version of Internet Explorer. To test other versions of Internet Explorer, you need to test on different machines or have various operating systems set up on your computer.

» **Check the links**—Dreamweaver has the capability to check your links. It's always a good idea to verify that your links all function properly after you make any changes.

» **Design professional buttons**—Use buttons that are not huge, but proportioned nicely with your site.

The following list is meant to be a quick checklist of some of the things that make a Web site scream "amateur" or are simply extremely irritating.

» **Everything is centered**—Beginners often center everything on a Web page. Don't use this method—it isn't professional looking.

» **All caps are used**—Do not for any reason write blocks of text using all caps. Not only is it unprofessional (and can appear as if you're shouting), it's also very difficult to read.

» **Includes counters**—Don't add one of those tacky counters to your pages—who cares? Have you ever seen one on a highly successful site? There are better ways to track visitors, such as using your Web log records.

» **Includes underlined text**—Don't underline text that is not a link. Underlines are used in print but not on the Web unless it's a link. You'll confuse users because they will be trying to click it.

» **Includes full screen text**—Don't run your text across the entire screen. Use a table to keep your text at a readable length, or use margins to keep the text off the edge of the browser. Long lines of text are very difficult to read.

» **Backgrounds are busy**—Don't use background images that interfere with the readability of your text. The only background images that work are textured types or very faded images. If you have to use a background with a busier print, put your text into a table that has a solid color background so it can be read.

» **Buttons aren't links**—Never make something look like a button if it's not clickable. Users are programmed to think that a beveled image that looks like a button will act like a button.

» **Includes bad graphics**—Items such as rainbow lines, animated lines, animated e-mail images, award icons, and huge buttons are all signs of an amateur site.

» **Includes graphics with halos**—*Halos* are the colors you see around an image. An anti-alias edged image blends into the surrounding color; when the image is removed from its background, pixels remain on the edges that were blended into the background. This usually occurs when an image is designed on one color background and then used on another color. You'll see it frequently on free images or images someone has snatched from someone else's Web site. The best way to avoid halos on your images is to place them on the same color background as the Web site before exporting. In Fireworks, you can set the Matte color to match the background color.

» **Includes blinking animations**—Don't use animations that constantly blink and never turn off. It will cause many potential users to leave.

» **Includes too many colors and fonts**—Don't use too many colors or too many fonts. A professionally designed site uses a few fonts at the most and a carefully selected palette of colors.

» **Uses splash pages**—Don't use an entry page unless there is an extremely good reason to do so (such as set the mood for a mood type site). When a user clicks your link to your site they expect to arrive at your site, not at a page that makes them click again to get in. Personal or special interest sites are the exception.

» **Excessively uses sound**—If you use sound, always give the users the choice to turn it off. Better yet, have an option to turn it on rather than be on automatically.

Installing PWS, IIS, and ColdFusion MX Developer

Tutorial

» Installing a Personal Web Server (Windows 98)

In this tutorial, Windows 98 users install Microsoft PWS (a scaled-down version of IIS) that runs on Windows 98 and NT Workstation, if you don't have it already. This is not the same as the Personal Web Server that ships with FrontPage.

To make dynamic pages, you must have a Web server and some sort of application server. To develop ASP pages, you need an application server that supports Microsoft Active Server Pages 2.0. Microsoft Personal Web Server (PWS — a scaled-down version of IIS) runs on Windows 98 and NT Workstation, and IIS runs on Windows 2000 and Windows XP.

Sun's Chili!Soft ASP may be used on Windows, Linux, and Solaris platforms. Macintosh users should use a Web hosting service with ASP 2.0 support or install IIS or PWS on a remote (Windows) computer. Macintosh users must (and Windows users may) use a Web hosting solution. Look for a company that supports ColdFusion MX and Access database.

1. **Check your C or D drives to see whether you have an Inetpub folder.**
   If not, you need to install PWS or IIS, or opt to use a hosting service.

2. **Double-click the PWS installation file on the Windows 98 CD.**
   Or double-click the file downloaded from the Microsoft Web site.

3. **Follow the Installation Wizard directions.**

4. **When asked for the default Web publishing home directory, accept the default C:\Inetpub\wwwroot.**

5. **Click Finish to end the installation.**

Tutorial

» Installing IIS

In this tutorial, Windows 2000 and Windows XP users install Microsoft IIS, which comes with Windows NT Server, Windows 2000, and Windows XP Professional. This is much preferred over PWS.

Before starting, if you happen to have ColdFusion MX installed already, please uninstall it. PWS and IIS do not function properly if ColdFusion is installed first.

1. **Check your C or D drives to see whether you have an Inetpub folder.**
   If not, you need to install PWS or IIS, or opt to use a hosting service for all testing.

2. **In Windows 2000 and Windows XP, choose Start→Settings→Control Panel→Add/Remove Programs.**

3. **Choose Add/Remove Windows Components.**

4. **Select the IIS box.**

5. **Click Next.**

6. **Follow the installation steps.**

Dynamic Pages

Dynamic pages require a connection to a Web server and a data source. There are many data source types; which one you use depends upon the nature of the pages you plan to build—the type of Web server used to host your pages. The Web server contains special application software that is used to process the scripts contained in a Web page. The software reads the code, and then removes it from the page and passes the page on with the processed results. When the users receive the page, all they see is the resulting HTML.

For all of this to work, you must first set up the correct information in your Site Definition. Dynamic pages require a live connection; this means that you must set up the proper access to a Web server with support for your application technology. Because this project uses ColdFusion and an Access database, your local Web server or your provider's Web server must have the latest Microsoft Access Drivers (4.0) and allow a connection to a database.

You need the latest MDAC drivers from Microsoft. You can download MDAC 2.5 and 2.6 for free. Be sure to install 2.5 first, and then 2.6. Windows 2000 with service pack 2 and Windows XP contain the latest drivers.

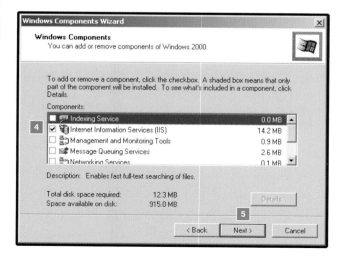

Tutorial

» Installing ColdFusion MX

After you install either PWS or IIS, you are ready to install ColdFusion MX. You can install ColdFusion on Windows, Unix, and Mac OSX. This tutorial covers Windows only. The Mac installation needs J2EE Run. Although it can be done and the instructions are on Macromedia's site (www.macromedia.com), it isn't an easy job and goes beyond the scope of this book.

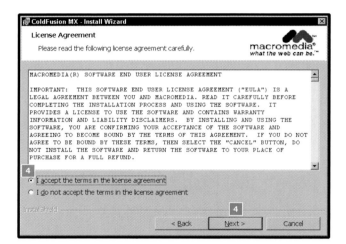

1. **Navigate to the Software→ColdFusion MX folder on this book's CD-ROM.**

2. **Locate the** `coldfusion-60-win-en.exe` **file and double-click it.**

3. **Click next in the Welcome window.**

4. **Click I accept the terms in the license agreement after you read it; then click the Next button.**

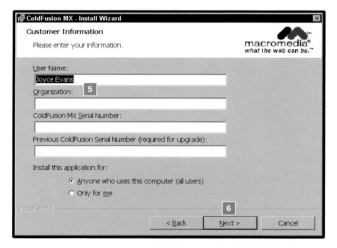

5. **Fill in the customer information. If you purchased the full version of ColdFusion, enter the serial number. If not, leave it blank, and it operates as the free developer edition.**

6. **Click Next.**

7. **In the Web Server dialog box, leave Standalone selected and click Next.**

<NOTE>
Because you installed IIS, you could choose that option instead of the standalone option. At least one tester had problems using the standalone option.

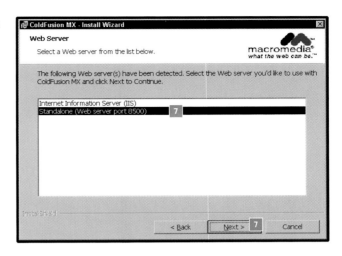

8. **The Webroot Folder dialog box opens. Change it if you want and click Next.**

9. **In the Custom Setup dialog box, you can choose to customize what is installed on your hard drive. Click Next when you are done.**

10. **Enter a password for the ColdFusion MX administrator and for RDS users and click Next.**
    The password enables you to access the Administrator portion of ColdFusion, so be sure to write it down.

11. **Click the Install button.**

12. **The Install Wizard Completed dialog box opens; click Finish.**

13. **Click the red x in the upper-right corner to close the install interface.**

14. **If the Administrator window opens, type the password you entered in step 10.**
    The window that opens next contains links to a lot of documentation and sample.

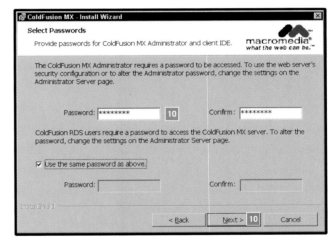

You are now ready to set up Dreamweaver to test with IIS, PWS, or ColdFusion. Session 14 walks you through the settings you need to make. The methods discussed are based on default installations of IIS, PWS, and ColdFusion, so if your path is different, you need to make those changes. If you find you need additional help for IIS and PWS, check Microsoft support (www.microsoft.com). For ColdFusion, you can go to Macromedia support (www.macromedia.com) if your system has "quirks" or variances that aren't covered here or in Session 14.

Resources

This appendix contains recommendations for tools that you might find useful. When designing, you often need other resources to enhance the design or to help you be more productive with your development time. None of these products is required; I just wanted to give a little input and help in finding things you might need or want.

ColdFusion MX Hosting Service

Crystal Tech

Crystal Tech (www.crystaltech.com) is hosting the www.stockimagenation.com site. I absolutely love it. They have superior customer service. You can contact support via e-mail and get quick responses or you can call an 800 number. They are always courteous and knowledgeable. They feature a fantastic Control Center where you control your site. Most servers require you to contact them to set up your DNS name for you—not so with Crystal Tech; you can do it yourself.

Crystal Tech supports a variety of scripting environments, including ColdFusion 5 or ColdFusion MX, ActiveState Perl, and PHP4.

Hosting Plans at Crystal Tech range from an entry-level package perfect for static HTML sites to a full-fledged semi-dedicated Plan supporting both ASP and ColdFusion on high end/low load servers. Crystal Tech also offers Dedicated Hosting, a Reseller Program, as well as partnerships with several well-respected vendors like Miva and payQuake.

Product Contributions

Web Assist

This is the company that supplied the free extension you used in Session 16. They also have a paid version with many more features, as well as other great products. Check them out at www.webassit.com.

SmartDraw

A trial version is on the CD. SmartDraw.com features more than 50,000 symbols, images, and templates as well as easy drag-and-drop drawing. I found this application extremely easy to use, much easier than the competing major product. SmartDraw is intuitive and immediately usable with no training, no manuals, and practically zero learning curve. For more information, visit www.smartdraw.com, or call 1-800-501-0314.

Color Schemer

A trial version is on the CD. Color Schemer (www.colorschemer.com) is an application that helps you come up with a color scheme. Some of the features include multiple color-matching modes, drag-and-drop colors, and sample pre-made color schemes. You can customize various schemes and change color values. It's simple to use. There is a sample tutorial using the trial version. The tutorial is in the Xtra Tutorials folder on the CD.

ColorWrite

A trial version is on the CD. ColorWrite (www.adaptiveview.com/cw) is a color chooser with an integrated CSS/HTML code generator. It allows you to define colors using RGB, HSV, CMY, and CMYK, and makes using Web-safe colors easy. ColorWrite runs on Macs (OS X), Linux, Solaris, and Windows systems.

Camtasia Studio

Camtasia Studio records full-motion video of your screen and produces the videos in Flash and streaming formats. You can edit the videos, as well as narrate and annotate with callouts, text boxes, and so on. You can also create flash menus for your videos with the Theater add-in. Camtasia Studio videos can be used to train, support, and demonstrate the best way to use PC software.

Sorenson Squeeze 3

Sorenson Squeeze 3 is a simple and powerful software application that provides an interface to Sorenson Media's professional video codecs—Sorenson Video 3.1 Pro, Sorenson Spark Pro, and Sorenson MPEG-4 Pro. The software application simplifies the compression process by providing the user with the presets to easily access the advanced features of the codecs. Sorenson Squeeze 3 is available in three versions—Sorenson Squeeze 3 Compression Suite, Sorenson Squeeze 3 for Macromedia Flash MX, and Sorenson Squeeze 3 for MPEG. All three versions are designed to meet the needs of both novice and professional content creators who want to encode and deliver high-quality video. To find out more about Sorenson Squeeze, visit www.sorenson.com.

Wildform

The Wildform Resource Center contains numerous Flash tutorials, FLAs, articles, and links, as well as sections on how to create Flash projectors, Flash players, and Flash ads and e-mails. Check out www.wildform.com/resources/. Wildform creates easy-to-use Flash products including the Flix Flash Video Encoders, the Linx Easy Flash Editor, and the SWfX Flash Text animator. With Wildform products you can create stunning Flash projects without knowing Flash, including Flash buttons, banners, navigation elements, tutorials, demos, slide shows, and multimedia presentations. Visit www.wildform.com/.

TopStyle Pro

You can get a trial version at www.bradsoft.com. Dreamweaver has wonderful new support for CSS, but if you want all the power and flexibility you can get, try the TopStyle editor. It's reasonably priced at $49 and is Dreamweaver MX compatible. CSS is actually quite simple, but getting it to work in multiple browsers is a challenge. This is where TopStyle is unique in that it checks your style sheets against multiple browser implementations, letting you know about bugs and incompatibilities that might affect your design. It also provides site management from a CSS perspective, providing you detailed style information about your entire site.

Project VII

Project Seven (PVII) is a leader in Dreamweaver development. The company was founded in 1997 by Al Sparber and Gerry Jacobsen. Its Web site (www.projectseven.com) attracts over 50,000 Dreamweaver visitors each week. I checked with Al and Gerry and as of June 2003, there have been over 600,000 PVII Dreamweaver extensions downloaded worldwide. PVII Dreamweaver Extensions, Extension Kits, Design Packs, and Tutorials are in a class by themselves—and they all work in Dreamweaver MX.

Dreamweaver Extension Kits, like Menu Magic and Geewizz, automate the creation of DHTML menus and scrollers from the comfort of the Dreamweaver interface. PVII Design Packs are not just templates, but learning tools that come with comprehensive user guides that lead you by the hand. I frequent the site's forum, and a lot of users get the packs to practice and learn different techniques.

Benson IT Solutions

Benson IT Solutions, Inc. (www.bensonitsolutions.com) provides ColdFusion developers with starter Web application products. Their Open Source forum product is called WebThreads. It is packed with features and provides a great beginning to those adding a Web forum/bulletin board system to their site. The open source availability of the product allows developers to integrate the product into any site's "look and feel." Forums can be password protected, open to a select group of users, or open to the public. Registered users can subscribe to specific forums or threads to be notified by e-mail as posts occur. Threads can have unlimited replies to replies, and there is a built-in option for users to use indenting with replies. A forum can also be marked read only to limit posting access to an administrator.

Clipart and Stock Images

Getty Images, Inc.

Getty Images (www.gettyimages.com) is focused on producing the most relevant, reflective, and "defining" pictures of today. Getty Images produces, preserves, and markets the largest collection of imagery in the world. You can find images from companies such as Photodisc, Digital Vision, Thinkstock, FoodPix, and many more.

Rubberball

The images used for stockimagenation were supplied by Rubberball. I love the fun and energetic images. Visit them to see the fun images of people. RubberBall uses silhouette style in themes, photographic angles, and people on white backgrounds.

RubberBall has a 500-image picture library. Children, teens, and adults in different environments and roles are portrayed throughout the 47-volume collection.

Hemera Technologies, Inc

Hemera's Photo-Objects (www.hemera.com) is my absolute favorite collection for quick photo images. They contain no backgrounds and have a fantastic browser.

Hemera Photo-Objects 50,000 Volumes I & II

Photo-Objects are photographic images of people, animals, and objects that have been isolated from their original backgrounds and pre-masked so they can be quickly and easily dropped into any design. These images are great for business and design professionals. Photo-Objects can enhance everything from presentations and annual reports to marketing collateral such as advertisements and brochures. Each collection of 50,000 Photo-Objects is available for Windows and Macintosh.

Photosphere

PhotoSphere Images is a premiere supplier of professional, royalty-free stock images (www.photosphere.com). It is fast and easy to access the library of more than 2,800. The keyword search engine will help you find specific images quickly. Each of the 30 collections of stock images includes 80-100 images.

All images are available online in JPEG format and on CD in Photo CD format. The pricing is very competitive.

Fonts

Following is a list of font resources. Many are free. You can always type "free fonts" into a search engine and get tons of returns.

Amazone and Dragonwick are the free fonts used in this book: www.fontmagic.com/cate/script1.html. Click on the number 5 at the bottom of the page for Dragonwick. The Mac versions can be found at www.masterstech-home.com/The_Library/Font_Samples/Font_Indices/D.html.

- » Larabie (www.larabie.com)
- » Adobe (www.adobe.com)
- » Garage Fonts (www.garagefonts.com)
- » Letterspace (www.letterspace.com)
- » Fonthaus (www.fonthaus.com)
- » t26 (www.t26.com)
- » P22 (www.p22.com)

Plug-Ins

Splat!

Created by Alien Skin Software (www.alienskin.com). I love this one; you can make some pretty great edges with it. What I especially like is the expandability of it. You can edit or make your own effects.

> » *Frame*: Adds realistic frames and mattes to any photo or other rectangle. Choose from 100 frames, including traditional wood frames, Dover, and geometric borders.

> » *Resurface*: Adds any of 100 high-resolution surface textures to an object or selection. Adds natural media with only a few clicks, distorting your image to match the surface. Textures include paper, concrete, leather, brick, stone, metal, wood, and more.

> » *Edges*: Adds versatile, decorative edge effects such as halftone dots, torn paper, and pixelated edges. This effect works with any selection and looks great applied to text.

> » *Fill Stamp*: Fills any selection with familiar objects. Choose from over 100 stamp files, and then scale the objects to fit. Fill Stamp adapts to any shape and works well on text. This effect can seamlessly tile and be colorized to match your image.

> » *Border Stamp*: Applies the power of Fill Stamp to borders, creating borders from everyday objects such as pebbles, pills, and tickets. Great for themed borders, Border Stamp includes realistic drop shadows and adapts to any shape.

> » *Patchwork*: Re-creates images as mosaics such as light pegs, ASCII art, ceramic tile, and cross-stitch. Simply browse the Patchwork libraries, scale your tiles, and apply.

Image Doctor

Image Doctor (www.alienskin.com) is a new set of powerful image-correction filters for Photoshop, Fireworks, Paint Shop Pro, and other image editors. Image Doctor removes blemishes and defects, repairs over-compressed JPEGs, and replaces unwanted details and objects. Professional and amateur photographers, photo editors, archivists, graphic designers, and Web designers can more quickly fix their images with Image Doctor.

Image Doctor delivers these effects in a clean, easy-to-use interface. Users can tweak their effects in a huge preview that includes a before/after toggle, command menus, keyboard shortcuts, and unlimited undo capability.

Image Doctor is the only filter set to offer selection-based image repair. Use the familiar selection tools of your image editor, and then correct large as well as small areas in one pass. The intelligent pattern matching of Image Doctor makes it the perfect complement to existing photo-editing tools.

Auto FX

Auto FX (www.autofx.com) has a great line of filters. Check out Mystical Lighting, which is a really great filter for special lighting effects, or Dreamsuite, which is a standalone application, but can also be used as a plug-in. It contains a ton of filters to do ripples, motion, metal effects and a lot more. There is also a filter named Gel for all kinds of gooey effects. Mystical Lighting and Dreamsuite I demos are on the CD.

Xenofex 2

Xenofex 2 (www.alienskin.com) is OS X–compatible and delivers 14 more effects. You can simulate natural phenomena such as lightning and clouds, and distortions such as Flag, Television, and Rip Open. You can also transform photos into jigsaw puzzles, constellations, and intricate mosaics with a single click. The hundreds of presets make adding effects very fast and easy.

Web Sites

There are many Web sites to help you learn Web design. Several are mentioned throughout this book. In addition here are a few more that you may find useful.

» Web Page Design for Designers, www.wpdfd.com, is a highly recommended site that I used a lot, especially when I was first learning Web design.

» Definitions of Words, www.whatis.com. The art of Web design includes a lot of jargon; this is a good place to get definitions.

» Google, www.google.com. Type **"web design tutorial"** (be sure to use the quotes to get the exact phrase).

Index

»E«

e-commerce. *See* data-driven pages; PayPal; shopping cart

edge options, 49

edges, sharpening, 49

editable template regions, 276

editing

    effects, 63

    a rectangle, 83–85

    rollover buttons, 206–208

effects

    adding, 120–123

    editing, 63

Effects panel

    glow, 103, 106

    shadows, 102

Ellipse tool, 83, 87–89

EPS format, 46

Eraser tool, 65, 69

events

    associating with behaviors, 208

    definition, 205

    triggering, 248

Expander arrow, 48

expanding/collapsing panels, 157

Export dialog box

    animated logo, 145–147

    HTML, 148–149

    menu images, 142–143

    page images, 144

    save-as type, 147

exporting

    animated logo, 145–147

    animation format, 145–147

    banners, 12–13

    home page, 144

    hotspots, 142

    HTML, 148

    images, 148

    navigation images, 141

    rollovers, 130–133

    sliced images, 141, 148

    submenus, 142–143

    visibility, 142–143

expressions, SQL, 306

Extension Manager, 216–217

extensions, 216–217

»F«

file and folder management, 155, 161–162

files

    copying from the CD, 38

    managing, 161

    naming conventions, 60

    organizing, 38

    read-only, unlocking, 38

    renaming, 161

    size, reducing *See* optimization

fill color, setting, 77

filters, 63

Fireworks MX. *See also* exporting

    on the CD, 352

    check boxes, 49

    color box, 49

    color palettes, 135

    custom layouts, 50

    definition, 38

    docking panels, 50

    Document window, 48

    edge options, 49

    Expander arrow, 48

    Gripper, 48

    Menu Bar, 48

    Options pop-up menu, 48–49

    Panel Groups, 48

    Property inspector, 48–49

    rearranging panels, 50

    saving a layout, 50

    scanning images, 51–52

    slider controls, 49

    Title Bar, 48

    user interface, 47–50

    vector graphics, 43

    workspace, 48

fixed-width tables, 167

Flash MX, 38

flattening images, 65

flowcharts, Web navigation, 26–27

fluid tables, 167

folders

    managing, 161

    renaming, 161

    synchronizing local and root, 345